Praise for *The Father of Us All*

"I have never read another book that explains so well the truth that 'war lies in the dark hearts of us all' but that history offers hope."
　　—William Shawcross, author of *Allies* and *Deliver Us from Evil*

"Victor Hanson brings to his writing a mixture of learning and reflection that is rare in any age, especially the ignorant one in which we live."
　　—Dr. Larry Arnn, president of Hillsdale College

"[A] lively collection . . . The writing is always elegant and erudite."
　　—*Foreign Affairs*

"Hanson has provided a thoughtful, wide-ranging look at the fundamental questions of war and peace."
　　—*MHQ: Quarterly Journal of Military History*

"A masterpiece of envelope pushing, and a comprehensive and dazzling analysis of why America fights as she does . . . Hanson's arguments may not convince everyone, but cannot be dismissed."　　**—*Publishers Weekly***

"Not a happy message to peace-studies idealists but one a balanced current-events collection should include."　　**—*Booklist***

"Hanson thinks we have become far too optimistic about the future and the potential for progress. War has been a prominent feature of all of human history, and is likely to remain so. I think he is right on this score."　　**—Larry DeWitt, HNN.us**

Praise for Victor Davis Hanson's work

"A small masterpiece of style and scholarship."
　　—*Economist* on *The Western Way of War*

"Enthralling . . . One closes this book wishing that its final verdict was as well known as more familiar tenets of Greek wisdom."
—**Christopher Hitchens,** *Newsday,* **on** *The Western Way of War*

"Vivid . . . Ambitious . . . Challenges readers to broaden their horizons and examine their assumptions . . . [Hanson] more than makes his case."
—*New York Times Book Review* **on** *Carnage and Culture*

"No one offers a more compelling picture of how wars reflect and affect the societies, including our own, that wage them."
—*National Review* **on** *Carnage and Culture*

"[Hanson] is becoming one of the best-known historians in America . . . [*Carnage and Culture*] can only enhance his reputation."
—**John Keegan,** *Daily Telegraph* **(London),**
on *Carnage and Culture*

"Victor Davis Hanson is courting controversy again with another highly readable, lucid work. Together with John Keegan, he is our most interesting historian of war."
—**Jean Bethke Elshtain, author of** *Women and War,*
on *Carnage and Culture*

"What [Hanson] brings to the public discussion—along with an unusually vigorous prose style and a remarkable erudition—is a philosophy of war not meant for the weak-kneed or faint-hearted. Hanson does not celebrate war, but he accepts it as a fact of life, a part of the human condition that no amount of idealistic preaching or good intentions can will away."   —*New York Times Book Review* **on** *Ripples of Battle*

"Victor Davis Hanson is refreshingly unabashed about being an old-fashioned military historian . . . He displays an exceptional chronological sweep."   —*Washington Post Book World* **on** *Ripples of Battle*

THE FATHER OF US ALL

War and History, Ancient and Modern

———

VICTOR DAVIS HANSON

*Co-director, the Group on Military History and
Contemporary Conflict, the Hoover Institution,
Stanford University*

BLOOMSBURY PRESS
New York Berlin London Sydney

Published by Bloomsbury Press, New York

All papers used by Bloomsbury Press are natural, recyclable products
made from wood grown in well-managed forests. The manufacturing processes
conform to the environmental regulations of the country of origin.

LIBRARY OF CONGRESS CATALOGING-IN-PUBLICATION DATA

Hanson, Victor Davis.
    The father of us all : war and history, ancient and modern / by Victor Davis Hanson.—1st ed.
        p.   cm.
    ISBN 978-1-60819-165-9 (hardback : alk. paper)
    1. War—History.   2. Military history.   I. Title.

    U27.H378 2010
    355.0209—dc22
    2009041714

First published by Bloomsbury Press in 2010
This paperback edition published in 2011

Paperback ISBN: 978-1-60819-410-0

1 3 5 7 9 10 8 6 4 2

Typeset by Westchester Book Group
Printed in the United States of America by Quad/Graphics, Fairfield, Pennsylvania

To the soldiers

of the American military—

for all that they do.

War is the father of all and king of all.

—*Heraclitus,*
  fragment 22B53

CONTENTS

S OME PORTIONS OF these essays have appeared in various pub-
lications or derive from transcripts of public lectures I delivered. In
every case, however, I have greatly expanded, rewritten, and updated
each chapter—and, in many instances, combined two or three earlier
shorter articles, along with entirely fresh material, to form these newly
titled longer essays.

Two themes resonate throughout the book: the unchanging face of
war and the tragic nature of its persistence over the ages. Despite the
purported novelty of today's so-called war on terror, and the public
furor and controversies that arose over the wars of this new millennium, conflict in the present age still remains understandable to us
through careful study of the past.

War is an entirely human enterprise. Even with changing technologies and ideologies, and new prophets of novel strategies and unconventional doctrines, conflict will remain the familiar father of us

all—as long as human nature stays constant and unchanging over time and across space and cultures.

War seems to be inseparable from the human condition. I do not wish to venture into the controversy about whether war is innate to the human gene pool, or whether aggression is characteristic of our evolution. Rather, as an empiricist, I note only that war—like birth, aging, death, politics, and age-old emotions such as fear, pride, and honor—has never disappeared. This so-called tragic view concedes that depressing fact about the human condition, and yet it steels the individual to the notion that suffering is a part of our human lot, and unfortunately cannot be entirely eradicated by any amount of well-intended nurturing.

Yet acceptance of the frequent horror of war does not equate to either an approval of or an abject inability to avert particular conflicts. If military history suggests that it is almost impossible to outlaw outright by statute, or eliminate entirely through progressive education, legalized killing on a grand scale, it nevertheless offers the hope that we can learn from the past in order to both lessen the frequency and mitigate the severity of particular conflicts. As the Athenian dramatist Sophocles teaches us, the stuff of tragedy is the endless struggle against something deep and persistent—and unpleasant—within ourselves.

In short, this book is a small attempt in these confusing times of high technology and intellectual haughtiness to remind us that past wars still best explain present conflicts.

I wish to thank the Hoover Institution, Stanford University, for help in preparing the manuscript. In particular I owe a debt of gratitude to Bill and Nancy Myers, and their children, Mary Myers-Kauppila and George Myers, for their support for my work, including the thinking contained in the essays herein. The Myers family has long demonstrated to the Hoover Institution its appreciation of scholarship in the classics, especially its application to contemporary history.

VICTOR DAVIS HANSON
November 1, 2009

PART I

Military History:
The Orphaned Discipline

CHAPTER 1

Why Study War?

*Military History Teaches Us About the Tragic Inevitability of Conflict**

Military History?—How Odd

TRY EXPLAINING TO a college student that Tet was, in fact, an American military victory. Or, in contrast, suggest that the Vietnamese offensive of 1968 was a stunning enemy success. Either way, you will not provoke a counterargument—let alone an assent—but a blank stare: Who or what was Tet?

When doing some radio interviews about the recent hit movie *300*, I encountered similar bewilderment about battles of the past from both listeners and hosts. Not only did most of them not know who the movie's eponymous three hundred Spartans were or what Thermopylae

---

* Portions of this essay originally appeared in the summer 2007 issue of *City Journal*.

was, but they also seemed clueless about the Persian Wars altogether. Was not Marathon a long-distance race, nothing more?

Americans tend to lack a basic understanding of military matters. Even when I was a graduate student, thirty-some years ago, military history—understood broadly as the investigation of why one side wins and another loses a war, and encompassing reflections on magisterial or foolish generalship, technological stagnation or breakthrough, and the roles of discipline, bravery, national will, and culture in determining a conflict's outcome and its consequences—had already become unfashionable on campus. Today, universities seem even less receptive to the subject.

This state of neglect in our schools is profoundly troubling. Democratic citizenship requires knowledge of war—and now, in the age of weapons of mass annihilation, more than ever.

I came to the formal study of warfare in an odd way at the age of twenty-four. Without ever taking a class in military history, I naively began writing about war for a Stanford University classics dissertation that explored the effects of agricultural devastation in ancient Greece, especially the Spartan ravaging of the Athenian countryside during the Peloponnesian War. The rather esoteric topic seemed far more complex than merely attacking farms. Was the Spartan strategy really all that effective? Why assume that ancient armies with primitive tools could easily burn or cut trees, vines, and grain on thousands of acres of enemy farms? On my family farm in Selma, California, it took me almost an hour to fell a mature fruit tree with a sharp modern ax, and it usually wasn't easy to burn grain, except during a brief dry period in late spring and summer.

Yet even if the invaders could not starve civilian populations, perhaps the destruction was still harmful psychologically, and to an extent to achieve military objectives of prompting an armed response. After all, soldiers would not persist in a tactic for centuries that did not work—or would they? I certainly saw farmers in my own environs outraged about even the most trivial damage to their crops and fields. So did the very idea of a Spartan arrogantly trampling through an Athenian vineyard goad proud agrarians to come out and fight in pitched battle—for matters of honor that far transcended any actual damage to their olive trees? And what did the practice tell us about the values of the Greeks—and of the generals who persisted in an operation that often must have brought few tangible results in terms of destroying the material resources of the enemy?

I posed these questions to my prospective thesis adviser, adding all sorts of further justifications. The topic was central to understanding the Peloponnesian War, I noted. The research would be interdisciplinary—a big plus in a field where jobs were scarce—drawing not just on ancient military histories but also on archaeology, classical drama, epigraphy, and poetry. I also could bring a wealth of practical experience to the study, having grown up around veterans of both world wars who talked constantly about battle. And from my upbringing on a farm, I wanted to add practical details about growing trees and vines in a Mediterranean climate.

Yet my adviser was skeptical. He knew better than I the prevailing attitudes in scholarship of the times. Agrarian wars, indeed wars of any kind, were not popular in classics Ph.D. programs—even though farming and fighting were the ancient Greeks' two most common pursuits, the sources of anecdote, allusion, and metaphor in almost every Greek philosophical, historical, and literary text. Few classicists seemed to remember that most notable Greek writers, thinkers, and statesmen—from Aeschylus to Pericles to Xenophon—had served in the phalanx or on a trireme at sea and that such experiences permeated their work.

Dozens of nineteenth-century French and German dissertations and monographs on ancient warfare—on the organization of the Spartan army, the birth of Greek tactics, the strategic thinking of Greek generals, and much more—by the 1970s went largely unread. Only a handful of essays were devoted to the role of war in the ancient world, despite the almost constant war making of the imperial Athenians and Romans.

Nor was the larger discipline of military history itself, once central to a liberal education, in vogue on campuses in the seventies. It was as if the academic community had forgotten that history itself had begun with Herodotus and Thucydides as the story of armed conflicts. Did Xenophon, Polybius, or Livy write about much other than wars and the brief hiatuses between them?

Why the Neglect of Military History?

WHAT LAY BEHIND this academic lack of interest, as opposed to the ongoing fascination of war among the public at large? An obvious explanation was the general climate of the immediate post-Vietnam era in the seventies. The public perception in the Nixon, Ford, and Carter years was that America had lost a war that for moral and practical reasons it should never have fought—a veritable catastrophe, thought many in the universities, that America must never repeat. The necessary corrective was not to learn from history how such unpopular wars started, went forward, and were lost or won. Instead, it was better to ignore anything that had to do with such an odious business in the first place—or at least to craft alternatives that might settle disputes without force or suggestions that the lessons of Napoleon in the Iberian peninsula could help explain Hue.

The nuclear pessimism of the Cold War, which followed the horror of two world wars, likewise dampened academic interest in different ways. The obscene postwar concept of "mutually assured destruction" had ensured an apocalyptic veneer to contemporary war. As President John F. Kennedy warned, "Mankind must put an end to war, or war will put an end to mankind."

Conflict had become something so destructive, in this view, that it no longer had any relation to the battles of the past. Even in the present, it seemed absurd to worry about a new tank or a novel doctrine of counterinsurgency when the press of a button, unleashing nuclear Armageddon, would render all military thinking superfluous. What did it matter whether Alexander the Great on the Indus or Stonewall Jackson in the Shenandoah Valley offered lessons about both strategic and tactical doctrine if a volley of nuclear missiles could make all such calculations obsolete? Harry Truman, after all, in conjunction with Secretary of Defense Louis Johnson, radically cut back American arms following the end of the Second World War. Johnson himself wished to dismantle the Marine Corps and felt nuclear weapons had made all such conventional arms unnecessary.

Further, the age of social upheaval and reform during the 1960s had ushered in a certain well-meaning pacifism deemed antithetical to formal academic thinking about war. The demise of the tragic view—the acceptance of suffering in the human experience and the need for heroic struggle against it—suggested that money, education, and better intentions could at last arrest the gory march of history. Government, the military, business, religion, and the family had conspired, the new Rousseauians believed, to warp the natural "make peace, not war," "give peace a chance" individual. The 1960s might rectify that by teaching us that we could make the world anew without war within a generation—and better use defense expenditures for pressing social programs hitherto sorely neglected.

For many, the Cold War also demanded an unthinking militaristic mind-set of "them or us." To assert that military history suggested that wars broke out because bad men, in fear or in pride, sought material advantage or status, or because sometimes good but naive men had done too little to deter them, was understandably seen as antithetical to a more enlightened understanding of human nature. "What difference does it make," in the words of the now much-quoted Mahatma Gandhi, "to the dead, the orphans, and the homeless whether the mad destruction is wrought under the name of totalitarianism or the holy name of liberty and democracy?"

It depends. Military history reminds us that those who died on behalf of democratic freedom to stop totalitarian killing were a different sort than totalitarians who died fighting against it to perpetuate killing. The sacrifice of the former meant that generations yet born might have a greater likelihood of opportunity, security, and freedom; the latter fought for a cause that would have increased the suffering of future generations. Most accept that those of the 101st Airborne at the Battle of the Bulge were a different sort from those of the Waffen SS, and that we today would also be different sorts had the latter won there and elsewhere as well.

In addition, the changing nature of the university ensured the decline of the formal discipline of military history. Race, class, and gender studies sought to deal with the anonymous masses of history, not its medaled grandees and deskbound planners. Within this new egalitarian emphasis on campus, it became more palatable to learn of how women struggled against patriarchal oppression, minorities endured white racism, and the poor were deprived of opportunity than to expand on John Keegan's face-of-battle descriptions of the horror of Agincourt, Waterloo, and the Somme for the thousands of nameless who were marshaled to fight there.

Of course, academic careerism and trendiness explain much as well. Military history is ancient; in contrast, the construction of racial identity and the rhetoric of masculinity are relatively new turf that offer new sources, new opportunities, and new exposure for the aspiring academic. An entirely new discipline is as sexy as a very ancient one is not.

So despite the growing frequency of wars across the globe, this academic neglect of the formal study of war has become even more acute today. Military history as a formal academic discipline has atrophied, with very few professorships, journal articles, or degree programs in ~parison with other areas of the humanities. In 2004, Edward M.

Coffman, a retired military history professor who taught at the University of Wisconsin, reviewed the faculties of the top twenty-five history departments, as ranked by *U.S. News and World Report*. He found that of more than one thousand professors, only twenty-one identified war as a specialty. In 2007 the American Historical Association noted that of some 15,487 history faculty in American universities, 1.9 percent were identified as primarily military historians. Military historians, of course, bitterly resent the notion of their own decline. Sometimes they suggest that the data mislead because war is often studied in ways that cannot be quantified, or they insist that three hundred military historians nationwide is not such a depressing figure after all.

Yet even when war does show up on university syllabi, it is so often not quite war as we knew it. The focus instead is frequently on the race, class, and gender of combatants and wartime civilians, and so our attention is turned away from the front to larger questions of ideology and identity. A class on the Civil War might focus almost entirely on the Underground Railroad and Reconstruction, not on the battles at Chancellorsville and Gettysburg. Understanding how heroic but neglected people dealt with oppressions is central to understanding the Civil War and must be welcomed as long overdue, but the conflict that ended chattel slavery is unfathomable without a sense of what Robert E. Lee was trying to accomplish militarily in 1863 against Union forces.

A course on the Second World War might emphasize Japanese internment, Rosie the Riveter, and the horrors of Hiroshima, not necessarily Guadalcanal, Midway, or Normandy. That too is understandable, as all three topics are critical to appreciating how the global war was more than just the action at the front between combatants. That said, victory or defeat was, after all, decided largely by action at the front among soldiers.

A typical survey of the Vietnam War will devote lots of time to the inequities of the draft, media coverage, and the antiwar movement at home, and less mention to the air and artillery barrages at Khe Sanh.

Current courses on Afghanistan and Iraq deal with American geopolitical interests in oil or the post-traumatic stress syndrome of veterans, rather than the heroism of the Marines at Fallujah or the nuts and bolts of the success of General David Petraeus in stifling the radical Islamic insurgency in Baghdad. Note here that in all three examples, contemporary academics wish to impart relevant present-day lessons by focusing on neglected social aspects of America's wars—forgetting that there are indeed rich lessons as well for today's students from learning why Americans landed on and endured Normandy Beach.

In contrast, those who want to study war in the traditional manner, which centers on combatants on the battlefield, face intense academic suspicion, as Margaret Atwood's poem "The Loneliness of the Military Historian" suggests:

Confess: it's my profession
that alarms you.
This is why few people ask me to dinner,
though Lord knows I don't go out of my way to be scary.

"Scary" historians of war must derive perverse pleasure, their critics in the university suspect, from reading about carnage and suffering—as if the oncologist somehow has an odd attraction to cancerous tumors, or the volcanologist perversely enjoys the destructive effects of magma.

Why not channel such interest to figure out instead how to outlaw war forever? society objects, as if it were not a tragic, nearly inevitable aspect of human existence. Hence, the recent surge of the noble-sounding discipline of "conflict resolution," which emphasizes the arts of diplomacy, negotiation, and arbitration strategies in eliminating the need for force altogether and establishing a perpetual peace, even between antagonists of quite different methods, values, and objectives. Admirable peace studies professors surely must not like war; dark and gloomy military historians obviously do.

War and the Popular Culture

T HE UNIVERSITIES' AVERSION to the study of war certainly does not reflect the public's lack of interest in the subject. Students—for both bad and good reasons—love old-fashioned war classes on those rare occasions when they are offered, usually as courses that professors sneak in when the choice of what to teach is left up to them. (I cannot imagine any dean, in today's climate, complaining to a history department chair that a major university's curriculum offered few, if any, classes on the history of war.) I taught a number of such classes at California State University, Fresno, and elsewhere. They would invariably wind up overenrolled, with plenty of students lingering after office hours to offer opinions on battles from Marathon to Lepanto. An absence of student interest does not explain the dearth of formal military history courses.

In short, popular culture displays extraordinary enthusiasm for many things military. There is now a Military History Channel, and Hollywood churns out a steady supply of blockbuster war movies, from *Saving Private Ryan* and *Das Boot* to *Enemy at the Gates* and *300*. Well after the Ken Burns documentary, the explosion of interest in the Civil War continues. Historical reenactment societies stage history's great battles, from the Roman legions' to the Wehrmacht's. Barnes and Noble and Borders bookstores boast well-stocked military history sections, where scores of new titles appear every month. Stephen Ambrose, Rick Atkinson, Max Hastings, John Keegan, James McPherson, David McCullough, and Cornelius Ryan collectively have sold millions of books on war and became public figures at large. A plethora of Web sites obsess over the minutiae of ancient encounters, and popular video games grow ever more realistic in their reconstructions of battles.

The public may feel drawn to military history because it wants to learn about honor and the ultimate sacrifice. Alternatively, some may have a more morbid interest in technology—wanting to know the muzzle velocity of a Tiger Tank's 88mm cannon or the difference between the AK-47 and M16 automatic rifles, for instance—or an innate need to experience violence, if only vicariously. Yet the importance—and challenge—of the academic study of war is to elevate such popular enthusiasm into a more capacious and serious understanding, a discipline in which one seeks answers to such questions as these: Why do wars break out? How do they end? Why do the winners win and the losers lose? How can wars be avoided or their worst effects be contained? Do wars have any utility and sometimes accomplish some good that diplomacy cannot?

The Price of Neglect

A PUBLIC THAT'S illiterate about the conflicts of the past can easily find itself confused during wartime. Without standards of historical comparison, people prove ill-equipped to make informed judgments when the dogs of war are unleashed. Neither U.S. politicians nor most citizens seem to recall the incompetence and terrible decisions that, in December 1777, December 1941, and November 1950, led to massive American casualties and, for a time, public despair. We assume military legends—Ulysses S. Grant, John Pershing, Dwight D. Eisenhower, and George Patton—experienced nothing of the acrimony that our present generals encounter and avoided the costly blunders we have seen made by our own generation of leaders in Afghanistan and Iraq.

Yet Grant was completely surprised at Shiloh, where Union forces were nearly routed on the first day of battle. Neither Eisenhower nor Omar Bradley fully comprehended the early days of the Battle of the Bulge—or, much later, the best way to force back the German salient. Patton repeatedly ordered frontal assaults against Metz that achieved little but high casualties. Such a lack of understanding of the realities of military history invariably leads to impossible demands on soldiers and officers when war breaks out. The Joint Chiefs of Stall had little idea what to do in Korea when the Communists invaded in June 1950.

It is no surprise, then, that today so many seem to think the violence in Iraq is unprecedented in our history. Some have frequently compared the war in Iraq to the Second World War on the strange logic that it has lasted longer than the American involvement from late 1941 to mid-1945. No one seemed to remember that the Philippine Insurrection (1899–1913) lasted, at least unofficially, much longer than either the fighting in Iraq or the Second World War.

The toll of more than four thousand combat deaths in Iraq after some six years of fighting is, of course, a terrible thing. And by 2007 this growing death toll provoked national outrage to the point that the government was considering withdrawal and an admission of defeat in stabilizing the Iraqi democracy. Public acrimony led to controversial responses over everything from up-armored Humvees to increased troop levels. Yet nothing so far in the present Middle East compares with an average month or two of violence in the Second World War.

A previous generation considered the ill-thought-out Okinawa campaign a stunning American victory and prepared to follow it up with an invasion of the Japanese mainland—despite losing three times as many Americans between April and July 1945 as we have lost in Iraq. Many were preventable casualties, due to faulty intelligence, poor generalship, and unimaginative suicidal head-on assaults against Japanese fortified positions. Indeed, Japanese kamikazes killed more Americans off Okinawa in a few weeks than Middle Eastern suicide bombers have in the last thirty years. Cries arose then, as now, that there was no defense against such zealots who were living to die—before a variety of innovative measures in fact nullified most of the airborne threat.

When more than three hundred thousand Chinese troops unexpectedly crossed the Yalu River into North Korea in November and December 1950, surprised American soldiers gave up most of all their hard-won gains of the prior three months and fled over three hundred miles southward—many throwing away their helmets and ammunition to expedite their flight from the supposed "hordes" of zealous Communists. Most in the media wrote off Korea as "lost"—for the second time in six months. Yet within four months, under the magnetic leadership of newly appointed reformist general Matthew Ridgway, American and Allied forces were back on the offensive. In spring 1951 they retook Seoul and recrossed the 38th parallel.

The Utility of Military History

WE SHOULD NOT study military history because it promises cookie-cutter comparisons with the past, or diagnostic wartime formulas, or hopes of salvation in dark times. Germany's 1917 victory over Russia in under three years apparently misled the military autodidact Hitler into thinking that the German army could overrun the Soviets in three or four weeks. After all, his Wehrmacht had brought down historically tougher France in just six weeks in the late spring of 1940. The führer, remember, grasping at historical straws just before his end, felt that his Reich would be saved after the death of Franklin Roosevelt—just as Frederick the Great had been given a reprieve from his anti-Prussian coalition that broke up on news of the sudden death of Empress Elizabeth of Russia.

Similarly, the conquest of the Taliban in eight weeks in 2001, followed by the establishment of a constitutional government within a year in Kabul, did not mean that the similarly easy removal of Saddam Hussein in three weeks in 2003, according to the prior formula, would ensure a working Iraqi democracy within six months. The differences between the countries—cultural, political, geographical, and economic— were too great to guarantee a predictable outcome.

Instead, knowledge of past wars establishes only wide parameters of what we can legitimately expect from new ones. The scale of logistics and the nature of technology changes, but themes, emotions, and rhetoric remain constant over the centuries, and thus generally predictable. Athens's disastrous 415 B.C. expedition against Sicily, the largest democracy in the Greek world, may not prefigure our war in Iraq. (A hypothetical parallel to democratic Athens's preemptive attack on the neutral, distant, far larger, and equally democratic Syracuse in the midst of an ongoing though dormant war with Sparta would be America's dropping its struggle with al-Qaeda to invade India). But the story of the Sicilian calamity and the changing Athenian public reaction to it, as reported and analyzed by the historian Thucydides, do instruct us on how consensual societies can clamor for war—yet soon become disheartened and predicate their support only on the perceived pulse of the battlefield.

Military history teaches us, contrary to popular belief, that wars are not necessarily the most costly of human calamities. The allied coalition lost few lives in getting Saddam out of Kuwait during the Gulf War of 1991, yet doing nothing in Rwanda allowed savage gangs and militias to murder hundreds of thousands with impunity. Bill Clinton stopped a Balkan holocaust through air strikes, without sacrificing American soldiers. His supporters argued, with some merit, that the collateral damage from the NATO bombing of Belgrade resulted in far fewer innocents killed, in such a "terrible arithmetic," than if the Serbian death squads had been allowed to continue their unchecked cleansing of Islamic communities. Hitler, Mao, Pol Pot, and Stalin killed far more off the battlefield than on it. The 1918 Spanish flu epidemic brought down more people than did the First World War. And more Americans—over 3.2 million—lost their lives driving cars over the past 90 years than died in combat in this nation's 230-plus-year history.

What bothers us about wars, though, is not just their occasionally horrific lethality; it's that people like ourselves choose to wage them. Such free will makes conflict seem avoidable—unlike a flu virus, a landslide, or a car wreck—and its toll unduly grievous. The contemporary global community can fathom that hundreds of thousands have been lost to earthquakes, tsunamis, and biblical floods; but given the element of human culpability, it is not so ready to accept that a few thousand have been lost in armed struggles. The earthquake in Bam, Iran, in December 2003 killed well over 25,000 innocents—and was largely ignored by a global media focused on the far-less-lethal ongoing fighting in Iraq.

We remember the 192 Athenians who died at Marathon and the 300 Spartans who fell at Thermopylae, both groups immortalized in Greek literature, but not the tens of thousands of anonymous ancient Greeks who perished when their mud-brick homes collapsed from earthquakes—a natural phenomenon that appears in our ancient sources almost as frequently as does war. Yet no ancient monograph is devoted to the murderous earthquake at Sparta in 464 that decimated the population, taking far more lives than King Xerxes ever did at Thermopylae.

Military history also reminds us that war sometimes has an eerie utility. As British strategist Basil H. Liddell Hart put it, "War is always a matter of doing evil in the hope that good may come of it." I would not agree with Hart's choice of "always." But wars—or the threat of war—at least put an end to American chattel slavery, Nazism, Fascism, Japanese militarism, and Soviet Communism. It is hard to think of any democracy—Afghan, American, Athenian, contemporary German, Iraqi, Italian, Japanese, ancient Theban—that was not an outcome of armed struggle and war.

Military history is just as often the tangential story of an appeasement that fails to head off warmongering as it is of an aggressive chest-thumping that prompts conflict. The destructive military careers of Alexander the Great, Caesar, Napoleon, and Hitler all would have ended earlier had any of their numerous enemies united when the odds favored them, had any listened to a Demosthenes, a Cato the Younger, or a Churchill.

Western air power, despite its clumsiness and the collateral damage that killed perhaps 1,500 Serbian civilians, stopped Slobodan Milošević's reign of terror at little cost to NATO forces—but only after a near decade of inaction and dialogue had made possible the slaughter of tens of thousands in a series of regional Balkan wars. Affluent Western societies understandably have often proved reluctant to use force to prevent greater violence in the future—an acceptance of constant preparedness that philosophers sometimes warn us is called for. "War is an ugly thing, but not the ugliest of things," observed the British philosopher John Stuart Mill. "The decayed and degraded state of moral and patriotic feeling which thinks nothing is worth a war, is worse." Mill, of course, wrote before the battles of Somme and Verdun—and the era of mutually assured destruction.

Indeed, by ignoring military history, those today are naturally liable to interpret war as a result of the failure of communication, of diplomacy—as if aggressors do not know exactly what they are doing. Who, after all, would knowingly start a violent, unnecessary war?

Speaker of the House of Representatives Nancy Pelosi, frustrated by President George W. Bush's supposed intransigence and archaic rhetoric in the so-called war on terror, flew to Syria in April 2007. In rather freelance diplomatic fashion, she was hoping to persuade President Bashar al-Assad to stop funding terror in the Middle East. Perhaps the Speaker assumed that Assad's belligerence resulted from American aloofness (we have no embassy in Damascus and had not recently spoken to the Syrian leader) and from Bush's intransigence—rather than from Assad's interest in destroying democracy in Lebanon and Iraq before such contagious freedom might destroy him. A few months after Pelosi's visit, Israeli jets flattened a partially finished Syrian covert nuclear reactor. Facts on the ground some day will determine which act, the Pelosi visit or the Israeli strike, diminished the chance of Syria's participation in a regional war.

For a generation more familiar with Oprah and Dr. Phil than with the letters of William Tecumseh Sherman and William L. Shirer's *Berlin*

Diary, the problems between states—like those between spouses, friends, and co-workers—ideally, should be discussed by equally civilized and peaceful rivals and solved without resorting to violence. Thus, in a more ideal world, serial apologies for past sins by American presidents to theocratic Iran, dictatorial Russia, socialist Latin American leaders, or postmodern Europe should at least convey that the United States is not unpredictable or occasionally bellicose—and therefore reassure possible belligerents that there will be greater opportunities for lasting peace in the contemporary age.

Yet it is hard to find many wars that have resulted from miscommunications or misunderstandings. Far more often they break out because of malevolent intent and the absence of deterrence, or because a prior war ended without a clear resolution or without settling disagreements—in a manner of Rome's first two wars with Carthage. Again, Margaret Atwood was empirical when she wrote in her poem, "Wars happen because the ones who start them / think they can win."

Hitler did. So did Mussolini and Tojo—and their assumptions were mostly logical, given the relative disarmament of the Western democracies at the time. In the summer of 1990, Saddam Hussein believed, after speaking with an American diplomat, that the territorial integrity of Kuwait was not a concern of the Western governments, at least not to such a degree that would prompt a military response from them.

Osama bin Laden did not attack on September 11 because there was a dearth of American diplomats willing to talk with him in the Hindu Kush. He did not think America denied its Muslim citizens the right to worship freely. He did not think his native Saudi Arabia was impoverished or short of lebensraum. Instead, he recognized that a series of Islamic terrorist assaults against U.S. interests over two decades had met with what he would judge as insignificant reprisals. And he therefore concluded, in rather explicit and public fashion, that the supposedly decadent Westerners would never fight, whatever the provocation—and that if the United States, the "weaker horse," ever should engage, it would withdraw as it had from Mogadishu once images of American killed and wounded blanketed our television screens.

"We also believe our war against the United States is much simpler than our war against the Soviet Union," bin Laden boasted to a journalist in March 1997, "because some of our mujahideen who fought here in Afghanistan also participated in the operations against the Americans in Somalia—and they were surprised at the collapse of the American morale. This convinced us that the Americans are a paper tiger." Over many years bin Laden cited dozens of concocted reasons about why he attacked the United States; the only valid one was that he attacked America because he thought—to paraphrase Margaret Atwood—with good reason, he could get away with it.

The More Wars Change . . .

WITHOUT GUIDANCE FROM the past, it is easier now more than ever to succumb to technological determinism, the idea that science, new weaponry, and globalization have altered the very rules of war. But military history teaches us that our ability to strike a single individual from thirty thousand feet up with a global-positioning-system-guided bomb and a jihadist's ability to have his propaganda beamed to millions in real time do not necessarily transform the conditions that determine who wins and who loses wars. Nor do they alter the thinking that prompts leaders to prompt or forgo wars.

True, the instant communications of the twenty-first century may now compress decision making in ways undreamed of in the past. Contemporary generals must be skilled at giving news conferences that can influence the views of millions worldwide. Yet these are really just new wrinkles on the old creased face of war. The improvised explosive device versus the up-armored Humvee is simply an updated take on the catapult versus the stonewall, or the harquebus versus the mailed knight. The long history of war suggests no static primacy of the defensive or the offensive. No law dictates one sort of weapon system over another, but just temporary advantages gained by particular strategies and technologies that go unanswered for a time by less adept adversaries.

So it is highly doubtful, the study of war again reminds us, that a new weapon will emerge from the Pentagon or anywhere else that will change the very nature of armed conflict—unless some sort of genetic engineering so alters man's brain chemistry that he begins to act in unprecedented ways. We fought the 1991 Gulf War with dazzling, computer-enhanced weaponry. But lost in the technological pizzazz was the basic wisdom that generals and their overseers need to fight wars with political objectives in mind.

In contrast, the result of "defeating" Saddam in four days in 1991 was subsequent wars between 1991 and the present to rid Iraq of the Baathists and their legacy. To conclude wars decisively and achieve prewar aims, the victor must defeat, and often even humiliate militarily, an enemy and force the loser to abandon prewar behavior before offering a magnanimous peace. "Humiliate," here, does not mean to gratuitously insult or ridicule a prostrate enemy but rather to show him that the wages of his unprovoked aggression are the end of his ability to make war on others.

In postmodern war, the word "victory" often appears in such quotation marks as a philosophical construct; it is supposedly mired in complexities and spoken only by the near savage, who insists that our intricate nuclear world is still fathomable in terms of nation-states and conventional armies. But the idea of winning will never disappear. It is an easily definable and timeless military concept of forcing an opponent to cease fighting, to abandon the real or imagined reasons for his bellicosity, and to agree to the conditions set down by those powers demonstrably able to so affect his thinking and behavior. Victory may now require a level of force deemed objectionable by civilized peoples, meaning that some, for justifiable reasons, may be reluctant to pursue it. But victory has not become an ossified concept altogether.

For some reason, no American general or diplomat seemed to understand that crucial point seventeen years ago—or perhaps they felt that United Nations troops had already inflicted an inordinate amount of damage on the Baathist state. The result was that on the cessation of hostilities, Saddam Hussein's supposedly defeated generals used their gunships to butcher Kurds and Shiites while the apparently victorious Americans looked on. And because we never quite understood or achieved the war's proper aim—ensuring that Iraq's dictatorship would not use its petro-wealth to destroy the peace of a globally critical region—we returned to fight a second war of NATO-enforced no-fly zones above Iraq. Then there was a third war to remove Saddam, and then again a fourth war, of counterinsurgency, to protect the fledgling Iraqi democracy.

Military history reminds us of important anomalies and paradoxes—especially the futility of most prewar wisdom. When Sparta invaded Attica in the first spring of the Peloponnesian War (431 B.C.), the historian Thucydides recounts, it expected the Athenians to surrender after a few short seasons of ravaging. But the Athenians had no intention of surrendering or conceding anything—and suffered little until a plague broke out and did more damage than thousands of Spartan ravagers had during five separate invasions. Twenty-seven years later, the maritime Athenians, deemed "lords of the sea," lost the war at sea to Sparta, an insular land power that started the conflict with scarcely a navy.

William Tecumseh Sherman was removed from command in October 1861, and accused of being "crazy," after suggesting that Union forces might need 200,000 troops to clear and hold Kentucky. Given the fact that the North had fielded some 2.5 million soldiers at Civil War's end, Sherman appeared in retrospect to have been clairvoyant. In the heyday of Allied victory in 1918–19, Marshal Ferdinand Foch predicted that the Versailles Treaty guaranteed a war with Germany in two decades: "This is not a peace. It is an armistice for 20 years," he said. Though he was scoffed at by utopians, he was off by only a few months. The 2003 removal of Saddam refuted the doom-and-gloom critics who had predicted thousands of deaths and millions of refugees, just as the subsequent messy six-year reconstruction has not yet ensured the anticipated quiet, stable democracy envisioned by proponents of the removal of the Baathist regime.

Other anomalies can be learned from studying military history, such as the fact that the size of an army does not always guarantee battlefield success: The victors of the landmark battles at Salamis, Issos, Mexico City, and Lepanto were all outnumbered. And war's most savage moments—the Allied summer offensive of 1918, the Russian siege of Berlin in the spring of 1945, the Battle of the Bulge, Hiroshima—often unfold right before hostilities cease. Democratic leaders during war—Winston Churchill, Harry Truman, Richard Nixon, George Bush—often leave office either disgraced or unpopular. Too often we use contemporary wisdom or innate logic to try to make sense of impending conflicts, rather than look to the history of past wars, which are frequently unpredictable and nearly inexplicable.

It would be reassuring to think that the righteousness of a cause, or the bravery of an army, or the nobility of a sacrifice would ensure public support for a war. At times, these reasons have and should. But military history shows that once a conflict begins, the perception of winning becomes far more important to the public. Citizens turn abruptly on any leader deemed culpable for losing. "Public sentiment is everything," wrote Abraham Lincoln. "With public sentiment nothing can fail. Without it nothing can succeed. Consequently, he who moulds public sentiment goes deeper than he who enacts statutes or pronounces decisions."

Lincoln knew that lesson well. Gettysburg and Vicksburg were brilliant Union victories that by summer 1863 had restored Lincoln's previously shaky credibility and strengthened his abolitionist aims. But a year later, after the losses at Wilderness, Spotsylvania, Petersburg, and Cold Harbor—Cold Harbor alone claimed seven thousand Union casualties in a few hours—the public reviled him and might well have been willing to live with a slaveholding Confederate nation next door. Neither Lincoln nor his policies had changed, but the Confederate ability to kill large numbers of Union soldiers had. And had General Sherman not taken Atlanta in spectacular fashion on September 2, 1864 ("Atlanta is ours, and fairly won"), President Lincoln—for all his rhetorical skills, his moral authority, and his strategic insight—would have lost the November election to General George McClellan and his copperhead supporters.

Ultimately, public opinion follows the ups and downs, including the perception of the ups and downs, of the battlefield, since victory excites the most ardent pacifist and defeat silences the most frothing zealot. After the defeat of France, Dunkirk, the losses to the Royal Air Force's Bomber Command, the U-boat rampage, and the fall of Greece, Singapore, and Tobruk, Winston Churchill took the blame for a war that was seemingly lost, until the brilliant prime minister's victories in North Africa, Sicily, and Normandy shortly after.

When the successful military action against Saddam Hussein ended in April 2003, more than 70 percent of the American people backed the invasion of Iraq, with politicians and pundits alike elbowing each other aside to take credit for their prescient support. By 2007, four years of insurgency later, Americans opposed the orphaned war by nearly the same margin. General George S. Patton may have been uncouth, but he wasn't wrong when he bellowed, "Americans love a winner and will not tolerate a loser."

The American public turned on the Iraq War not because of the antiwar oratory of Cindy Sheehan or the cinematographic propaganda of Michael Moore or the lack of nerve gas in Saddam's bunkers, but because it felt that the battlefield news had become uniformly bad and that the price in American lives and treasure for ensuring Iraqi reform had become too dear. The public grew tired of seeing Americans blown up in Humvees each night on television, tired of Iraqis shouting "Death to America," and tired of being told that our blood and treasure was worth "their" freedom. When General David Petraeus promised that a surge of American troops could salvage Iraq, critics pilloried him as "General Betray Us"; when his soldiers did just what he had promised, pundits were suddenly talking of his presidential timber.

General Douglas MacArthur's peers initially laughed at his proposal for a daring landing at Incheon when Americans were about to be pushed off the Korean peninsula far to the south at Pusan. Then the general was deified when he pulled it off and all but won the war— only to be finally demonized for recklessly pursuing the defeated North Koreans far to the north, where rough terrain, freezing temperatures, and hundreds of thousands of Chinese ensured American catastrophe. Few American commentators evaluated MacArthur's strategic sense at various stages in his generalship in Korea; it was instead the perception of whether he was winning or losing that mattered most to the public.

The Morality of Military History

MILITARY HISTORY HAS a moral purpose: educating us about past sacrifices that have secured our present freedom and security. If we know nothing of Shiloh, Belleau Wood, Tarawa, and Chosin, the crosses in our military cemeteries are reduced to just pleasant white markers on lush green lawns. The gaunt faces in the windows of the Veterans Administration hospitals become no different from the faces of those hospitalized because of illness, infirmity, and age. These sacrifices no longer serve as reminders that thousands endured pain and hardship for our right to listen to what we wish and to shop in safety—and that the departed expected future generations, links in this great chain of obligation, to do the same for those not yet born.

The United States was born through war, reunited by war, and saved from destruction by war. No future generation, however comfortable and affluent, can escape that terrible knowledge. Our freedom is not entirely our own; in some sense it is mortgaged from those who paid the ultimate price for its continuance. My own life of security, freedom, opportunity, and relative affluence certainly has been made possible because a grandfather fought and was gassed in the Argonne; an uncle in the Marines died trying to stop Japanese imperialism on Okinawa; a cousin in the Army lost his life at twenty-two trying to stop Hitler in France; and my father in the Army Air Force flew forty times over Japan hoping to end the idea of the expansive Greater East Asia Co-prosperity Sphere. I have spent some time these past decades trying to learn where, how, and why they and their generations fought as they did—and what our own obligations are to acknowledge their sacrifices.

What has changed in our perceptions of war in and outside the university over the more than thirty years since I first studied war in an esoteric dissertation on the ravaging of farms in the classical Greek world? War, like agriculture, certainly has not disappeared, although its superficial face has seemingly changed as much as family farming has been superseded by corporate agribusiness.

Instead, there have been ever more varieties of war, large and small, nearly bloodless and nearly genocidal, insurgencies and conventional conflicts—in Afghanistan, the Balkans, Chechnya, the Congo, East Timor, Grenada, the Falklands, Iran, Iraq, Panama, Pakistan, Rwanda, and other landscapes too numerous to cite. The public interest in reading about these conflicts, whether measured through books sales or television ratings, has seldom been higher. And yet as popular culture, research institutions, and journalists explore conflict as never before, the formal study of military history remains the orphaned child of the college and university, as if we academics could wish away what we fear to be inescapable.

Does that even matter? And if so, what, then, can we do to restore the study of war to its proper place in the life of the American mind? The challenge is not just to reform the graduate schools or the professoriate, though that would help, since the universities offer a collective common learning experience to millions of young Americans who will inherit self-governance in the decades ahead, and may one day decide when, how, and why their children are to fight.

On a deeper level, we need to reexamine the larger forces that have devalued the very idea of military history—of the understanding of war itself. We must question the well-meaning but naive faith that with enough money, education, or good intentions we can change the nature of mankind so that conflict, as if by fiat, becomes a thing of the past. Such entrenched academic thinking if sanctioned by our university elite, may well encourage some to begin wars. In the end, the study of war reminds us that we will never quite evolve into gods but simply remain mere mortals. And that means some will always prefer war to peace; and other men and women, hopefully the more numerous and powerful who have learned from the past, will have a moral obligation to stop them.

Studying War: Where to Start

THE BEST PLACE to begin studying war is with the stories of soldiers themselves. E. B. Sledge's memoir *With the Old Breed: At Peleliu and Okinawa* is nightmarish, but it reminds us that while war often translates to rot, filth, and carnage, it can also be in the service of a noble cause. Elmer Bendiner's tragic retelling of the annihilation of B-17s over Germany, *The Fall of Fortresses: A Personal Account of the Most Daring, and Deadly, American Air Battles of World War II*, is an unrecognized classic.

For a different wartime perspective, that of the generals, Ulysses S. Grant's *Personal Memoirs* is justly celebrated as a model of prose. Yet the nearly contemporaneous *Memoirs of General W. T. Sherman* is far more analytical in its dissection of the human follies and pretensions that lead to war. Likewise, George S. Patton's *War as I Knew It* is not only a compilation of the eccentric general's diary entries but also a candid assessment of human nature itself. Xenophon's *Anabasis*, the story of how the Greek Ten Thousand fought their way out of the Persian Empire, begins the genre of the general's memoir.

Fiction often captures the experience of war as effectively as memoir, beginning with Homer's *Iliad*, in which Achilles confronts the paradox that rewards do not always go to the most deserving in war. The three most famous novels about the futility of conflict are Stephen Crane's *The Red Badge of Courage*, Erich Maria Remarque's *All Quiet on the Western Front*, and Aleksandr Solzhenitsyn's *August 1914*. No work has better insights on the folly of war, however, than Euripides' *Trojan Women* or Thucydides' *History of the Peloponnesian War*.

Although many contemporary critics find it passé to document landmark battles in history, one can find a storehouse of information in *The Fifteen Decisive Battles of the World: From Marathon to Waterloo*, by Edward S. Creasy, and *A Military History of the Western World*, by J. F. C. Fuller. Hans Delbrück's *History of the Art of War* and Russell F. Weigley's *The Age of Battles: The Quest for Decisive Warfare from Breitenfeld to Waterloo* center their sweeping histories on decisive engagements, using battles like Marathon and Waterloo to illustrate larger social, political, and cultural values. A sense of high drama permeates William H. Prescott's *History of the Conquest of Mexico* and *History of the Conquest of Peru*, while tragedy more often characterizes Steven Runciman's spellbinding *The Fall of Constantinople, 1453,* and Donald R. Morris's massive *The Washing of the Spears: A History of the Rise of the Zulu Nation Under Shaka and Its Fall in the Zulu War of 1879.* The most comprehensive and accessible one-volume treatment of history's most destructive war remains Gerhard L. Weinberg's *A World at Arms: A Global History of World War II*.

Relevant histories for our current struggle with Middle East terrorism are Alistair Horne's superb *A Savage War of Peace: Algeria 1954–1962*, Michael B. Oren's *Six Days of War: June 1967 and the Making of the Modern Middle East*, and Mark Bowden's *Black Hawk Down: A Story of Modern War*. While anything John Keegan writes is worth reading, his *The Face of Battle: A Study of Agincourt, Waterloo, and the Somme* remains the most impressive general military history of the last fifty years.

Biography too often winds up ignored in the study of war. Plutarch's lives of Pericles, Alcibiades, Julius Caesar, Pompey, and Alexander the Great established the traditional view of these great captains as men of action, while weighing their record of near-superhuman achievement against their megalomania. Elizabeth Longford's *Wellington* is a classic study of England's greatest soldier. *Lee's Lieutenants: A Study in Command*, by Douglas Southall Freeman, for all its detractors, remains spellbinding.

If "war is the continuation of politics by other means," as Carl von Clausewitz stated, then study of civilian wartime leadership is critical. The classic scholarly account of the proper relationship between the military and its overseers is still Samuel P. Huntington's *The Soldier and the State: The Theory and Politics of Civil-Military Relations*. For a contemporary j'accuse of American military leadership during the Vietnam War, see H. R. McMaster's *Dereliction of Duty: Lyndon Johnson, Robert McNamara, the Joint Chiefs of Staff, and the Lies That Led to Vietnam*.

Eliot A. Cohen's *Supreme Command: Soldiers, Statesmen, and Leadership in Wartime*, purportedly a favorite read of George W. Bush's, argues that successful leaders like Ben-Gurion, Churchill, Clemenceau, and Lincoln kept a tight rein on their generals and never confused officers' esoteric military expertise with either political sense or strategic resolution.

In *The Mask of Command*, Keegan examines the military competence of Alexander the Great, Wellington, Grant, and Hitler, and comes down on the side of the two who fought under consensual government. In *The Soul of Battle: From Ancient Times to the Present Day, How Three Great Liberators Vanquished Tyranny*, I took that argument further and suggested that three of history's most audacious generals—Epaminondas, Sherman, and Patton—were also keen political thinkers, with strategic insight into what made their democratic armies so formidable.

How politicians lose wars is also of interest. See especially Ian Kershaw's biography *Hitler, 1936–1945: Nemesis*. Mark Moyar's first volume of a proposed two-volume reexamination of Vietnam, *Triumph Forsaken: The Vietnam War, 1954–1965*, is akin to reading Euripides' tales of self-inflicted woe and missed chances. Alistair Horne's *To Lose a Battle: France 1940* is also noteworthy.

Few historians can weave military narrative into the contemporary political and cultural landscape. James M. McPherson does in *Battle Cry of Freedom: The Civil War Era*, a volume that ushered in the most recent renaissance of Civil War history. Barbara W. Tuchman's *The Guns of August* describes the first month of the First World War in riveting but excruciatingly sad detail. Two volumes by David McCullough, *Truman* and *1776*, give fascinating inside accounts of the political will necessary to continue wars amid domestic depression and bad news from the front. So does Martin Gilbert's *Winston S. Churchill: Finest Hour, 1939–1941*. Donald Kagan's *On the Origins of War and the Preservation of Peace* warns against the dangers of appeasement, especially the lethal combination of tough rhetoric and little military preparedness, in a survey of wars from ancient Greece to the Cuban missile crisis. Robert Kagan's *Dangerous Nation* reminds Americans that their idealism (if not self-righteousness) is nothing new, but rather it helps explain more than two centuries of intervention—wise or ill-considered—abroad.

Any survey on military history should conclude with more abstract lessons about war. *Principles of War* by Clausewitz remains the cornerstone of the science. Niccolò Machiavelli's *The Art of War* blends realism with classical military detail. Two indispensable works, *War: Ends and Means*, by Angelo Codevilla and Paul Seabury, and *Makers of Modern Strategy: From Machiavelli to the Nuclear Age*, edited by Peter Paret, provide refreshingly honest accounts of the timeless rules and nature of war.

CHAPTER 2

Classical Lessons and Post-9/11 Wars

Peace—the Parenthesis[*]

IN ADVOCATING MORE military history in the university, I first confess to an odd bias about the proper foundation for studying wars of the past. I was a Greek and Latin language professor for twenty-one years. After eight prior years of undergraduate and graduate training in the classical languages, I was indoctrinated to believe that starting at the beginning of anything is always good advice. Consequently, reading a historian of wars such as Edward Gibbon, W. H. Prescott, or Stephen Ambrose can make more sense once one has read what Thucydides or Xenophon wrote about conflict centuries earlier.

---

[*] Portions of this article are based on a transcript of a public lecture delivered ex tempore at Hillsdale College, two months after the September 11 attacks, parts of which in turn were later published in the February 2002 issue of *Imprimis*.

Classical explanations and accounts of war take us far from the politics, noise, and fashions of the contemporary world. They allow us to think in terms of larger blueprints, abstract ideas, and age-old paradoxes about war in general that in turn elevate and enrich the modern debate about particular recent wars.

The study of classics—the literature and history of Greece and Rome—can also offer moral insight in the post–September 11 world, as well as a superb grounding in art, literature, history, and language. By the same token, the absence of familiarity with the foundations of Western culture in part may explain many of the odder and more emotional reactions to recent wars that we have seen expressed in popular American culture.

War in classical antiquity—and for most of the past 2,500 years of Western civilization—was seen as a tragedy. But it was one that was innate to the human condition, recurrent, and terribly familiar. Conflict was seen as a time of human plague. The historian Herodotus said of war that fathers bury sons rather than sons bury fathers. Killing humans over disagreements should not happen among civilized people, but predictably will occur.

War, the poet Hesiod lamented, was "a curse from Zeus"— something of near divine parentage that mere men must endure. Of course, in a preindustrial world without nuclear weapons or conventional machines of mass annihilation, the Greeks' seasonal war making did not necessarily translate into modern notions of battlefield genocide.

More died in the siege of Stalingrad than probably perished on all sides in all theaters during the twenty-seven-year-long Peloponnesian War. The Greeks could fight seasonally for decades on end (the Athenians on average waged war three out of four years in the fifth century) and called their bloodletting, in the words of the philosopher Heraclitus, "the father, the king of us all." We moderns, after three seasons of Hiroshimas, or four or five battles of Kursk, would know war instead as "the end of us all."

Nevertheless, the preindustrial Greeks are to be listened to when they warn that conflict will always break out—and very frequently so—because we are human, and thus not always rational. Even the utopian Plato agreed: "War is always existing by nature between every Greek city-state," one of the characters in his *Laws* matter-of-factly remarks. How galling to us moderns that Plato, of all people, once called peace—not war—the real "parenthesis" in human affairs. Similar tragic acknowledgments can be found in the works of the historians Polybius, Thucydides, and Xenophon, who assumed wars among the city-states would always be breaking out somewhere. The Greeks, of course, wrote down unenforceable rules of war making on stone, proclaimed fifty-year truces and alliances, produced plays about the insanity of war, looked at times to strongmen to enforce a perpetual peace among squabbling city-states—and all the while usually kept right on fighting.

Warfare could be terrifying—"a thing of fear," as the poet Pindar summed it up—and senseless, but not therein unnatural or in every instance wholly evil. The Greeks would remind us that evil genocide in Darfur did not stop because of elevated global oratory or the impassioned pleas of nongovernment organizations. It continued because the Western public (whose militaries alone had the resources to stop the ethnic and religious bloodletting) did not wish to endanger hundreds of its pilots and tank commanders in a far distant land to save hundreds of thousands who could be more easily forgotten by switching the television channel—and thereby ensure that their children would not be trying to stop a Rwanda a year from Africa to Latin America.

While for the Greeks all wars presented only bad and worse choices, and were tragic in the sense of destroying the lives of young men who in peacetime had no intrinsic reason to murder one another, conflicts could still be judged as more or less good or evil depending on their causes, the nature of the fighting, and the ultimate costs and results. Some wars then were deemed better than others, and it was not all that difficult to make the necessary distinctions.

The Greek defense against the overwhelming Persian attack in 480 B.C., in the eyes of the playwright Aeschylus (who chose as his epitaph mention of his service at the battle of Marathon, not his masterpiece the *Orestia*), was "glorious." Yet the theme of Thucydides' history of the internecine Peloponnesian War was self-destructive folly, and sometimes senseless butchery from Corcyra and Melos to the revolting mess at the Assinarus River in Sicily. Likewise, language of freedom and liberty is associated with the Greeks' naval victory at "divine" Salamis, but not so with the slaughter at the Battle of Gaugamela—Alexander the Great's destruction of the Persian army in Mesopotamia that wrecked Darius III's empire and replaced eastern despots with Macedonian autocrats.

The Greeks tried to define plenty of just wars while establishing the basis of both legitimate and unfair war making. Those who employed missile weapons—arrows, catapults, sling bullets—at times were felt to be either uncivilized or unfair for killing randomly from afar. Others who killed Greeks rather than *barbaroi* (foreigners) were deemed murderous (Alexander the Great probably killed more Greeks in Asia than Xerxes ever did in Greece). Some who conscripted slaves, or hired mercenaries, or butchered civilians were relegated to the status of near murderers rather than war makers. Nonetheless, wars of all sorts went on and were judged as bad or good by their perceived conduct, results, morality, and utility.

Indeed, in matters military, the greatest difference between our own world and the ancients' is this present-day notion that war itself—rather than particular wars per se—must be inherently evil. Aristophanes' *Peace* is a screed against the Peloponnesian War, as is Euripides' *Trojan Wars*. Neither playwright, however, would have objected to the Persian wars and the "Marathon men" who fought them.

The Greek mind had little in common with either "The Sermon on the Mount" or Immanuel Kant's idealistic guidelines for how to ensure perpetual peace between nations. Few Greeks trusted in expressed good intentions or shared notions of brotherhood to keep the peace—although writers as diverse as Plato and Isocrates outlined ways in which the city-states could curtail internecine conflicts. What usually stopped wars from breaking out for a season or two was more likely the notion of an enemy's larger phalanx, bigger fleet, or higher ramparts, which created some sort of perceived deterrence—and with it the impression that any ensuing war for an adventurous state could be too unprofitable, costly, or drawn out.

I emphasize "more likely," since hubris, miscalculation, greed, misplaced honor, and an array of other emotions often led *strategoi* (generals)—like Alcibiades, Pelopidas, Cleombrotus, and Pyrrhus—to roll the knucklebones when reason advised otherwise. Disastrous wars were common because-less-than-competent leaders often misjudged the likely outcome or felt the costs would be worth the desired benefits.

The Roots of War

WHILE WAR WAS innate to the ancients, and its morality more often defined by particular circumstances, fighting was not necessarily justified by prior exploitation or legitimate grievance. Fifth-century Greek historians largely introduced into the Greek vocabulary the binary *prophasis and aitia*—the pretext and the real cause—often to emphasize that what military leaders claimed were understandable provocations were not, or at least not believable ones.

Nor did aggression have to arise from poverty or inequality. States, like people, the historian Thucydides demonstrates, could be envious—and unpredictable and aggressive without apparent reason. Theban oligarchs in spring 431 had no ostensible reason to attack tiny, neighboring Plataea at a time of peace, a provocation that helped to start the Peloponnesian War. I should say "no logical reason," inasmuch as the Thebans entertained a long-standing hatred of the isolated Athenian ally, a belief that they could take the city at little cost, and, in the fashion of Mussolini in 1940, a hunch that they should stake a quick claim to spoils since a powerful ally (in this case, Sparta) was about to prevail in a far larger war.

If megalomaniacal assailants like King Xerxes of Persia could sense there was little cost to enacting their agendas, they surely would persist in seemingly unnecessary aggression until convinced otherwise. Again, I emphasize words like "unnecessary," in the sense that a Persia of more than twenty million had no real reason to absorb tiny, materially poor, relatively underpopulated, and distant Greece—other than to make an example of an upstart people who had humiliated the Great King during the earlier Ionian War and the disastrous Persian landing at Marathon. It certainly did not need more lebensraum for the Persian peoples.

The Athenians in Thucydides' history claim that they acquired and kept their empire largely out of "honor, fear, and self-interest"—more than any rational calculation of profit making or the acquisition of valuable foreign territory. Sparta preempted and attacked Athens in spring 431, Thucydides says, because of a "fear" of growing Athenian power— and apparently without a desire to annex Attic farmland, or a detailed plan to confiscate the rich Athenian silver mines at Laurium, or a plot to raise bullion by enslaving and selling off the population.

We of the present do not quite understand this idea of simple "fear" causing wars. Indeed, we of the post-Marxist age of materialism, wedded as we are to the supremacy of reason, often search in vain for a magic oil field or strategic concession that would explain the inexplicable wars in Vietnam or Iraq. We insist that there is a shady pipeline that must "really" account for the intervention in an otherwise impoverished Afghanistan, and that some sort of offshore treasure near the Falklands Islands made the desolate atoll of some strategic or economic value to the British navy. In truth, Greek catalysts like anger, pride, honor, fear, and perceived self-interest often better explain the desire to wage such conflicts, big and small. When asked why one-billion-person-strong China would consider invading much smaller but similarly communist Vietnam—and to the benefit the genocidal regime in Cambodia—Chinese paramount leader Deng Xiaoping matter-of-factly said to his American hosts in January 1979, "It's time to smack the bottom of unruly little children."

According to the canons of such self-acknowledged Hellenic cynicism, the Japanese and Germans in 1941 were not starving, or short of land, or unable to acquire strategic materials on the open market. Hitler received far more strategic materials through purchase from a compliant Stalin before June 1941 than he was ever as able to extract through violence from an occupied and bitterly hostile Soviet Union. Rather they were proud peoples, stung by past slights and perceived grievances, who wanted deference from those whom they deemed inferior and weak. Both countries, after all, now seem nonthreatening, and content enough with larger populations and smaller territories in peacetime than they did in 1939 on the eve of the Second World War. Both have consensual governments as well, which apparently understand the bitter wages of attacking neighbors in wars of aggrandizement.

Does China, with trillions of dollars in foreign reserves, really need the few extra million Taiwanese as a part of its citizenry, or the rather mountainous terrain of the island of Formosa to add to its agricultural potential? Is the allure of blackmail money—or fear and a distorted sense of honor—what makes a bankrupt North Korea, whose people are often reduced to eating grass, serially threaten to annihilate South Korea, Japan, and the United States with expensive nuclear missiles? Much of the justification for the Russian invasion of Georgia in August 2008 transcended worry about Russian speakers in Georgian-controlled South Ossetia and instead seemed to focus on Russian "dignity" and "honor"—especially the sense of exasperation that a once tiny republic of the former Soviet Union now had the audacity to consider itself an equal to, and rival of, Mother Russia herself.

To a student of classics who gleans from a Thucydides or a Plato some notion of war, the present crisis that grew out of September 11, I think, might be interpreted in reductive fashion: The United States, being a strong and wealthy society, and with unrivaled global influence, invites envy. The success of its restless culture of freedom, constitutional democracy, self-critique, secular rationalism, and open markets provokes the resentment of both weaker and less-secure theocracy and autocracy alike. Who we are, how we think, and the manner in which we act, ipsis factis, are considered obnoxious, dangerous, and unpalatable to many fundamentalist Muslims around the globe, who endure manifestations of our power and influence daily, from DVDs in Kabul to text-messaging ads in Yemen.

In emblematic fashion, America stands as a protector of the global system of market capitalism and constitutional government, and of the often reckless modernist culture that threatens so much of tribal and indigenous custom and protocols. That we are therefore often to be hated by the authoritarian, the statist, and the tribalist—and periodically to be challenged by those who want to diminish our power, riches, or influence—is regrettable but nevertheless conceded.

Diplomacy and humility abroad can encourage friendship. And such good manners and deference are vital in improving our global image and lessening tensions. Yet, unfortunately, pleasantness and magnanimity are not always enough to ensure good relations with rival states and interest groups that look more to what we represent than to what we might say or do on any one occasion.

It is a tragedy of the human character that a Hugo Chávez of Venezuela and a Mahmoud Ahmadinejad of Iran say they predicate relations with the United States on notions of goodwill, deference, mutual respect, past apologies, and benevolent diplomacy, even as they tend to interpret our outreach as weakness and treat deterrence with respect. Having a hundred-thousand-ton nuclear carrier in the Persian Gulf, more lethal than the combined militaries of most nations, probably does more to keep the calm in that region than sending a presidential video to the Iranian theocracy, no matter how artfully phrased.

Perhaps the strangest barometer of the rise of the therapeutic mindset is the growing prevalence of old-style piracy. Criminals based in Somalia, using just a few thugs equipped with small arms, routinely hijack and commandeer large oceangoing merchant vessels. Such overt piracy is a symptom of the erosion of international order—not merely in the example of the perpetually failed state of Somalia, but more so by the general global indifference to the piratical encroachment into the world's vital sea lanes. Likewise, the classical antidote of going ashore to demolish the homes, bases, and dockyards of the miscreants—known from the days of Pompey's successful efforts against Cilician piracy— seems to be taboo to Western navies in the age after the American "Black Hawk Down" humiliation in Mogadishu. Instead of a military response, we are likely to run a cost-benefit analysis of the piratical threat, to consider the mitigating circumstances of poverty and oppression that turn erstwhile fishermen into seaborne criminals, and to blame the victim in wondering out loud why seagoing vessels don't carry their own security teams or why such profit-mongering shipping companies must skirt so close to hostile coasts.

The same confusion is often true of hostage-taking, whether the takeover of the American embassy in Tehran in 1979 or the Iranians' capture of fifteen British sailors in disputed waters off Iraq in 2007. Kidnapping regimes are no longer issued ultimatums to release captured diplomatic or military personnel—or else. Instead, the detained are paraded on international television and coerced into signing affidavits admitting guilt or testifying to superb treatment from their captors—while state propaganda airs accusations of espionage, coupled with threats of trials and worse.

Western powers place a peaceful resolution of the crisis and a safe return of the hostages above all other considerations—even when they privately accept that public signs of humiliation and weakness will lead to further aggression and more hostage-taking. The ultimate result of the Iranian hostages crises was not better understanding between the Iranian theocracy and Western powers; rather it was increased Iranian terrorism after 1980, and, in the British case, an arrest in 2009 of British embassy employees on charges of espionage and treason.

Yet who in the affluent West would have wished for an American president in November 1979 to issue a warning along the following lines: "If the Iranian government does not release the fifty-two captured, and illegally detained, American diplomatic and military personnel, the United States will soon begin a systematic aerial destruction of all of its military assets. If the personnel are harmed in any way, the government of the United States will further ensure the destruction of the Iranian power grid, refinery capacity, and general infrastructure"?

On hearing such an ultimatum, the Iranians might well have released the hostages, might well have abandoned further provocative acts, and might well have so lost public face that their credibility in the radical Islamic world would have eroded and their position among Iranians at home weakened. But all those "mights" would have been predicated on two unfortunate possibilities: an American president would have had to gamble that fifty-two Americans could be executed and that in retaliation he would have had to endure Western criticism for using the vast power of the United States inordinately against a weaker, third world "revolutionary" regime.

The past failure of both Democratic and Republican administrations to strike back hard and consistently at Osama bin Laden's early terrorist acts against Americans abroad did not bring us respect for our forbearance, much less sympathy from jihadists for our reason and faith in the powers of adjudication. Rather, human nature being what it is, our restraint tragically invited ever more contempt and audacity on al-Qaeda's part—and more dead as the bitter wages of a certain self-righteous morality and tragic miscalculation.

Sparta crossed the Athenian border in spring 431 B.C. despite the majestic Parthenon, and without any concern that Aristophanes, Euripides, Pericles, Socrates, and Sophocles walked the streets of Athens. Its army advanced northward because King Archidamus calculated *rightly* that Athens had never before by force stopped a Spartan army from entering Attica, and certainly gave no indication of doing much about it this time—and *wrongly* that the ensuing Spartan attack on Attica's agriculture would either end the war or lead ipso facto to Sparta's own strategic advantage.

The enemies of free speech and intolerance—German Nazis, Italian Fascists, Japanese militarists, Stalinist Communists, and Islamic fundamentalists—have just as often attacked us (when they calculated that it could be done without major losses) for what we are or will do, rather than for what we have done, inasmuch as they innately detest freedom and the liberality that is its twin as notions lethal to their own authoritarianism. Again, call the Greeks reductionist, but they did not believe the Achmaenid king Xerxes had legitimate prior grievances arising from their participation in the Ionian revolt, or that he even saw Greece as integral to the administration of the vast Persian Empire, or that he concluded that Hellenic olive trees were essential to the Persian economy. Instead, they saw the conflict as one of an arrogant autocracy, in hubristic fashion, seeking the destruction of its far smaller and free neighbor, for understandable reasons of pride, vengeance, and honor.

Only our moral response—not our status as belligerents per se—determines whether contemporary war is just. If we butcher a weaker opponent for no good cause, as the Athenians did neutral Melians, or if we gratuitously torture our captives, then our battle against the enemy becomes tainted, and we may well not win it. But if we are trying to preserve freedom against its tyrannical aggressors, like the Greeks at Thermopylae and the G.I.s on the beaches of Normandy, then war may be the right and indeed often the only thing we can do to preserve our larger culture. The point is not that moral purpose always ensures victory. Nor should we assume even that the ethical high ground justifies the resort to arms. We can only console ourselves that democracies by their very nature usually cannot win the wars they choose to enter when their own free people are not convinced that their collective efforts have any humane foundation.

Caught in such a tragedy—where efforts at reason and humanity had fallen on the deaf ears of killers, and where those who professed a desire to avoid war had to inflict more costs on the enemy than they themselves suffered—the United States apparently wished to send a message to its enemies after September 11, 2001. Their defeat and loss of face in the Middle East would serve as a harsh teacher—for at least a generation or two—that it is wrong and very dangerous to kill thousands of civilians in the streets of our cities. For all the domestic acrimony over Afghanistan and Iraq, for all the anger at the United States in the Middle East, for all the blunders committed in the conduct of recent wars, the terrorists for nine years have not been able to repeat the events of September 11—and the popularity of bin Laden and his tactic of suicide bombing has plummeted rather than risen in polls taken throughout the Middle East.

Indeed, a 2005 Pew Global Attitudes Project poll of Middle East public opinion suggested the paradoxical: Bin Laden's and suicide bombers' popularity alike showed a marked decline. Yet attitudes toward George W. Bush's America in many Middle East countries remained negative. Or were such results all that divergent? Many in the proverbial Arab street of public opinion might well have despised America for warring against radical Islam, but despised bin Laden and his acolytes even more for losing—and bringing disrepute and misery to all in their midst. Public opinion in Germany by winter 1945 was neither favorable to the America that had ignited German cities nor to the führer whose policies had both earned Allied attacks and failed to thwart them.

It would be unwise, years after 9/11, to suggest that the so-called war on terror is over—to the extent of outlawing the provocative phrase "war on terror" altogether and replacing it with the kinder, gentler "overseas contingency operations" taken in response to "man-made ca-tastrophes." Or to insist that we are really not at war with anything so remote as "Islamic extremism," even as we continue to target jihadists on the Afghan border, deploy in Iraq, and execute suspected terrorists through drone missile attacks. In such a contradictory scenario, Ameri-cans would do plenty enough to incite enemies to continue their belli-cosity, while at the same time assuring them that we no longer see the struggle in quite such existential terms—a strange passive-aggressive medley that could ensure a dangerous climate indeed.

In sum, study of the Greeks in this sophisticated age of high tech-nology, and deeply embedded sociology and psychology, is a reminder that wars—and the emotions and mentalities that fuel them—are trag-ically eternal. And the wisdom of the past concerning how conflict begins, is deterred, and ends is more critical now than ever, however unwelcome such lessons may be.

The Anticlassical View

DESPITE THE ADMONITIONS of Edward Gibbon, it was not the advent of Christianity and "turn the other cheek" that ended the classically tragic view of the constant need for military pre-paredness to ensure the peace, and so brought down Rome. Well before hundreds of thousands crossed the Rhine and the Danube, Christian philosophers and theologians developed the doctrine of "just war," hav-ing realized that passivity and nonresistance could translate into sui-cide. Nor did the Enlightenment and its god Reason end the insanity of war—inasmuch as most philosophers soon conceded that global courts, broadly educated publics, and enlightened elites could not dissuade Frederick the Great, Napoleon, or Wellington from the use of armed force.

More likely, it was the horror of the two world wars—Verdun, the Somme, Hiroshima—that led to our own era's questioning of the tragic view of war. Such a reaction was certainly true and understandable in a Europe that nearly destroyed itself in two devastating industrial wars within a roughly twenty-year period. Yet out of such numbing losses we may have missed the lesson of the horror. The calamity of sixty million dead was not just because nationalistic Westerners went to war in an industrial age of weaponry of mass annihilation, but rather because the liberal democracies were unwilling to make moderate sacrifices to keep the peace well before 1914 and 1939—when real resolve could have stopped Prussian militarism, and then Nazism without millions of the blameless perishing.

Increased affluence, entertainment, and leisure of the past half century in the relatively quiet and postmodern West also has made it easier to pronounce a war of any type as retrograde and of no utility. It is, after all, hard to convince young people to forgo the beach for basic training. It was one thing for parents to send one of five children from the backbreaking work on the farm to serve "over there" in France in 1917, but quite another for today's parents to risk losing an only child—the beneficiary of braces, SAT camps, and college-prep courses—on patrol in the Hindu Kush, adjudicating tribal feuds among the pro- and anti-Taliban factions.

The legacy of the British and French Enlightenments, of course, gave birth to popular social sciences that sought to "prove" to us that war was always irrationally evil and therefore surely preventable. Indeed, during the 1986 International Year of Peace, a global commission of well-meaning academics (See "The Seville Statement on Violence, Spain, 1986") concluded that war was innately unnatural and humans themselves unwarlike—the implication being that war itself was entirely preventable with proper thinking and global preventive medicine.

Seeing war as "Zeus's curse" in this age of our greatest learning and wealth—and pride—is to descend into savagery, when our more educated trust that prayer, talk, or money can prevent conflict. But if Westerners deem themselves too smart, too moral, or too soft to stop aggressors in this complex nuclear age, then—as Socrates and Aristotle alike remind us—they can indeed become real accomplices to evil through inaction. We forget sometimes that the philosopher Socrates— citizen of the world, critic of the disastrous Sicilian Expedition, foe of frenzied mob rule, skeptic of fashionable sophistic relativism—fought as an Athenian hoplite (a heavily armored and armed infantryman) in battle at least three times on the eve of and during the Peloponnesian War, at Potidaea, Delium, and Amphipolis, all on foreign soil in campaigns deemed "imperial" by the enemies of Athens and "optional" by many Athenians themselves. The playwright Sophocles commanded triremes against the revolting tributary island of Samos (pitted against the Samian Eleatic philosopher Melissus) and served late in life as a commissioner in the wake of the catastrophe at Sicily—roughly the ancient equivalent of Philip Roth being appointed to a 9/11 commission or a middle-age Rick Warren being assigned to the 101st Airborne.

Western Exceptionalism

WAS SUCH ABSTRACT speculation about war unique in the early West? Was it uncommon elsewhere to debate wars and to ratify decisions to go to war by majority votes, as was true in the polis and Roman Republic? In large part, yes. Classics should remind us that the Greeks and Romans were anti-Mediterranean cultures, in the sense of being at odds with much of the political heritages of Persia, Egypt, and Phoenicia. While Hellenism was influenced—and enriched—at times by Near Eastern, Egyptian, and Persian art, literature, religion, and architecture, its faith in consensual government and free markets was unique. Greek and Latin words for "democracy," "republic," "city-state," "constitution," "freedom," "liberty," and "free speech" have no philological equivalents in other ancient languages of the Mediterranean (and few in the contemporary languages of the non-West as well).

We have forgotten this ancient truth of Western exceptionalism. In the age of cultural studies, Americans have often made the common mistake of assuming that our enemies are simply different from us, rather than far different from us. Perhaps the hesitancy to appreciate the singularity of the West results from guilt over European colonialism. Or it may be laudable humility. Or it could reflect an ignorance of cultures in general and Western civilization in particular. Or we may live in an interconnected global age where all narratives are complementary rather than antithetical—no one "truth" having any absolute currency.

Nonetheless, Athens was a democracy; Sidon was not. Farmers owned property in Greece, voted, and formed the militia of the polis; that was not the case in Persia and Egypt. King Xerxes sat on a throne at Salamis and recorded the names of brave and cowardly subjects battling in the straits below. His counterparts, the Spartan general Eurybiades and the Athenian admiral Themistocles, debated the wisdom of fighting at Salamis, led their own sailors into the sea battle, and heard their rowers shout cries of "freedom" as they rammed the enemy.

Thucydides was able to criticize his mother polis, Greece; Persian clerks who recorded Darius's res gestae on the walls of Persepolis could not. Such differences were not merely perceived but also real and critical, for they affected the manner in which people conducted their daily lives—whether they lived in fear or in safety, in want or in security.

If the public today would study the classics, they might rediscover the origins of their culture—and in doing so learn that we are not even remotely culturally akin to the Taliban or the Saudis, but are, in fact, profoundly different in the manner we craft our government, treat our women, earn our living, and set the parameters of our religion. The point is not that bias, oppression, and subjugation didn't exist during the Dark Ages, Middle Ages, or the ages of overseas conquest and imperialism in the West. But rather there was also the blueprint of personal freedom and consensual government that survived the darkest moments of Western civilization and resprouted at the most unexpected moments in classical Athens, Republican Rome, Renaissance Italy, and Enlightenment Western Europe. It is unwise perhaps in triumphalist fashion to chest-thump in our globally connected world about past Western achievement; but in a transnational war of ideas, it is equally unwise to deny the radically different cultural attitudes toward religiously driven suicide bombing and the relationship between religion and secular government.

Modern cultural anthropology, social linguistics, cross-cultural geography, and sociology in theory could contextualize the Taliban's desecration of the graves of the infidel, destruction of ancient statues of Buddha, clitoridectomies of infants, torture of the accused, murder of the untried, and hounding out of the non-Islamic as something not quite "evil." Yet a world run according to the dictates of the Taliban or its supporters, like the satrapy that Xerxes envisioned for a conquered Greece, would mean no cultural anthropology at all. There would be no real voting and scant protection from arbitrary and coercive government. Instead, theocracy, censorship, and brutality would invade every facet of daily life. Such were the stakes at Salamis. And so too is the contest with the radical worldview of Islamic fundamentalists, who are as akin to ancient absolutists as Westerners are to the Greeks.

Such neglect of one's own past can, I think, ultimately weaken a powerful society such as ours that must project confidence, power, humanity, and hope to those less fortunate abroad. The new species of often upscale and Internet-savvy terrorist hates America for a variety of complex reasons. (Ayman al-Zawahiri has listed dozens of grievances for al-Qaeda's war on America that commenced on September 11,

2001—among them, our lack of campaign finance reform and the supposed presence of Jewish women in the holy city of Mecca.)

The terrorist despises, of course, his own attraction toward our ease and liberality, explaining why some of the most virulent Islamists are precisely those, who chose to be educated in the West. Mohammed Atta, the tactician of 9/11, and Khalid Sheik Mohammed, its strategic architect, studied at the Technical University of Hamburg and North Carolina Agricultural and Technical State University, respectively.

The terrorist recognizes that our freedom and affluence spur on his appetites more than Islam can repress them. But just as important, the al-Qaedist perceives that there is a sort of aristocratic guilt within a minority of influential Americans, who are too often ashamed of, or apologetic about, their culture—or have lost any ability even to articulate it. And in this hesitance, our enemies sense not merely our unfamiliarity with our own foundations but perhaps weakness as well—and at times wrongly believe that their assaults on America are simply an extreme reification of what many inside the West, in the abstract, do not like about the West.

Apologizing for our past sins may reveal character and for a time lessen anti-Americanism abroad, but if it is done without acknowledging that the sins of America are the sins of mankind, and that our remedies are so often exceptional, then it only earns transitory applause—and a more lasting contempt that we ourselves do not believe in the values we profess.

To sum up the Hellenic view of war and the lessons we may learn from the Greeks: Conflict is omnipresent. It is often irrational in nature and more a result of strong emotions than of material need. Preparedness is more of a deterrent than is empathy, understanding, or demonstrations of good intentions. War is sometimes won or lost as much by confidence in one's culture as by military assets themselves. It is often not a question of a choice between good or bad but between bad or worse. And war should be judged moral or immoral by the circumstances in which it breaks out and the conditions under which it is waged, rather than by the fact that violence is employed.

We may not like such a bitter message, but recent events have shown the empirical Greeks of the past are still more relevant to present warfare than what passes for much of the wisdom of the contemporary age.

CHAPTER 3

Raw, Relevant History:
From the 300 Spartans to the
History of Thucydides

*Why the Public Is Still Fascinated by the Wars of the Past**

Real, Imagined, or Stylized Spartans?

WHILE, AS I argued in chapter 2, the study of classics can serve as a valuable foundation of military history, Greek and Latin nevertheless are difficult languages that require hundreds of hours of study, apart from the study of military history itself. And even in translation, the themes and ideas found in classical history, philosophy, and literature are not easy to digest. To study the Persian Wars is to enter a distant world of esoteric place names, unpronounceable nomenclature, and weird protocols presented by Herodotus or Plutarch as if they were second nature to the reader. A knowledge of the arcane

---

* Parts of this essay derived from an article in the April 18, 1998 *New York Times* and an article in the March 7, 2007 *City Journal* (online edition).

disciplines of archaeology, art history, epigraphy, numismatics, and philology is often necessary just to make one's way through the written record of the Greek past.

The result is that classics is often a mandarin discipline, as poorly understood by the general public as it is fascinating. Almost any effort, then, that brings the Greeks to the general public—vulgarization, as it is sometimes called—is to be welcomed. The public's innate interest in our classical heritage sometimes manifests itself in surprising ways.

For example, on a Monday night in Hollywood in March 2007, I attended an advance screening of the Zack Snyder–directed movie *300*, starring Gerard Butler as Leonidas, king of Sparta. The prior October, I had watched an earlier uncut working version of the film at the request of screenwriter Kurt Johnstad, who drove a copy down to my farm. I liked much of what I saw, and then wrote an introduction to the book accompanying the film. So I am not a disinterested observer.

I thought from the outset that many critics would dislike the final version of the film, for a variety of reasons, even aside from its unabashed defense of the Spartan notion of martial excellence and the superiority of a free Hellas over a subservient Persian East. At earlier prescreenings, for example, some Europeans apparently bristled at such Western chauvinism, came to the strange conclusion that the movie was an allegory for George Bush and Iraq, and were appalled that the Persians appeared both bent on conquest and less valiant, man for man, than the free Spartans guarding the pass. Quite understandably, the autocratic, authoritarian contemporary Iranian government subsequently railed that the film depicted ancient Persia as an autocratic authoritarian government.

The movie is certainly violent, with beheadings and lopped limbs aplenty. The characters are one-dimensional, with little complexity and no self-doubt or evolution in their thinking. And, of course, *300* does not claim to be the true story of the battle at Thermopylae but rather an adaptation from a comic book that is itself an adaptation from secondary books and films about the battle. While there are plenty of direct quotations from the accounts of Plutarch and Herodotus, we are nevertheless a long way from the last stand of the Spartans, Thespians, and Thebans in the late summer of 480 B.C. If you wish to learn the story of what actually happened at Thermopylae, this movie won't necessarily help you do it.

But the impressionism of *300* is oddly Hellenic in spirit; the buff bare chests of the Spartans holding the pass are reminiscent of the "heroic nudity" of stylized warriors on Attic black- and red-figure vase paintings. Even in its surrealism—an ahistorical rhinoceros, futuristic odd-shaped swords, and an effeminate, Mr. Clean–esque Xerxes (Rodrigo Santoro), who gets his ear flicked by a Spartan spear cast—it is not all that different from some of Euripides' wilder dramatic adaptations, like his tragedy *Helen* or *Iphigeneia at Taurus*, in their strange deviation from the mythological party line of the Homeric epics.

Like the highly formalist Attic tragedy—with its set length, three actors, music, iambic and choral meters, and so forth—*300* consciously abandons any claims of realist portrayal. The film's actors may not seem believable, but remember that ancient Greek actors wore masks. Men played women's roles. They chanted in lyric meters, broken up by choral hymns. The audience understood that dramatists reworked common myths to meet current tastes and to offer commentary on the human experience in stylized drama.

Again, *300* does not claim to follow exactly ancient accounts of the battle of Thermopylae in 480 B.C. Instead, it is an impressionistic take on a graphic novel by Frank Miller, intended first to entertain and shock, and second to instruct. Indeed, at the real battle King Xerxes was bearded and sat on a throne high above the fighting; he wasn't, as in the movie, bald and sexually ambiguous, and he didn't prance around the killing field. And neither the traitor Ephialtes nor the Spartan overseers, the Ephors, were grotesquely deformed.

When the Greeks were surrounded on the battle's last day, there were seven hundred Thespians and another four hundred Thebans who fought alongside the three hundred Spartans under King Leonidas. But these non-Spartans are scarcely prominent in the movie. All that said, the main story line mostly conveys the general truth of Thermopylae. A small contingent of Greeks at Thermopylae (which translates to "the hot gates") really did block the enormous Persian army for three days before being betrayed. The defenders, as they are portrayed in the history of Herodotus and canonized in lyric poetry, claimed their fight was for the survival of a free people against subjugation by the Persian Empire.

Many of the film's corniest lines—such as the Spartan dare "Come and take them," when ordered by the Persians to hand over their weapons, and the Spartans' flippant reply, "Then we will fight in the shade," when warned that the cloud of Persian arrows will blot out the sun—are literal translations from ancient Greek accounts by Herodotus and Plutarch.

The warriors of *300* look like comic book heroes because they are based on Miller's drawings, which emphasize bare torsos, futuristic swords, and staged fight scenes. In other words, director Zack Snyder tells the story not in the fashion of the mostly failed attempts to recapture the ancient world in costume dramas, such as *Troy* and *Alexander*, but in the surreal manner of a comic book or video game. Overt suspension of belief at the outset relieves the viewer from wondering whether the usual British-accented actors playing Greeks are all that close to their ancient counterparts.

The movie also demonstrates surprising affinity with Herodotus in two other areas. First, it captures the martial ethos of the Spartan state, the notion that the sum total of a man's life, the ultimate arbiter of all success or failure, is how well he fought on the battlefield, especially when it becomes clear at last that bravery cannot prevent defeat.

Second, the Greeks, if we can believe Simonides, Aeschylus, and Herodotus, saw Thermopylae as a "clash of civilizations" that set Eastern centralism and collective serfdom against the idea of the free citizen of an autonomous polis. The ancient morality tale emphasized that a haughty imperious Xerxes was punished by the gods for trying, in hubristic fashion, to subjugate self-reliant and rather pious Greeks, whose creed was moderation, not superciliousness. That Hellenic-centric view comes through in the movie, especially in the fine performances of Butler and Lena Headey (who plays Leonidas's wife, Gorgo). If the Spartans seem too cocky and self-assured in their belief that they are the more effective warriors of a superior culture, blame Herodotus, not necessarily Zack Snyder or the influence of cardboard comic heroes like Superman and Batman. The cinematography, acting, and computer-generated special effects are often quite stunning. The Spartans' mood of defiance is chilling, especially when we remember that their gallant last stand ended in the greatest defeat in the history of Greek city-states— until Alexander ended their freedom 140 years later, at Chaironeia.

Some reviewers argue that the film's graphic violence is gratuitous and at times revolting. But Thermopylae was no picnic. Almost all the Spartans and Thespians were killed, along with several hundred from other Greek contingents. Some of the film's most graphic killing—such as Persians being pushed over the cliff into the sea—derives also from the text of Herodotus. And the filmmakers omitted the mutilation of King Leonidas, whose head Xerxes ordered impaled on a stake.

Some have suggested that *300* is juvenile in its black-and-white plot and character depiction—and glorification—of free Greeks versus imperious Persians. Yet that good-bad contrast comes not entirely from Snyder or Miller, but again is based on accounts from the Greeks themselves, who saw their own society as antithetical to the monarchy of imperial Persia.

True, 2,500 years ago, almost every society in the ancient Mediterranean world had slaves. And all relegated women to a relatively inferior position. Sparta turned the entire region of Messenia into a dependent serf state. But in the Greek polis alone, there were elected governments, ranging from the constitutional oligarchy at Sparta to much broader-based voting in states like Athens and Thespiae.

Most important, only in Greece was there a constant tradition of unfettered expression and self-criticism. Aristophanes, Sophocles, and Plato questioned the subordinate position of women. Alcidamas lamented the notion of slavery. Such openness was found nowhere else in the ancient Mediterranean world. That freedom of expression explains why we rightly consider the ancient Greeks as the founders of our present Western civilization—and as millions of moviegoers seemed to sense, far more like us than the ancient enemy who ultimately failed to conquer them. In the end, *300* went on to earn nearly five hundred million dollars in global box-office receipts, making it among the top one hundred grossing films of all time—a testament not only to its comic book splashy violence and video game imagery but also to an action-packed retelling of an ancient tale in which free men prevailed over their far more numerous oppressors.

Thucydides for Everyone

POPULAR INTEREST IN the Greeks at war occurs at a more serious level as well. As a teacher of classics for some twenty-one years in the Central Valley of California, I was often surprised that the ancient Greek historian Thucydides was among the most popular authors I assigned to undergraduates, the vast majority of whose parents had not attended college. "An Athenian, who wrote the history of the war between the Peloponnesians and the Athenians"—with those words of introduction, the disgraced Athenian admiral matter-of-factly opens *The History of the Peloponnesian War*, his monumental, though unfinished, narrative of the twenty-seven-year war (431–404 B.C.) between Athens and Sparta that left the Athenian empire and the entire culture of the Greek city-state in ruins.

Because he had lived through and participated in the events he described, Thucydides had an advantage over later historians, who have had to dig through unreliable records and consult secondary sources about the war. But even as he set down his record of contemporary events, Thucydides was eyeing posterity. His work, he boasted, was "not an essay to win applause of the moment, but a possession for all time."

If his contemporaries failed to appreciate his true genius, perhaps people like ourselves would fathom it two and a half millennia in the future. And so we do. Studying how a seafaring democratic Athens fought an insular oligarchy like Sparta teaches us a lot about current world crises and the fickleness of public opinion. Thucydides knew nothing about conflict-resolution theory, God's will, or the United Nations, but he could declare for all time that people—as the Athenians did to acquire and preserve their empire—go to war for reasons of "honor, fear and self-interest." Period.

Thousands of paperback translations of Thucydides are sold each year, bearing out his extraordinary boast. But if his book, like other great works, is timeless, it is also very difficult, in places even obscure. A page of Thucydides takes as long to read as five of Tom Clancy. Thucydides doesn't dispense easy virtues and won't do a thing to get you into heaven. And his disturbing ideas turn every modern bromide on its head.

So it's surprising that so many people read him at all—and in surprising places. There's no reason to think a book by an ancient Greek would interest students at the California State University campus in Fresno, home to the wayward Bulldogs basketball team—once coached by the much maligned Jerry Tarkanian.

To generalize, most students are the children of farmworkers and the working poor from places like Bakersfield and Tulare. They are neither privileged nor well prepared for college. Their reference points come from television, not ballet, computer camp, or prep school. Many have never been outside the Central Valley—Thucydides' Athens might as well be Athens, Georgia. Students here confuse Cleon, the Athenian demagogue, with a warrior race in *Star Trek* and think the Spartans are a rival San Jose football team, not dour foot soldiers from the Peloponnese.

At Stanford, where I did graduate work, Thucydides was an entirely different historian from the one I came to know in Fresno. The Thucydides of the graduate seminar is often now Michel Foucault, Jacques Derrida, and Hayden White all rolled into one. His book is the subject of many pages of jargon in which, for example, Pericles' funeral oration is discussed as a dry rhetorical exercise that reflects subjective, not absolute, "truth," or that can serve as a valuable "construction" that reveals the gender, class, and ethnic biases of Thucydides himself.

I prefer the analysis of the text offered by a Fresno State student I taught in a night class. "Sure, he might have lied a little," he said. "Who doesn't? And what do you expect? Thucydides with a tape recorder?"

Scholars and graduate students talk grandly of Thucydides "the realist," whose bleak assessment of human nature was a valuable antithesis to romanticism. But this remote, literary language takes us far from the actual Thucydides, a hardheaded admiral whose judgments derive from firsthand experience and profound career disappointment. As a working mother at Fresno put it, "Thucydides might like Carter better, but he'd want Reagan dealing with the Russians." Another student, an immigrant, agreed: "Be trusting with someone else's life—not mine."

Students in Fresno come to savor Thucydides as the disgraced commander too late to save the Athenian outpost at Amphipolis. In time they soak up the street fighting at Plataea, where the women and slaves "yelled from the houses and threw stones and tiles," and root for the blood-hungry Athenians at the slaughter near Delium, who in their fury "fell into confusion in surrounding the enemy and mistook and killed each other."

"I bet he killed a few himself to write like that," observed one student, tattooed and scarred, in a humanities class. "It gets crazy like that in a free-for-all," another added. When we discussed the slaughter of the Athenians on Sicily, which brought a pathetic end to the greatest generation of the greatest Greek city in its greatest age, one student urged me on: "Check it out. Don't be afraid. Read it to us out aloud." So I did:

The Peloponnesians also came down and butchered them, especially those in the water, which was thus immediately spoiled, but which they went on drinking just the same, mud and all, bloody as it was, most fighting to have it.

If we're to keep the ideas of ancient Greece alive, we must first rekindle the Hellenic spirit, for the two are inseparable. That spirit, though it may already be lost in the Ivy League, thrives here among students working at Burger King and among night-school returnees, who, once hooked on Thucydides' blood and guts, then—but only then—begin to appreciate the power of his thought.

Students working off their tuition in places like Fresno, of course, don't need the university to tell them how unique their own lives are and how richly diverse their past experiences are. But they welcome a tough guy like Thucydides, who shows how their brutal experiences are universal, even banal, and thus explicable through abstract canons that exist "for all time." He is a storyteller first, an obtuse philosopher a distant second.

In an age like ours, in which setbacks and disappointments are often dealt without acceptance of the tragic nature of our existence, Thucydides' honesty comes as a welcome touch of realism. With him there is no "feeling your pain," no pretense of cheap compassion, and no easy apologies for what we are and what we have done. His description of the horrific plague at Athens is both scientific and gruesome, as he chronicles the social chaos in the manner of a physician reviewing symptoms, formulating a diagnosis, and offering a bleak cultural prognosis. His noble hero Pericles, Thucydides reminds us soon after his description of the plague, will die from the disease as well—ironic since the old man's own inspired plan of withdrawing the population inside the walls of Athens will ensure the subsequent squalor that births the epidemic. Thucydides offers students of all races and classes the reassurance that, as humans, in many respects we are all more alike than we think. And in so doing, he offers wisdom about the present, but relief from it as well.

In central California, students naturally assume that Thucydides wrote his history from what he saw and did rather than from what he read, that he became a historian only because he could no longer be a warrior—that he was a man more like themselves than like their professors.

In Thucydides there is a soul every bit as powerful as his ideas. What has nearly killed classical learning is not too little but rather too much scholarly information, at the expense of unbridled enthusiasm about the unscholarly Greeks. In our eleventh hour of classics, we can often learn the most about Thucydides from those who still remain very much Thucydidean in their own lives.

PART II

Writing About War

CHAPTER 4

Thalatta! Thalatta!

*The timeless attraction of Xenophon**

Xenophon was no Thucydides. He clearly lacked the latter's ability to offer universal human truths from the often mundane events of the Peloponnesian War and subsequent city-state conflicts. But Xenophon (ca. 430–454) traveled, fought, wrote, and hobnobbed more than almost any other Greek of his age. He also had a multi-faceted ability to relate such a rich life through the art of storytelling—and nowhere better than in his gripping tale of thousands of Greek mercenaries abandoned and trapped in hostile Persia.

In spring 401 B.C., amid the detritus of the recently ended twenty-seven-year-long war between Athens and Sparta, about thirteen thousand

---

* I have expanded here on reviews that appeared in the October 2005 issue of the *New Criterion* of *The Long March: Xenophon and the Ten Thousand*, edited by Robin Lane Fox (New Haven, CT: Yale University Press, 2004), and *"The Sea! The Sea!": The Shout of the Ten Thousand in the Modern Imagination*, by Tim Rood (London: Duckworth, 2004).

Greek mercenary soldiers marched eastward in the pay of the Persian prince and would-be usurper of the throne at Persepolis, Cyrus the Younger. The Greeks weren't quite sure where they were ultimately headed. And as out-of-work veterans happy to receive gold for the use of their spears, most of them at first didn't seem to care—even if it was unlikely that they were simply hired, as told, to put down some quarreling among insurrectionist Persian satraps.

Instead, the so-called Ten Thousand—the majority of whom were from the Peloponnese—put their trust in their Spartan drillmasters, chiefly the brutish paymaster Clearchus, and kept pressing ahead. Most wanted money, and many were inured to military adventure after long experience fighting for all sides in the Peloponnesian War. Indeed, this ancient Wild Bunch figured that any one of them in a fair fight could lick ten Persians, and there were lots of coins to be made and little to fear. Most had been nursed on stories of the Greek victories at Marathon and Plataea, and rightly figured that in such numbers they could do pretty much as they pleased in Asia.

Not too long after starting out from Sardis, the Ten Thousand discovered that Cyrus really meant to use them to depose his brother King Artaxerxes II, and wrest away kingship of the vast Persian Empire. No matter—money was still money, and Cyrus, always a reliable friend to Greeks, could deliver on promises of even more. By September 401, after a leisurely six-month march, Cyrus's invading army ended up on the Euphrates at the plain of Cunaxa, not far from present-day Baghdad, where they finally ran into the much larger forces of the king. Cunaxa soon proved why these clumsy, heavily armed, and querulous Greek foot soldiers were worth bringing along on a 1,500-mile trek from the Aegean.

The Greek spearmen easily broke Artaxerxes' far larger but variegated forces, had only one wounded in the bargain, and, at the moment of their victory, figured they were going to be rich beyond comprehension. But then catastrophe struck, as a rash Cyrus—posted on the other side of the army from the Greeks—wildly rushed out at the sight of his panicking brother, was swarmed, and perished.

Not long after, both former friends and old enemies, now united into the royal Persian army under King Artaxerxes, turned in unison on the mercenaries. What followed—unlike later disastrous retreats in the Western collective memory, such as Romans slaughtered after Crassus's disaster at nearby Carrhae or Napoleon's apocalyptic flight from czarist Russia—was a gallant nine-month trek over some 1,500 miles northward to the Black Sea, and then west along its shore toward European Byzantium. Somehow, the Ten Thousand, through snow, ice, ambush, and famine, saved three quarters of their force and proved to be folk far more resolute and innovative than mere hired thugs. Indeed, their organization, egalitarianism, and consensual decision making more resembled a "moving polis" of free citizens and voters than a mercenary army, and explained in large part how they were able to either outsmart or outfight an array of enemies.

We know all this because in his old age, Xenophon the Athenian—the prolific author of histories, biography, and how-to manuals—wrote a comprehensive memoir of his own youthful role, thirty-something years earlier, in saving the Greek army. Although he employed the optimistic title *Anabasis* (the first-leg "march up" into the interior of Iraq), in fact, Xenophon's account really gets going only after the Greeks were dry-gulched at Cunaxa. So the core of the work is really a katabasis, detailing the heroic slog through the cold and snows of upper Iraq, Kurdistan, and Armenia to the safety of the Black Sea, ending with a parabasis, along the southern coast of the sea back toward Byzantium and Europe.

Classicists used to be fascinated with the *Anabasis*. The adventure proved an instructive primer for subsequent Greek generals, from the Spartan king Agesilaos to Alexander the Great, who prepped their armies for their own later, successful invasions of Persia. And whatever the brutish nature of the combatants, how the Ten Thousand survived—voting on critical decisions, assigning work by committee, creating new weapons and tactics—seemed to be a testament to Hellenic genius and innovation itself, and were felt to be antithetical to the authoritarianism of their imperial Persian opponents.

———

THE LATE TWENTIETH century has not been so kind to either Xenophon or his march up country. The past few decades especially have seen an understandable resurgence in the study of Thucydides and Herodotus, brilliant authors of histories that also far better meet modern postmodern and anthropological tastes. Despite his philosophical pretensions, Xenophon does not stack up as such a seminal thinker, as one who could employ his narrative of warring Greeks for higher purposes. You seem to get only what you see in the *Anabasis*—and it is not quite a monumental war between Athens and Sparta (unlike his *Hellenica*, which takes up and completes Thucydides' incomplete narrative) or the salvation of Greece from Eastern autocracy, much less Thucydidean insight on the interplay between culture and man's nature.

Xenophon's Greek, also, is straightforward, lacking long antitheses and elaborate subordination. The speeches serve the events at hand and are not used as larger explications of human nature. The narrative of the *Anabasis* moves along in predictable chronological fashion. For all those reasons the work is often the first prose text assigned to second-year Greek students—which has only seemed to cement the author's reputation for pedestrian thinking and facile expression without much grammatical complexity.

The arrival of the politically correct age was no help. The very notion that thousands of greedy Greek male killers would invade eastern peoples, bent on plunder and profit, was bad enough. But when a Westerner chronicled the entire fiasco, informed by Eurocentric prejudices about effete Persians and duplicitous Armenians, there was even less romance in survival over terrible odds. In our skeptical age, recollections referring to the author in the third person, whether Xenophon's or

Caesar's, naturally earn charges of self-serving fabrication or at least conceit. And so much of what has been written in the past two decades about the *Anabasis* uses Xenophon as a locus classicus to take off on Western triumphalism, male supremacy, and colonialism.

Perhaps September 11, and the subsequent toppling of the Taliban and Saddam Hussein, reignited some interest in this otherwise obscure tale of Western adventurism come to naught—even if bin Laden did not include Xenophon and company with the Crusades and the Reconquista in his litany of still-unpunished Western sins. In any case, in March 2003, the heavily armed Americans trudged up the Tigris-Euphrates corridor, not far from sites like Cunaxa (and Alexander's later master-piece battle at Gaugamela), in relatively small numbers, intent on top-pling a despot, and otherwise supremely confident, despite their relative ignorance of what they were getting into.

Robin Lane Fox, best known for an engaging biography of Alexander the Great, organized a symposium on the *Anabasis* in Octo-ber and November 2001 at Oxford University. Yale University Press published the subsequent twelve essays in 2004 under the somewhat confusing title *The Long March*—while the trek was long, it little re-sembled Mao's more famous escape.

It should be admitted at the outset that there is little chance non-classicists will read *The Long March*. Besides the fact that few Americans now know who Xenophon was, the essay titles range from "Sex, Gen-der and the Other in Xenophon's *Anabasis*" (by Fox) to "You Can't Go Home Again: Displacement and Identity in Xenophon's *Anabasis*" (by John Ma), and they reflect the university seminar rather than the inter-est of the general readers. Yet, compared with most such collections in the contemporary academic genre, *The Long March* turns out to be an engaging read.

Thomas Braun, in "Xenophon's Dangerous Liaisons," gives a nice portrait of both the Spartan mercenary warlord Clearchus and the Persian prince Cyrus. But the charm of his essay, aside from his constant references to having studied classics with the greats (like Tony Andrewes and Russell Meiggs), is how it politely strips away the sometimes warm and fuzzy Xenophonean veneer from the tyrannical Clearchus and the would-be fratricide Cyrus—and from Xenophon himself, who, after all, went to kill others largely in pursuit of profit. They were not nation-builders, nor imperialists, but rather simply contractors, like their modern counterparts working for a private company like Blackwater that provides veteran mercenaries for various tasks in the Middle East for a set price. That they were not Persian grandees in the hire of a despotic Artaxerxes does not quite make them Hellenic liberators either.

In "Xenophon's Ten Thousand as a Fighting Force," Michael Whitby explains how the march offers a valuable prognosis of an evolving Greek warfare to come. While hoplite crashes no longer constituted the main arena of war, phalanxes of heavy infantry still could change an entire theater—if generals were wise enough to incorporate light-armed cavalry and archers into a multifaceted army without worrying about the social connotation or past tradition that often hampered military efficacy.

The Ten Thousand, then, really were a precursor to Alexander, who crushed his enemies at four set-piece battles with phalangites, but who also got to those battlefields only through the use of almost every other type of troops imaginable. One of the great stories of ancient military history was the divorce of infantry organization, tactics, and weaponry in the fourth-century B.C. from the original agrarian moral landscape of its birth. That evolution saw small farmers of the phalanx in heavy bronze panoplies give way to hired phalangites with eighteen-feet-long pikes. Somewhere in between lie the hired hoplites of the Ten Thousand, who ventured into exotic terrain against untraditional enemies, requiring changes in organization, armament, and tactics.

James Roy, in "The Ambitions of a Mercenary," reminds us that most of the Ten Thousand were Peloponnesians, and then, again, mostly

Arcadian hoplites. Neither rich nor poor, they were probably recruited from hardscrabble farming families on the rocky plateaus of Arcadia, who went east not so much to escape poverty as to find wealth in good wages and booty that might earn them, like Xenophon himself, a nice retirement estate back in rural Greece. Xenophon, like Wellington in India, came home from Asia a relatively rich man. The Ten Thousand may now seem like romantic explorers, but almost all of them went east for money, either in wages from Cyrus or in booty from Artaxerxes—or both.

TIM ROOD, WHO contributes an essay to the Fox volume on the speeches in the *Anabasis* and the resurgence of Panhellenism, offers in a new book almost everything that we might have wished—and perhaps far more besides—about just two immortal words, "The Sea! The Sea!" (*thalatta, thalatta*), that famous chorus of exultation that Xenophon's men hollered after catching a glimpse of the Black Sea. The survivors were almost done in after their harrowing winter escape from Iraq. From atop Mount Theches, near Trapezus, they caught unexpected sight of the coast far below, which meant salvation and a return to civilization among the Hellenic communities along the southern shore.

Rood exhaustively traces how the refrain came to symbolize both a universal sigh of relief after an impossible ordeal survived and, more specifically, became a theme in almost every European adventure story of survival in the East. Because so many Edwardians and Victorians, in addition to American and continental elites, had been nursed on the *Anabasis* as part of their obligatory Latin and Greek childhood education, it was no surprise that the adventure story stayed with them for life, whether they evoked it at the desk or out in the wilds of the British Empire.

And what a gallery of illustrious men (and women) Xenophon's march has inspired, from fiction writers and poets like Daniel Defoe,

Louis MacNeice, and Mary Shelley, to the real men of action like the Norwegian adventurers of the Arctic, T. E. Lawrence, and the desperate at Dunkirk. Novels and stories were titled "Thalatta," and "O, You Xenophon!" The painter Benjamin Robert Haydon's *Xenophon*—a re-creation of the shouters from the heights of Mount Theches—was for a time inspiration for the Philhellenic romantics of early-nineteenth-century London.

Of course, Rood acknowledges that, more recently, the image of Xenophon's story has devolved from that of confident Western triumpha-lism to the postmodern angst of ending up where you don't belong and so deserve what you get. But the sheer richness of his examples—and the wide variety of both leftists and imperialists who were inspired by the *Anabasis*—reflects the timeless power of human ordeal and triumph.

After Rood's (often mind-boggling) catalog of Xenophonisms, one wonders: If Thucydides and Tacitus were the superior ancient his-torians, why is it that the ripples of the *Anabasis* proved far broader over some 2,500 years of Western creative experience?

The answer is that for all the brutality of the Ten Thousand, Alexander at the Indus, or Hernan Cortés burning his ships at Vera Cruz, Xenophon, along with Arrian and Bernal Díaz, captures a de-sire for something big, something heroic against all odds—however dark the heart—in all of us.

CHAPTER 5

The Old Breed

The brilliant but harrowing narrative of E. B. Sledge*

Until the millennium arrives and countries cease trying to en-
slave others, it will be necessary to accept one's responsibilities
and to be willing to make sacrifices for one's country—as my
comrades did. As the troops used to say, "If the country is good
enough to live in, it's good enough to fight for." With privilege
goes responsibility.

So E. B. sledge ends his memoir of the horrors of the Marines' fighting in late 1944 and spring 1945 against the imperial Japanese on
Peleliu and Okinawa. Like Xenophon, Sledge, even at a young age, was
a reflective man—a writer and a warrior, who went East and endured

---

* I have updated and adapted this chapter from an introduction I wrote for a new edition of
E. B. Sledge's classic memoir, *With the Old Breed: At Peleliu and Okinawa* (New York: Random
House, paperback, 2007).

unimaginable suffering against enemies as brutal as they were different from those his early in life in the American South. We should recall these concluding thoughts in his memoir about patriotic duty because *With the Old Breed* has now achieved the status of a military classic—in part on the perception of Sledge's blanket condemnation of the brutality and senselessness of war itself.

Although there are horrors aplenty in the graphic accounts of the First Marine Division's ordeal in these two invasions in the Pacific, Sledge's message is still not so darkly condemnatory. The real power of his memoir is not just found in his melancholy. Even in his frequent despair over the depravity seen everywhere around him, there is an overriding sense of tragedy: Until human nature itself changes, reluctant men such as E. B. Sledge will be asked to do things that civilization should not otherwise ask of its own—but must if it is to survive barbarity.

Sledge, a previously unknown retired professor, late in life published his first book, which was originally drawn from contemporary notes taken during battle and intended only as a private memoir for his family. Yet within two decades of publication that draft became acknowledged as the finest literary account to emerge about the Pacific war.

Despite the still-growing acclaim given to *With the Old Breed*—first published in 1981 by the Presidio Press of Novato, California—the death of Sledge at seventy-seven, in March 2001, garnered little national attention. After his retirement, Sledge, the master memoirist of the Second World War, had remained a mostly private person who rarely entered the public arena.

Who, in fact, was Eugene Bondurant Sledge? Even with his perfect Marine name, E. B. Sledge might have seemed an unlikely combat veteran. Born to a prominent local physician in Mobile, Alabama, the articulate, slight, and shy Sledge spent only a year at Marion Military Institute and then enrolled at the Georgia Institute of Technology—before choosing instead to leave the officers' training program there to enlist in late 1943 in the U.S. Marine Corps as a private. This early intimate and ambiguous experience with officer training, together with the subsequent decision to serve with the enlisted corps, colors much of the narrative of *With the Old Breed*. Sledge repeatedly takes stock of officers, and both the worst and best men in the corps prove to be its second lieutenants and captains.

After the defeat of Japan, Sledge served in the American occupying force in China; his account of that tour was published posthumously as *China Marine*. Sledge later remarked that he found the return to civilian life difficult after Peleliu and Okinawa, as did many veterans of island fighting in the Pacific who could not "comprehend people who griped because America wasn't perfect, or their coffee wasn't hot enough, or they had to stand in line and wait for a train or bus." Yet Sledge adjusted well enough to graduate in 1949 with a B.S. degree. By 1960 he had completed his Ph.D. in zoology and settled on an academic career; at thirty-nine he joined the University of Montevallo, where he taught microbiology and ornithology until his retirement.

His scholarly expertise and precision of thought and language, gained from nearly thirty years as a teacher and scientist, perhaps explain much of the force of *With the Old Breed*. The narrative is systematic and peppered with wide-ranging empirical observations of his new surroundings—and Thucydidean philosophical shrugs about the incongruity of it all: "There the Okinawans had tilled their soil with ancient and crude farming methods; but the war had come, bringing with it the latest and most refined technology for killing. It seemed so insane, and I realized that the war was like some sort of disease afflicting man."

The look back at the savagery of Peleliu and Okinawa—based on old battle notes he had once kept on slips of paper in his copy of the New Testament—is presented with the care of a clinician. Sledge's language is modest; there is no bombast. The resulting autopsy of battle is eerie, almost dreamlike. Dispassionate understatement accentuates rather than sanitizes the barbarity. Seemingly random observations prompt abstract philosophical summations—in between descriptions of abject savagery. Sledge describes a dead Japanese medical corpsman torn apart by American shelling thusly: "The corpsman was on his back, his abdominal cavity laid bare. I stared in horror, shocked at the glistening viscera bespecked with fine coral dust. This can't have been a human being, I agonized. It looked more like the guts of one of the many rabbits or squirrels I had cleaned on hunting trips as a boy. I felt sick as I stared at the corpses."

We readers are dumbfounded by the first few pages—how can such a decent man have endured such an inferno, emerged apparently whole, and now decades later bring us back to these awful islands to write so logically about such abject horrors? On the eve of the invasion of Peleliu, the ever-curious Sledge matter-of-factly asks an intelligent-looking but doomed Marine what he plans to do after the war, and then he describes the reply, "'I want to be a brain surgeon. The human brain is an incredible thing; it fascinates me,' he replied. But he didn't survive Peleliu to realize his ambition."

The Pacific ground theater of the Second World War from Guadalcanal to Okinawa that nearly consumed Sledge, as it did thousands of American youths, was no bad dream, but a nightmare unlike any other fighting in the nation's wartime history. It was an existential struggle of annihilation. And the killing was fueled by political, cultural, and racial odium in which no quarter was asked or given: "A brutish, primitive hatred," Sledge reminds us decades later, "as characteristic of the horror of war in the Pacific as the palm trees and the islands."

The sheer distances across the seas, the formidable size of the imperial Japanese fleet, and the priority of the United States in defeating Nazi Germany, all meant that the odds, at least at first, were often with the enemy. In particular theaters the Japanese had advantages over the Americans in numbers, choice of terrain, and even supply. We now might underestimate the wartime technology of imperial Japan, forgetting that it was often as good as, or even superior to, American munitions. On both islands Sledge writes in detail of the singular Japanese mortars and artillery that wheeled out, fired, and then withdrew in safety behind heavy steel doors. Especially feared was "a 320-mm spigot-mortar unit equipped to fire a 675-pound shell. Americans first encountered this awesome weapon on Iwo Jima."

As Sledge relates, the heat, rugged coral peaks, and incessant warm rain of the exotic Pacific islands, so unlike the European theater, were as foreign to Americans as the debilitating tropical diseases. Land crabs and ubiquitous jungle rot ate away leather and canvas—and flesh. "It was gruesome," Sledge the biologist writes of Peleliu, "to see the stages of decay proceed from just killed to bloated to maggot-infested rotting to partially exposed bones—like some biological clock marking the inexorable passage of time." He adds of the stench, "At every breath one inhaled hot, humid air heavy with countless repulsive odors."

The awfulness was not just that the fanatical nature of the Japanese resistance meant that America's Depression-era draftees were usually forced to kill rather than wound or capture their enemy. Rather, there grew a certain dread or even bewilderment among young draftees about the nature of an ideology that could fuel such elemental hatred of the Americans. On news of the Japanese surrender after Hiroshima and Nagasaki, the veteran Sledge remained puzzled: "We thought the Japanese would never surrender. Many refused to believe it. Sitting in stunned silence, we remembered our dead. So many dead. So many maimed. So many bright futures consigned to the ashes of the past."

E. B. Sledge's story begins with his training as a Marine in Company K, Third Battalion, Fifth Marine Regiment, First Marine Division. The memoir centers on two nightmarish island battles that ultimately ruined the division. The first was at Peleliu, Operation Stalemate II (September 15–November 25, 1944), where in ten weeks of horrific fighting some 8,769 Americans were killed, wounded, or missing. About 11,000 Japanese perished—nearly the entire enemy garrison on the island. Controversy raged about whether General Douglas MacArthur really needed the capture of the Japanese garrison on Peleliu to ensure a safe right flank on his way to the Philippines—and still rages about the wisdom of storming many of the Pacific islands.

Yet such arguments over strategic necessity count less to Sledge. His concern is instead with the survival of his 235 comrades in Company K, which suffered 150 killed, wounded, or missing. And so there is little acrimony over the retrospective folly of taking on Peleliu. Sledge's resignation might be best summed up as something like, "The enemy held the island; we took it; they lost, and we moved on."

Operation Iceberg (April 1, 1945–July 2, 1945), launched the next year to capture Okinawa, was far worse. Indeed it was the most nightmarish American experience of the entire Pacific war—with more than 50,000 American casualties, including some 12,500 soldiers and sailors killed, and the greatest number of combat fatigue cases ever recorded in a single American battle.

My namesake, Victor Hanson, of the Sixth Marine Division, Twenty-ninth Regiment, was killed near the Shuri Line in the last assault on the heights, a few hours before its capture on May 19, 1945. His letters, and those of his commanding officer notifying our family of his death, make poignant reading—including the account of his final moments on Sugar Loaf Hill. I continue to wear the ring that was taken off his finger after his death, and mailed to me by his fellow surviving Marines in 2002, some fifty-eight years later. Indeed, the very name Okinawa has haunted the Hanson family, as it had Sledge's and thousands of other American households, for a half century hence. For decades in the United States no one really knew—or no one wished to know—what really went on at Okinawa.

In fact, neither of Sledge's two battles, despite their ferocity and the brutal eventual American victories—being in obscure, distant places and in the so-called second theater—garnered the public attention of Normandy Beach or the Battle of the Bulge. In the case of Okinawa, the savagery was overshadowed, first by the April 12 death of Franklin

Roosevelt and the May 8 German surrender in Europe, and later by the dropping of the atomic bombs on Hiroshima and Nagasaki (August 6 and 9), just over five weeks after the island was declared finally secured on July 2.

Sandwiched in between these momentous events, tens of thousands of Americans in obscurity slowly ground their way down the island. They accepted that they might have to kill everyone in most of the last crack Japanese units, led by the most accomplished officers in the Japanese military, the brilliant but infamous generals Mitsuru Ushijima and Isamu Cho and the gifted tactician Colonel Hiromichi Yahara.

When the battle was over, the U.S. Navy had suffered its worst single battle losses in its history. The newly formed Sixth Marine Division and Sledge's veteran First Marine Division were wrecked, with almost half their original strength either killed or wounded. The commander of all U.S. ground forces on Okinawa, General Simon Bolivar Buckner Jr., became the highest-ranking soldier to die in combat in the Second World War. The destructive potential of thousands of kamikaze suicide bombers, together with the faulty prebattle intelligence that had sorely underestimated the size, armament, and ferocity of the island resistance, created a dread about the upcoming November 1 scheduled assault on the Japanese mainland (Operation Olympic).

Controversy still rages over the morality of dropping the two atomic bombs that ended the war before the American invasions of Kyushu and Honshu. But we forget that President Truman's decision was largely predicated on avoiding the nightmare that Marines like E. B. Sledge had just endured on Peleliu and Okinawa. If today Americans in the leisure of a long peace wonder whether our grandfathers were too hasty in their decision to resort to atomic weapons, they forget that many veterans of the Pacific wondered why they had to suffer through an Okinawa when the successful test at Alamogordo, New Mexico, on July 16 came just a few days after the island was declared secure. Surely the carnage on Okinawa could have been delayed until late summer to let such envisioned weapons convince the Japanese of the futility of prolonging the war.

There are fine memoirs of Okinawa and narrative accounts of the battle's role in the American victory over Japan, most notably William Manchester's beautifully written, but controversial and sometimes unreliable, *Goodbye, Darkness*, and George Feifer's comprehensive *Tennozan: The Battle of Okinawa and the Atomic Bomb*. But E. B. Sledge's harrowing story remains unmatched, told in a prose that is dignified, without obscenities or even much slang—all the more memorable since the author was not a formal stylist nor given to easy revelations of his own strong passions. John Keegan, Paul Fussel, and Studs Terkel have all praised Sledge's honesty, especially his explicit acknowledgment that he experienced the same hatred but fought daily against the barbarity that drove others to nearly match the atrocities of their Japanese enemies.

Unlike the case of many postwar memoirs, the accuracy of Sledge's facts has never been called into question. He does not magnify his own achievements or those of his own Company K. Sledge sometimes uses a few footnotes of explication; often they are heartbreaking asterisks that apprise the reader that the wonderful officer Sledge has just described in the text was later shot or blown up on Peleliu or Okinawa. He reminds his readers that his Marines, being as human as any other soldiers, were capable of great cruelty—"a passionate hatred for the Japanese burned through all Marines I knew." But that being said, Sledge's own moral censure reveals a certain American exceptionalism that such barbarism should be, and usually was, condemned as deviance rather than accepted as the norm—quite different from the Japanese:

> In disbelief I stared at the face as I realized that the Japanese had cut off the dead Marine's penis and stuffed it into his mouth. My emotions solidified into rage and a hatred for the Japanese beyond anything I ever had experienced. From that moment on I never felt the least pity or compassion for them no matter what

the circumstances. My comrades would field strip their packs and pockets for souvenirs and take gold teeth, but I never saw a Marine commit the kind of barbaric mutilation the Japanese committed if they had access to our dead.

What I find most haunting about *With the Old Breed* is Sledge's empathy with those whom he might not have been expected to share a natural affinity, among them even at times the enemy—whom he often wishes not to kill gratuitously and whose corpses he refuses to desecrate. His is a very mannered Southern world where the martial chivalry of Alabama, Louisiana, and Texas shine through; implicit is a pride in the stereotyped manhood of the Old South, but also love for his Yankee comrades, who, he knows, fight as well as his kinsmen. Sledge admits fear, occasionally acknowledging that his courage was only the result of desperation or rational calculation. He only incidentally notes his skill as a Marine. Yet through his own matter-of-fact descriptions the reader easily surmises why his comrades nicknamed a man of 135 pounds "Sledgehammer."

Sledge's heroes amid the desolation of the charred islands—Sergeants Baily and Hanney, Lieutenant "Hillbilly" Jones, and the beloved Captain Haldane—are singled out for their reticence, reflection, and humanity. Of Jones, Sledge writes, "He had that rare ability to be friendly yet familiar with enlisted men. He possessed a unique combination of those qualities of bravery, leadership, ability, integrity, dignity, straightforwardness, and compassion. The only other officer I knew who was his equal in all these qualities was Captain Haldane."

While the reader is astonished at the élan and skill of Sledge's young compatriots, Sledge nevertheless describes them as apprentices in the shadows of the real "old-time" Marines—a near mythical generation that came of age between the wars and was made of even sterner stuff, fighting and winning the initial battles of the Pacific at Guadalcanal and Cape Gloucester on New Britain against the supposedly invincible and ascendant Japanese of 1942 and 1943. Of Gunnery Sergeant Elmo Haney, who scrubbed his genitals with a bristle brush and cleaned his M1 and bayonet three times daily, Sledge concludes, "Despite his personal idiosyncrasies, Haney inspired us youngsters in Company K. He provided us with a direct link to the 'Old Corps.' To us he was the old breed. We admired him—and we loved him."

Indeed, in Sledge's Pacific, there are Homeric heroes of all sorts of an age now long gone. Bob Hope, at the height of his Hollywood career, turns up as the devoted patriot at out-of-the-way Pavuvu, flying in at some danger to entertain the troops. And the future Illinois senator Paul Douglas—noted author and University of Chicago economics professor—appears in the worst of combat at Peleliu as a gray-haired, bespectacled fifty-three-year-old Marine enlistee, handing out ammo to the young Sledge. Douglas later becomes severely wounded at Okinawa and receives the Silver Star and Purple Heart. Again, if modern readers are amazed at the courageous breed of young Marines who surround Sledge, he advises us that we are even more removed than we think from these earlier Americans, since the real "old breed" antedated and was even superior to his own.

Sledge shares a hatred for the brutality of the Japanese, but it never blinds him to their shared horrible fate of being joined together in death at awful places such as Peleliu and Okinawa. So he is furious when he sees a fellow Marine yanking the gold teeth out of a mortally wounded but very much alive, Japanese soldier on Okinawa: "It was uncivilized, as is all war, and was carried out with the particular savagery that characterized the struggle between the Marines and the Japanese. It wasn't simply souvenir hunting or looting the enemy dead; it was more like Indian warriors taking scalps. Such was the incredible cruelty that decent men could commit when reduced to a brutish existence in their fight for survival amid the violent death, terror, tension, fatigue, and filth that was the infantryman's war."

Indeed at the heart of Sledge's genius of recollection is precisely his gift to step aside to condemn the insanity of war, to deplore its bloodletting, without denying that there is often a reason for it, and that a deep love results among those who share its burdens.

> War is brutish, inglorious, and a terrible waster. Combat leaves an inedible mark on those who are forced to endure it. The only redeeming factors were my comrades' incredible bravery and their devotion to each other. Marine Corps training taught us to kill efficiently and to try to survive. But it also taught us loyalty to each other—and love. That esprit de corps sustained us.

There is a renewed timeliness to Sledge's memoir. *With the Old Breed* has never been more relevant than after September 11—war being the domain of an unchanging human nature and thus subject to predictable lessons that transcend time and space. It is not just that American Marines of the new millennium also face a novel strain of suicide bombers, or fanatic enemies emboldened by a frightening anti-Western creed, or once again the similar terror of Sledge's mines, mortars, and hand-to-hand battle in places like Iraqi's Haditha or Ramadi.

Rather, Sledge reminds us of the lethality of what we might call the normal American adolescent in uniform, a grim determination that we also recognized in the Hindu Kush and Kirkuk. Raised amid bounty and freedom, the American soldier seems a poor candidate to learn ex nihilo the craft of killing. How can a suburban teenager suddenly be asked to face and defeat the likes of zealots, whether on Okinawa's Shuri Line or at Fallujah in the Sunni Triangle? "Would I do my duty or be a coward?" Sledge wonders on his initial voyage to the Pacific. "Could I kill?"

But read *With the Old Breed* to be reminded how a certain American reluctance to kill and the accompanying unease with militarism have the odd effect of magnifying courage, as free men prove capable of almost any sacrifice to preserve their liberty. Or as E. B. Sledge once more reminds us thirty-six years after surviving Okinawa:

In writing I am fulfilling an obligation I have long felt to my comrades in the 1st Marine Division, all of whom suffered so much for our country. None came out unscathed. Many gave their lives, many their health, and some their sanity. All who survived will long remember the horror they would rather forget. But they suffered and they did their duty so a sheltered homeland can enjoy the peace that was purchased at such high cost. We owe those Marines a profound debt of gratitude.

We owe the same to the late E. B. Sledge. He reminds us in a "sheltered homeland" that America is never immune from the "insanity" of war. So he brings alive again the names, faces, and thoughts of those who left us at Okinawa and Peleliu, but who passed on to us what we must in turn bequeath to others to follow.

CHAPTER 6

The War to Begin All Wars
*Athens Meets Sparta**

O NE REASON WHY E. B. Sledge's magnificent memoir, *With the Old Breed*, did not immediately win a large audience following its initial publication in 1981 was perhaps the public's weariness, if not disgust, with American military action in southeast Asia, especially tales of infantry brutality. But in general, military history has not been very popular after the controversial Vietnam War. In a larger sense, the unease may be because war itself, under any circumstances, is felt to have little utility in a postmodern world.

When it comes to our martial past, we especially of the present academic culture tend to cast moral aspersions on history's Cro-Magnons: those benighted combatants who, unlike ourselves, resorted to war out

---

* An earlier version of this review of *The Peloponnesian War*, by Donald Kagan (New York: Viking, 2003), appeared in the April 2003 issue of the *New Criterion*.

of stupidity, greed, exploitation, vanity, or a quest for power. And more often, we in the university simply do not want to read about war at all. Thus in the most recent *Oxford Classical Dictionary* (third edition, 1996)—the classicist's invaluable guide to the people, places, and ideas of the ancient Greek and Roman worlds—the entry for "Peloponnesian War" earns a pitiful twenty-one lines, far fewer than for "Gynaecology" at eighty-one lines, "Magic" at 122, "Homosexuality" at 337, or "Literary Theory" at 435. In that authoritative dictionary's single short paragraph about the war, we read that the twenty-seven-year-long conflict, which wrecked fifth-century Athens and altered the course of the Greek city-states, "was recorded by the great historian Thucydides *and that is the most interesting thing about it*" (emphasis added).

So without Thucydides' *Peloponnesian War*, was the real Peloponnesian War—the fact, the event, what we might call the non-text version—just an uninteresting few thousand dead here and there, an unimportant democracy wrecked, and a minor renaissance ended? Forget that a quarter of the population of Athens (including Pericles) died within four years from a mysterious plague; forget that entire cities, including Potidaea, Mytilene, Plataea, Scione, and Melos, were either brutally conquered or simply razed; forget that almost forty thousand Athenians and their allies perished on Sicily; or that dramatic masterpieces—*Trojan Women*, *Oedipus Rex*, *Acharnians*, and others—grew out of the ordeal. Put all that to one side, because now "the most interesting thing" about that great conflict was the fact that Thucydides *wrote* about it.

Thucydides was brilliant, of course—perhaps the greatest mind the ancient world produced, given his ability to translate confused and often absurd events of his time into abstract laws of human behavior, as he put it, "for all time." His history did not merely chronicle the war but also analyzed it as a vehicle to explain to us the unchanging nature of man and our tenuous grip on civilized life.

Nevertheless, the Peloponnesian War—the actual battle, not the book—*is* the seminal historical event of the Greek city-state. It transcended even the genius who wrote about it and the lesser chroniclers such as Xenophon, Plutarch, and Diodorus who rounded out the story. (Thucydides' unfinished account breaks off amid the events of 411 B.C.) Facts really do exist without texts.

We have heard a lot about Thucydides in the new century, both explicitly and through vague, indirect references to his supposed thought and message. In the immediate aftermath of September 11, 2001, Americans at war worried about the outbreak of plague in their cities. Newspaper columnists warned that sending troops abroad to Afghanistan or Iraq was tantamount to dispatching them to perish like the Athenian armada in Sicily. Newscasters admonished us not to bully neutrals as if they were poor Melians. In turn, defenders of the war argued that the United States was a democratic, open society—an Athens fighting for its life against those who preferred hierarchies and various castes of subservience. Neither side could agree whether America was an ascendant civilization or one at the brink of an Athenian-like collapse, so exhausted and demoralized by a culture of excess that it no longer believed in or could defend itself. Nevertheless, most agreed that the so-called war on terror was "new" and could drag on for "decades."

The Peloponnesian War, then, is not really so ancient. Even if some classicists think that Athens's war with Sparta was relatively uninteresting, outsiders still write books with titles like *War and Democracy: A Comparative Study of the Korean War and the Peloponnesian War* and *Hegemonic Rivalry: From Thucydides to the Nuclear Age*. The conflict continues to be evoked in the present—its supposed lessons both astutely and clumsily applied to most of our own wars of the last century.

Russia—or was it really Hitler's Germany?—purportedly was like oligarchic Sparta in its efforts to destroy a democratic, seafaring America. Did not the Cold War, after all, similarly divide the world into two armed camps, with former allies who had united against a common enemy only a half century later facing off in decades of hostilities? Modern observers still recall that Victorian and maritime England (read:

imperial Athens) went to war twice against the great land armies of autocratic Germany with its Prussian warrior code (read: modern Sparta). Do democracies—with their moral laxity and messiness—ultimately lose fights against more authoritarian states? Or was Thucydides right in concluding that democracies are more resilient and imaginative than other governments at war? Was the Sicilian expedition a lesson for the Boer War, Gallipoli, Vietnam, or any proposed great democratic crusade abroad?

Why is this ancient war between tiny Athens and a smaller Sparta still so often used as a historical primer and yet misused? First, it was long—twenty-seven years—and it lined up the entire Greek world into opposite armed camps. Second, the two antagonists were antithetical in nearly every respect, and thus the bipolar fighting was proclaimed to be a final arbiter of their respective values—political and cultural values that still divide us today. Third, it started in Greece's great golden age, and its attendant calamity was felt to have ended for good that period of great promise. Fourth, players in the war were the greats of Hellenic civilization—Socrates, Pericles, Euripides, Alcibiades, Sophocles, Aristophanes, and others—and their lives and work reflect that seminal experience. Fifth, Athens lost, casting into doubt ever since not merely the power but also the morality of democracy, especially when it executed Socrates in the war's aftermath. Sixth—and at last we arrive at the theme of the *Oxford Classical Dictionary*'s brief entry on the war—Greece's preeminent historian, Thucydides, was not merely an analytical and systematic writer of a great extant history; he was also a brilliant philosopher who tried to lend to the events of the war a value that transcended his own time, making his history of ideas "a possession for all time" that could furnish lessons for men at war in any age. Thucydides' man of the ages is a pretty savage creature whose known murderous proclivities are kept in check—albeit just barely—by an often tenuous and hard-to-maintain veneer of civilization.

"A great war and more worthy of relation than any that had pre-

ceded it," Thucydides wrote, contending at the outset of his history that
the struggle between the two opposing city-states would be cataclysmic
because both belligerents were at the height of their powers and were
eager to draw the rest of the Greek world into the equivalent of an
ancient Hellenic World War. "The greatest disturbance in history," he
soberly added of the conflict that consumed his own adult life. Even
2,500 years later we tend to agree that it sabotaged much of what Greece
could have accomplished.

"It is," the classicist Donald Kagan concludes in his newly condensed history of the war,

> both legitimate and instructive to think of what we call the Pelo-
> ponnesian War as "the great war between Athens and Sparta," as
> one scholar designated it, because, like the European war of
> 1914–18 to which the title "the Great War" was applied by an
> earlier generation that knew only one, it was a tragic event, a
> great turning point in history, the end of an era of progress, pros-
> perity, confidence, and hope, and the beginning of a darker time.

Most wars, of course, do not end like they start. Before Shiloh
(April 6–8, 1862), for example, Grant thought one great battle would win
the Civil War. After the battle, he realized that years, thousands of lives,
and millions of dollars in capital were needed to ruin rather than defeat
a recalcitrant Confederacy. So too the Spartans marched into Attica in
spring 431 B.C., thinking that a year or two of old-style ravaging of fields
would bring them victory; seven years later neither side was closer to victory, and they still had another twenty far-worse seasons to go.

If the earlier united victory over the Persian king Xerxes (480–479
B.C.) marked the inauguration of the triumphant golden age, this classical century that started with such great promise finally crashed with the
self-inflicted wreckage of the city-states. Thousands of free Greeks who
had once united to fight Persians now killed one another and aided

Persians. The carnage that Darius and Xerxes once could only hope for at Marathon and Salamis, Greeks like Pericles, Cleon, Alcibiades, Brasidas, Gylippus, and Lysander a half century later brought about, killing more of their own people in a year than the Persians had in a decade.

Thucydides felt strongly that Spartans had invaded the Athenian countryside in spring 431 because "they feared the growth of the power of the Athenians, seeing most of Hellas already subject to them." Of course, there were various other, more immediate pretexts for war: Athens had imposed economic sanctions against Megara, a Spartan ally; both sides sought to draw the neutral island of Corcyra into their respective alliances; they each quarreled over the loyalty of the key northern city of Potidaea; the Boeotians wished to eliminate the outpost city of Plataea, which brought fear of Athenian imperialism to their doorstep. And so on.

But Thucydides stuck to his thesis about the "clash of civilizations," believing that the larger underlying differences between the two powers—perhaps not always perceptible to Athenians and Spartans themselves—ensured that the more immediate and minor disagreements would eventually lead to a cataclysm. After all, if Sparta ignored the pretexts of Corinthian and Megarian grievances, the sheer dynamism of Pericles' imperial culture—majestic buildings, drama, comedy, intellectual fervor, an immense fleet, radical democratic government, an expanding population, and a growing overseas empire—would eventually spread throughout the Peloponnese and offer incentives to Sparta's friends that she could not hope to match. Who could win a war of attrition against the world's first America—especially when you could offer only massive iron ingots as money, a ramshackle hovel as a national capital, and a Gestapo-like storm corps in lieu of an army of liberation?

Still, scholars argue over Thucydides' glum appraisal that war was inevitable and overrode what individual Spartan and Athenian leaders might do or not do in any given crisis. Yet few now—in part thanks to the work of Professor Donald Kagan—question his keen appraisal that states can war over ideas, perceptions, fears, and honor as well as particular material grievances. Sparta's fault in breaking the peace of 431 was not so much that it was culpable in any given context, but rather that it was all too human—and thus prone to all the wild emotions that sometimes make men do what is not in either their own or the general interest. In the post-Marxist era, we still find it hard to believe men will fight for reasons other than exploitation, colonialism, or to take someone else's money or land.

The Peloponnesian War itself proved to be a colossal paradox. Sparta had the most feared infantry in the Greek world. Yet it was Sparta's newly created navy that finally won the great battles of the war. Democratic Athens sent almost forty thousand allied soldiers to their deaths trying to capture far-off Syracuse, the largest democracy in the Greek world—even as thousands more of her enemies were soon to plunder her property with impunity less than twenty miles outside her walls from the base at Decelea. Alcibiades at times proved the savior of Athens, Sparta, and Persia—and their collective spoiler as well. Athens started the war off with gold piled high in its majestic Parthenon; it ended the conflict broke and unable even to flute the final columns of the Propylae, the monumental gateway to the still-unfinished temples on the acropolis. Sparta fielded the most terrifying army in Greece, and yet most of its opponents fell not in pitched battle but rather either to disease, at sea, or in guerrilla-style killing.

Pericles planned the war and reminded his countrymen of what was required to see them through, but he did not even survive the conflict's third year—a victim of a plague that he helped to induce by ordering all of Athens's rural population to evacuate inside the crowded city's walls. The philosopher Socrates had doubts about democratic Athens's hubris and megalomania, but not enough reluctance to prevent him from fighting heroically in her cause in his potbellied middle age. Thucydides used the broad message of the war's senselessness to explore his bleak views about human nature, but no Athenian fought more un-questioningly and without cynicism in service to his country.

No ancient war—not Xerxes' invasion of Greece, Alexander the Great's grandiose invasions, or Hannibal's romp into Italy—is more contradictory than the three decades of intramural fighting between Athens and Sparta: a land power versus a maritime power; the Dorian starkness contrasted with Ionian liberality; oligarchy pitted against democracy; ostentatious wealth set against practiced dearth; a majestic imperial city dethroned by a rural hamlet; and a humane imperialism that killed the innocent even as a garrison state championed the cause of state autonomy abroad. No wonder classicists tend to avoid the whole and focus on its bits and pieces—treaties, generals, decrees, finances, rhetoric, and the like. It is all too big and confusing, and so by our experts better relegated to a standard reference work in a single paragraph of twenty-one lines.

In contrast, Donald Kagan set out to chronicle the entire war in all its complexity. He did just that for much of his scholarly career while teaching at Cornell and Yale. His four volumes, *The Peloponnesian War*, were published over nearly twenty years, beginning with the 1969 work on the origins of the conflict and ending with the 1987 work on the utter defeat of Athens. Kagan ranges widely throughout European history, invoking ancient wars to elucidate Spartan or Athenian strategy. He frequently poses counterfactual questions and often doubts Thucydides (most famously about the latter's judgment that the war was inevitable and arose from Spartan fear over growing Athenian power). Kagan asks practical questions about the financing of the war, criticizes Pericles' judgment, and occasionally labels Thucydides a revisionist whose sober grand assessments did not always reflect the data of his own narrative.

It was not especially prudent of Kagan to begin a career by starting a grand multivolume narrative about an ancient war—especially at Cornell at a time of another unpopular war and general campus unrest, and when most scholars were more interested in social, economic, and cultural history, turning out scads of articles and monographs for promotion and tenure rather than sober four-volume masterpieces. But Kagan persevered, and more than forty years after the first volume appeared, his work endures for a variety of reasons besides its proven reliability, accuracy, and comprehensiveness. He went toe to toe with the great triad of German historians of the nineteenth and early twentieth centuries, Georg Busolt, K. J. Beloch, and Eduard Meyer—most of whose work remains untranslated—and helped to reintroduce them, not always with approval, to a modern American audience. Kagan reminds us of the role of factions within the city-states: Athens did not simply execute the Melians or Spartans seek a break in the hostilities, but rather particular groups of Athenians and Spartans did so, and in constant friction that reflected their own wide disparities of wealth, property, and lineage.

But Kagan's greatest achievement is to remind us of the personal—the irrational—element in war, what Thucydides himself called "the human thing." (This is also a theme of Kagan's later book *On the Origins of War.*) It is not always cosmic ideas or profit or ideology that start wars, but often very human urges of real people transferred to a grand scale—urges like honor, fear, prestige, and perceived (rather than real) grievances. The result is that his Peloponnesian War, like Thucydides' own, serves a wider didactic purpose than the preservation of old facts and ancient men's lives.

Kagan's history reminds us that fickle and weak people often say one thing precisely so that they can act on another. I wish our current observers would read the professions and excuses of the hurt Spartans and aggrieved Athenians and then ask in a similarly skeptical mood why we should listen to what bin Laden says caused his jihad. For Kagan, Sparta was no more doomed to go to war than Hitler needed lebensraum. Sparta went to war primarily because it thought it might win a cheap victory over an imperial Athens, and thereby increase its stature without much cost; and it knew that if it crossed the Attica border in spring 431 B.C., there was not one thing Athenian hoplites could do to keep its army out.

The Thebans attacked Plataea not simply because it posed a danger, or because they needed more Boeotian farmland, but because the likely capture of Plataea would prove a testament of Theban power, and so offered an easy opportunity—an opportunity more psychological than material. Britain needed the Falklands no more than did Argentina, but the dictatorship of the latter saw a chance for a quick, cheap victory that could placate domestic unrest, while England for its future security could not afford the dangerous precedent of letting a second-rate power attack a great nation with impunity. States then do, as Kagan reminds us, fight over perceptions with plenty of professions (*prophaseis*)—not always for sheep and rocky windswept islands in the South Atlantic.

In the 2003 single-volume edition, condensed by 75 percent from the four-volume original, Kagan tries to make the Peloponnesian War come alive as a story, derived for the most part from a judicious reading of Thucydides, Xenophon, Plutarch, and Diodorus. The astute comparisons to later wars, the footnotes, and the scholarly controversies of the earlier volumes are gone. They are replaced by a fast-paced narrative, with plenty of maps, that presents the Peloponnesian War year by year in very short titled subsections. His earlier perceptions and judgments remain, but they are implicit and fade into the narrative. It is now the train of events that must take center stage.

Kagan's abridged *Peloponnesian War* is still important because the solid judgment of its author remains evident throughout. No one—not a majestic Pericles, a fiery Cleon, or the chameleon Alcibiades—can fool Don Kagan; he appreciates the genius of bad men he does not like, and he praises the inspiration of rogues he despises. Bad plans, like capturing Sicily, can work if implemented well; good ideas of good men can fail, as in the Delium campaign, for bad luck and the simple want of common sense. Things about radical Athens bother him, but not to such a degree that he denies its energy and dynamism. He admires

Spartan discipline but not the blinkered society that was at the bottom of it all. Democracy was often murderous, but oligarchy and tyranny brought the same violence, only without the grandeur.

Finally, and most important, Kagan has no condescension for his subjects. Cleon and Brasidas, Nicias, and Lysander are not silly squabbling ancient peoples in need of modern enlightenment. They are men of universal appetites to be taken on their own terms, just like us, whose occasional crackpot ideas, fears, jealousies, and sins can sometimes—if the thin veneer of civilization is suddenly stripped away—lead to something absolutely god-awful. If you don't agree, ask the Serbians, Rwandans, or Afghans—or, if we could, those with cell phones and briefcases who politely boarded planes to butcher thousands.

CHAPTER 7

Don Juan of Austria Is Riding to the Sea

A Clash of Civilizations in the Sixteenth-Century Mediterranean*

TWO MILLENNIA AFTER the Peloponnesian War, the entire Mediterranean witnessed a clash of civilizations far greater than the Aegean rivalry between the Spartan and Athenian alliances. The old ethnic, political, geographic, and cultural antitheses were now overshadowed by a religious divide beyond anything in the ancient world, an irreconcilable rift between a growing Islamic empire and its embattled Mediterranean Christian rivals.

The Gospel of Matthew is a long way from the Koran, but the Christian soldiers of the sixteenth century knew well enough that weakness in the face of the Ottoman galleys sweeping the Italian coast

---

* The original version of this review of Niccolò Capponi's *The Victory of the West: The Great Christian-Muslim Clash at the Battle of Lepanto* (New York: Perseus, 2007) appeared in the August–September 2007 issue of *First Things*.

meant death or conversion. Until the next world, violence alone ensured the survival of a divided, poorer, and more vulnerable Christendom in the Mediterranean. And so, after their victory at the great Battle of Lepanto, Spanish and Italians butchered scores of defeated Turkish seamen thrashing in the bloody seas, determined that the sultan would lose all his skilled bowmen and rowers.

In their way of thinking, any jihadist left alive would mean only more Christians dead in the near future. The clash on the Mediterranean between the West and Islam often turned even more horrific. In the months before the battle near Lepanto, the Venetian captain Marcantonio Bragadin surrendered the garrison at Famagusta to an overwhelming Turkish invasion force. Despite Turkish promises of safe passage out of Cyprus, mass slaughter and rape ensued, with the heads of the Venetian lords lined up for display in the town square. Bragadin first had his ears cut off, then he was forced to carry earth as a captured slave. After having Bragadin hanged from a galley yard, the Ottoman commander Lala Mustafa ordered him flayed alive. He expired about halfway through the grisly torture, but his tormentors continued. His hide was stuffed with straw, clothed, and paraded as a trophy before being sent to Istanbul.

After the attacks on the United States on September 11, 2001, the landmark Christian-Muslim clashes of the past were continually evoked—often crudely and inexactly so—in popular dialogue, as if they were apparent ancient precursors to the current Western struggle against radical Islam. So Poitiers, the Crusades, the fall of Constantinople, Grenada, the sieges of Vienna, and Omdurman were all referenced—not just by Westerners, but perhaps more often by Osama bin Laden and his associates, whose fatwas blared grievances about the lost "al-Andalus" and the infidel "Crusader kingdoms" in the Middle East.

Yet no East-West clash resonates more than Lepanto, the great sea battle of October 7, 1571, which involved more than four hundred ships and eighty thousand seamen, and, along with Actium, Salamis, and

Ecnomus, may well have been one of the most deadly single-day naval battles in history. Fought off the northwest coast of Greece near the Curzolaris Islands—not far south from Augustus's great victory over Marc Antony and Cleopatra at Actium—Lepanto proved to be the last great clash of oared ships that resulted in a surprising victory of Christendom over the sultan's feared Ottoman fleet.

But while Christian Europeans at the time saw their victory as a divine gift that saved their civilization, its geopolitical significance has always underwhelmed modern historians. The Christian League was an ad hoc alliance of convenience, riddled with internecine fighting and intrigue. It was never really much more than the galley fleets of Spain, the Papal States, and Venice. England and France kept clear; both had long ago cut their own deals with the Ottomans. Indeed, during the winter of 1542 the French had even allowed the Ottoman corsair Barbarossa the use of their harbor at Toulon to refit as he conducted raids along the Italian coast. For most countries with ports on the Atlantic, it was far better to get rich trading with the Turk than to fight him.

As Niccolò Capponi writes in his 2007 book, *The Victory of the West: The Great Christian-Muslim Clash at the Battle of Lepanto*:

> By the beginning of the sixteenth century Christendom was in a very sorry state. Gone were the crusading ideals of old; people turned deaf ears to the alarmed utterances of preachers and popes about the necessity of stopping the Turkish advance. For most European governments the Ottoman threat was low on their list of concerns—they were more interested in maintaining their positions in the rich eastern markets—while a few states were quite ready to abet, or at least not hinder, the sultan's expansionist policies for the sake of their own commercial interests.

So the battle was not quite an epic struggle of a consolidated Europe against the Eastern threat. While the Ottomans had united most of the

Muslims of the Middle East under the Grand Porte, Europe was trisected by Orthodoxy, Catholicism, and Protestantism. The most effective admirals in the Turkish fleet were often Italian renegades. Galley rowers were in no small part chained Christian slaves. The best Turkish galleys themselves were either copied from Italian designs or captured from the Spanish and Venetians and refitted.

On the voyage out to meet the Ottoman fleet, Don Juan of Austria—the bastard son of King Charles V of Spain, half brother of King Philip II, and the nominal head of the allied Christian fleet—almost arrested some of his allied Venetian admirals. One, Sebastiano Venier, had hanged some murderous seamen employed by the Spanish, which nearly precipitated a war between the two allied fleets on the eve of the battle.

It was never quite clear how many Christian ships would actually show up to sail eastward toward Lepanto, the winter port of the Ottomans, or how the galleys were to be provisioned and their crews paid. By October and the onset of rough seas, many admirals in the fleet thought the season to go chasing the huge Ottoman fleet was long over.

Even when the Christians won and nearly destroyed the Ottoman armada, Europe was too disunited to capitalize on the enemy's setback. It never recaptured the lost Cyprus, much less sailed up the Dardanelles to retake Constantinople. In contrast, the Ottomans quickly replaced their galleys, hired new crews, and went on the offensive again in the eastern Mediterranean, recapturing most of their fortresses in North Africa within a year. A little over a century later, the Ottomans would head up the Danube on their way to Vienna and the center of European culture.

So what is it about Lepanto that, more than six hundred years later, still makes it a symbol of a supposedly indomitable Christian West? The heroic efforts of an aged, obsessed Pope Pius V to cobble together a makeshift fleet of last resort to put a stop to the continuous westward surge of Islam? The singular calm of the twenty-six-year-old Don Juan, who danced a jig on his flagship *Real* in the very seconds before the battle—after offering one of the tersest pre-battle harangues in military history: "Gentlemen, this is not the time to discuss but to fight"?

Is the battle's immortality due to its popularity in literature and art? The young Cervantes was wounded in the battle and later wrote that Lepanto was the "most noble and memorable event that past centuries have seen or future generations can ever hope to witness." Massive canvasses by Titian and Tintoretto commemorated the victory. Or was Lepanto enshrined by the raw courage of the mortally wounded Antonio Barbarigo; the brilliant performance of the unshakeable Don Álvaro de Bazán, marquis of Santa Cruz; or the fire of seventy-five-year-old Sebastiano Venier, later doge of Venice?

Surprisingly, there has not been an accessible, scholarly one-volume history of the battle in English until this book by the Italian Renaissance scholar Niccolò Capponi. Drawing on new archival work and reexamining contemporary letters and inventories, Capponi offers a fresh view of both the fighting (he eschews the battle's traditional nomenclature of Lepanto for the more geographically accurate Curzolis) and its strategic significance, rejecting the common opinion that the victory had few lasting consequences. His title, *Victory of the West*, thus refers to Western triumph in both the fullest tactical and strategic sense.

Only about thirty of the book's four hundred pages are devoted to a narrative of the fighting. Capponi instead has given an account of the rise of the Ottomans and of the divisiveness and the bickering rampant in Western Europe. He also provides meticulous information about the mechanics and horrendous expense of galley warfare on the Mediterranean.

Capponi is no triumphalist. Indeed, he announces at the outset, "I also admit to having something of a soft spot for the Turks as fighters, my great-great-grandfather, a Crimean War veteran, describing them as the best soldiers in the world." In the midst of describing serial Turkish atrocities, he quotes an Ottoman official who deplored such savagery and notes that sometimes Christians were as likely to execute prisoners as were Ottomans.

How then did the Christians win the battle? They were probably outnumbered, both in ships and men. Lepanto was fought in Turkish-controlled waters near the Ottoman winter port at the mouth of the Gulf of Corinth opposite Patras, the present-day Nafpaktos. The Venetians had lost Cyprus and were demoralized from increasingly bold attacks on the coast of Italy.

Capponi summarizes the usual reasons for the incredible victory, previously outlined by others. The use of six galleasses—huge artillery platforms that were towed to the front of the Christian fleet—devastated many of the Ottoman armada's first lines before they even engaged. These monsters fired from between forty and fifty cannon of various calibers, often blowing apart the light Ottoman galleys, which rarely had more than five or six guns, and sometimes even fewer.

Capponi draws on contemporary scientific accounts to emphasize the deadliness of these new contraptions. But in general, the rest of the Christian galleys had far more guns, composed of better-cast bronze, and superior training and discipline in ballistics. Their marines were armed with harquebuses in far greater numbers, and armor plate made them almost invincible to Ottoman archery.

Spanish and Italian captains tried to avoid fighting hand to hand with the more numerous Turkish swordsmen and instead relied on small- and large-arms fire to thin out the enemy galleys before boarding them. These advantages testify to the growing sixteenth-century technological gap between Western Europe and the Ottomans. The Turks' lack of a sophisticated banking system and the unfettered intellectual pursuit of the Europeans, together with a changing maritime world outside the Mediterranean, made it ever more difficult to match the West in munitions and naval prowess. The Ottoman answer instead was usually more janissaries and more galleys, at precisely the time that lucrative East-West overland trade was drying up and a westward-looking Europe was increasingly unconcerned with what the sultan to the east had to offer.

The canard survives that Lepanto did not change a thing—a century later the Turks were still able to mount a great offensive against the West that would reach to the gates of Vienna, and the Ottoman Empire survived into the twentieth century. In the words of the Ottomans, they merely had their beard shaved at Lepanto rather than their arm lost like the Christians at Cyprus.

But Capponi emphasizes the battle's more insidious psychological consequences. Before Lepanto, the Turks cruised with impunity along the southern coast of Europe; afterward, they were uncertain whether their galleys would be attacked and defeated anywhere in the Mediterranean.

More important still, galley warfare itself was coming to an end, as those European states with Atlantic ports—Britain, France, the Netherlands, Portugal, and Spain—found no need of either Mediterranean transit or Ottoman overland routes to tap the great natural wealth of the Orient and the newly opened Americas. In just a few years, a single galleon, crammed with cheaper iron cannon, could blast apart an entire Turkish fleet of galleys that were ill-equipped to venture out of the Mediterranean into the Atlantic, where the action increasingly was found.

As Capponi makes clear, galleys were ingeniously designed for the relative calm of the Mediterranean, where East and West were often only a few days—or hours—apart. So the problem was not so much with galleys but rather that the sea on which they traveled had lost its global centrality and proved a barrier, instead of a bridge, to the wealth of the ever more powerful West. In other words, Lepanto was the Ottomans' last gasp. When the courage and numbers of the Turkish fleet at its zenith still failed to stop a divided southern Europe, then the future was set, as a parasitic Ottoman Empire increasingly lost its host.

It is to Capponi's credit that he tells the riveting, human story of the battle while keeping in mind its larger historical and strategic implications. And while he is always sensitive to the often bizarre nature of the Ottoman Empire, with its *devsirme* (the conscription of Christian boys into imperial Ottoman service), harem, imperial court fratricide, and janissaries, he never falls into the politically correct fallacy that Istanbul's religious and political values were just different from, rather than antithetical to, the worldview of a freer and more vibrant West. Indeed, it is the divide that we still see today.

PART III

The Postmodern Meets the Premodern

CHAPTER 8

The End of Decisive Battle—For Now

Have the RPG and AK-47 trumped tanks and bombers?*

Late, Great Battle

HAVE WE SEEN in our time the end of decisive battles between conventional armies and navies in the long tradition of Cunaxa, Lepanto, and Okinawa? Will any nation at war continue to marshal huge forces, determined to settle the issue head-to-head, in an overt contest of massed arms against like kind that has characterized Western warfare since Marathon?

John Keegan, in his classic *Face of Battle* (1976), suggested more than thirty years ago that it would be increasingly hard for the modern European state to engage in the slugfests on land that resulted in something like the infantry holocaust at the battle of the Somme. "The

---

* This essay was written in spring 2009, and a version appeared in a fall 2009 issue of *City Journal*.

suspicion grows," Keegan argued of a new cohort of affluent and leisured European youth—rebellious in spirit and reluctant to give over the good life to mass conscription—"that battle has already abolished itself."

Two decades ago I concluded *The Western Way of War* with the suggestion that since Western decisive battle had become so lethal, and had raised the specter of nuclear escalation, I thought it doubtful that two Western states could any longer engage in large head-to-head conventional battles: "Have we not seen, then, in our lifetime the end of the Western way of war?"

Events of the past half century seem to have confirmed the notion that decisive battles between two large, highly trained Westernized armies clashing openly, with sophisticated arms, whether on land or sea, have become increasingly rare. War planners at the Pentagon now talk more about counterinsurgency training, winning the hearts and minds of civilian populations, and "smart" interrogation techniques—and less about old-fashion "blow 'em up" hardware like the Crusader artillery platform and the F-22 Raptor interceptor jet that has proven so advantageous to winning a conventional set battle.

While perhaps the most stunning manifestation of combat and the prominently mentioned events of military history, set-piece engagements, it should be said at the outset, were never quite the norm of war. More often, armed conflict was less dramatic, intermittent, and played out in landscapes not conducive to conventionally marshaled armies and navies, and it involved civilians. We associate the battles of Granicus, Issus, and Guagamela and the fight on the Hydaspes River with the military genius of Alexander the Great, but he spent far more time fighting irregular forces in counterinsurgency efforts throughout the Balkans, the Hindu Kush, and Bactria.

Nevertheless big battles—or so generals dreamed—could sometimes change entire conflicts in a matter of hours, which in turn might alter politics and the fate of millions for decades. It is with history's rare battle, not the more common dirty war, insurgency, or street fighting, that we typically associate war poetry, commemoration, and, for good or evil, radical changes of fortune and the martial notions of glory and honor. Winston Churchill supposedly said Admiral John Jellicoe, commander of the British Grand Fleet in the First World War, who alone ensured the British expeditionary army could be supplied and the homeland kept alive with imports, was "the only man on either side who could lose the war in an afternoon." Had Jellicoe lost the Battle of Jutland, Churchill might well have been proven right.

Had the Greeks lost their fleet in an afternoon at "Holy" Salamis (480 B.C.), the history of the polis may well have come to an end, and with it a vulnerable Western civilization in its infancy. Had the Confederates broken the Union lines at the epic battle of Gettysburg, and swept behind Washington, D.C., Abraham Lincoln would have faced enormous pressures to settle the Civil War according to the recognized status quo ante bellum. If the "band of brothers" had been repulsed at Normandy Beach on the morning of June 6, 1944, it is difficult to envision them replaying an enormous amphibious invasion soon after—but easier to imagine the Red Army within a year or two at the Atlantic Coast.

So there is something dramatic, frightening even, about two opposing forces intent on dueling each other with a sizable percentage of their aggregate strength, determined to plow through an adversary and crush its will to resist—and, with such victory, often end the ability of an enemy culture at the rear to retain its independence. We forget that powerful nations, and even empires, so often depend, in both a real and a psychological sense, on their far-distant armies to keep them safe at home. Should such forces abroad fail in a day, then there may be no other ramparts or reserves to keep the oncoming enemy at bay. It is indeed no wonder that we do not have a genre of books with titles like "The 100 Great Insurgencies of All Time," "History's Landmark Urban Fights," or "Fifteen Decisive Terrorist Acts of the World."

Wars Without Battle

THE RARE PERIODS of big battles—such as the bloodletting years between 1799 and 1815, the carnage of 1861–65, the Great War of 1914–18, or the six-year nightmare of 1939 to 1945—seem long distant in our modern era. Except for the daring American landing at Incheon (September 1950) and the subsequent first liberation of Seoul, not many battles of the past seven decades were anything like Jutland and the Somme of the First World War or the Second World War's Battle of the Bulge and Kursk.

Amid the murderous fighting between well-organized armies during the Vietnam War, North Vietnamese forces as a matter of practice did not attempt to engage Western forces in formal set engagements. The sieges at Khe Sahn and, earlier, against the French at Dien Bien Phu were the exceptions rather than the rule, and themselves not quite traditional collisions of infantry.

The Soviet army may have killed more than a million Afghans in its failed attempt in the 1980s to take over Afghanistan—without once engaging in a set collision with tens of thousands of jihadist insurgents. In two Chechen wars, the Russians all but leveled Grozny—and yet never met in pitched battle the forces of their Islamic enemy. We still do not know all the gory details of that horrific Iran-Iraq war (1980–89), in which more than a million combatants and civilians on both sides perished. And despite the brutality and bloodshed that characterized that existential struggle between Saddam Hussein and the Ayatollah Khomeini—especially in murderous confrontations over the Iraqi city of Basra—there were rarely set engagements between two massed armies across the battlefield. At least we know of no particular name associated with such a putative showdown of massed forces.

Even the "Mother of all Battles" in the 1991 Gulf War was largely a rout. The tank battle at Medina Ridge involved hundreds of armored vehicles but lasted little more than an hour—the Americans suffering neither casualties to enemy fire nor the loss of a single Abrams tank while obliterating 186 Iraqi tanks. Most of Saddam's army disintegrated before advancing American armor rather than fought—as was commonly the case during the three-week war of 2003. Today only a handful of Americans even know what the Medina Ridge was.

Given the open terrain and conventional forces involved, there was some decisive fighting on the ground between British and Argentine units during the Falklands War of 1982, but on a minuscule scale in comparison to the twentieth-century's other bloody engagements. Tank battles raged in the Golan Heights in the Six-Day War in 1967 and the Yom Kippur War of 1973. And for a few days the Israelis and the Egyptian Third Army fought quite openly in the desert expanse of the Sinai Peninsula—in contrast to the sixty years of terrorism, intifadas, bombings, and missile strikes that have characterized the inconclusive Israeli-Arab conflicts.

Far more common in the modern world are the insurgencies that characterize the present Afghan and Iraq wars, as well as rapid surprise takeovers, such as Grenada and Panama; bombing campaigns, such as those against Mu'ammar Gadhafi and the sustained air assault that forced Slobodan Milošević out of Serbia; and messy police actions, like those in Somalia or Haiti.

This is not to say that hundreds of thousands do not die violently in these often vicious insurgencies, air campaigns, civil strife, genocides, and shellings of our age. The spring 1994 bloodletting in Rwanda saw five hundred thousand Tutsis butchered, and three hundred thousand Chechnyans and Russians perished in their two wars of the 1990s. Nor is the return of set-piece battles impossible. The U.S. military still prepares for the possibility of all sorts of conventional challenges. We hold thousands of tanks and artillery pieces in constant readiness, along with close-ground support missiles and planes, in fear that Kim Song Il's People's Army of Korea might someday quite brazenly try to swarm across the demilitarized zone into Seoul, or that conventional forces of the Chinese Red Army might storm the beaches of Taiwan.

Conventional clashes can be a part of every war. But again, decisive, sustained collisions, involving thousands of like combatants in relatively open terrain, are not. Sometimes entire wars are decided in theaters outside decisive battle. The present absence of set battles is hardly novel in the cyclical course of military history. The twenty-seven-year-long Peloponnesian War saw only two major ground engagements, at Delium (424 B.C.) and Mantinea (418 B.C.), and a few smaller infantry clashes at Solygeia and outside Syracuse. In such an asymmetrical struggle between Athenian naval power and premier Spartan infantry, far more common were hit-and-run attacks, terrorism, sieges, a constant ravaging of agriculture, and amphibious assaults, along with some large sea battles off the coast of Asia Minor.

During the murderous Roman Civil War (49–31 B.C.) frequent and savage battles at Dyrrhacium, Pharsalus, Utica, Ruspina, Thapsus, Munda, Mutina, Philippi, and Actium claimed more than a quarter-million Roman lives. Yet after the creation of the Principate by the new emperor Augustus—except for the occasional frontier disasters such at Teutoberg Wald (A.D. 9) or Adrianople (A.D. 378), or the periodic internecine battles for imperial succession—much of the Mediterranean world was relatively united, and thus relatively free of major battles for nearly half a millennium.

After the fall of Roman Empire, the more impoverished Middle Ages saw mostly sieges and low-intensity conflict, not larger campaigns like the famous engagements at Poitiers (732), Hattin (1187), or Crécy (1346). The eminent military historian Russell Weigley writes of an "Age of Battles." He argues that there was a uniquely murderous two centuries of pitched battles—between Gustavus Adolphus's victory at Breitenfeld (1631) and Napoleon's defeat at Waterloo (1815)—in which European armies of multifarious rivals sought, often in vain, to decide entire wars in a few hours of head-to-head fighting. Scholars as diverse as David Bell and Frederick W. Kagan have chronicled the new age of battle in which Napoleon fought more decisive engagements in his twenty-year career than would transpire in Europe over the subsequent century.

Indeed, the agreements following the Congress of Vienna and military deterrence kept a widespread peace in Europe for nearly a century, which might explain why something like Sedan (1870) was the exception rather than the rule. In general, set battles of the era, on land or sea, were more a colonial experience (Tel el-Kebir, Omdurman) and more common in Asia (Tsushima) and the Americas (the decisive battles of the Mexican-American, Spanish-American, and American Civil War).

The era from the beginning of the First World War to end of the Second saw the most destructive battles in the history of arms. The details of Iwo Jima, Kursk, Marne, Meuse-Argonne, Okinawa, Passchendale, the Somme, Stalingrad, and Verdun are still chilling. Most Westerners know little of the horror of the battles of the Huaihai campaign (late 1948 to early 1949), in which the Nationalist Chinese lost an entire army of six hundred thousand to the Communists in mostly conventional fighting.

Why—Why Not—Decisive Battle?

WHY IN THE long cycles of military history, does the frequency of decisive battles wax and wane? The political landscape certainly explains much. The establishment of empire of any sort can lessen the incidence of regional warring in general. Unified, central political control transmogrifies the usual ethnic, tribal, racial, and religious strife into more-internal and less-violent rivalries for state representation and influence.

Sometimes repression of nationalist chauvinism, which so often leads to war, is accomplished violently and in authoritarian fashion, as in the case of the unification of Russia and its surrounding republics into the Soviet Union. On other occasions, such unification is mostly consensual, such as the American frontier expansion of settler movements that turned Western territories of provincials into mostly brotherly states. Either way, the resulting enormous confederation makes major battles in the region less likely. The contemporary European Union for now lacks the interstate rivalry that plunged Europe into battles for much of the first half of the twentieth century. Once Philip unified Greece under a Macedonian hegemony after Chaeronea (338 B.C.), engagements like the prior fourth-century B.C. set battles between the city-states— Coronea, Haliartos, Leuctra, Mantinea, Nemea, and Tegyra—became a rarity.

True, when the world is divided into such larger blocs that have sizable, competent conventional forces—such as the Soviet and American spheres during the Cold War—there is the risk that confrontation can turn catastrophic, given the vast resources available to each side. Yet there is also the likelihood that frequent battling along nationalist lines among a variety of state players will be less frequent. No nation of the Warsaw Pact fought a Soviet republic; and nominal American allies like Iran did not threaten American allies like Israel. Tito and Yugoslavian communism for a while kept Bosnians, Croats, Kosovars, Macedonians, and Serbs from killing each other. There were no more Punic Wars once the Romans established a "Roman peace" and Carthago Nova as the capital of the new Latin-speaking province of Africa. The constant tribal fighting so common in Caesar's Gallic Wars largely quieted down once the Romans annexed the entire region as the Roman province of Gaul.

In the current age, many of the most powerful economies in the world are united under the loose rubric "the West," which includes the former nations of much of the British Commonwealth (Australia, Canada, New Zealand, etc.), the transatlantic NATO alliance (most of the European Union and the United States), and democratic nations of the Pacific (Japan, the Philippines, South Korea, Taiwan, etc.), along with miscellaneous kindred allies that are capitalist and democratic such as India and Israel. At present there is virtually no likelihood that we will see decisive battles between any of these similarly minded states, even though a mere seventy years ago most of them squared off in various temporary alliances against one another in terrible battles at places like the Ardennes, Arnheim, the Falaise Gap, Leyte Gulf, and Okinawa.

While consensual states such as ancient Athens, the mercantile Venetian Republic, and the contemporary United States proved to be both ferocious and relentless warmakers, these democratically inclined states rarely fought like kind. The Athenian attack on democratic Syracuse was an anomaly. The periodic Venetian rivalry against the Florentine Republic and the War of 1812 were the exceptions rather than the rule. There now are more democratic states in existence than at any time in civilization's history, suggesting that while they may continue to attack nondemocratic rivals with some frequency, they are less likely to turn on one another.

The Future of Battle

IN THE IMMEDIATE present, we can imagine two scenarios for decisive, conventional battle. One is between rival nations that have formidable armored and infantry forces of roughly the same size and that are in rough proximity to one another—India and Pakistan, North and South Korea, Taiwan and the Peoples' Republic of China. Such matchups, however, are rare in the scope of contemporary world rivalries. More important, those states most likely to engage in such conventional battles are precisely the same contestants that might be deterred by fears of an escalation of their fights into a nuclear confrontation.

The world at large—but especially the immediate neighbors of

India and Pakistan—has an interest in ensuring that sudden flare-ups along the Kashmir borderlands do not evolve into monstrous conventional set battles that themselves evolve into a nuclear exchange. If North Korean armored divisions, under a protective volley of supporting missile and artillery fire, cross into South Korea, the vastly outnumbered American forces might consider the option of tactical nuclear weapons to save the prosperous and democratic south. All these nightmarish scenarios are known to interested regional parties, and may explain the recent absence of conventional battles between such bitter rivals.

A second scenario is perhaps more common, but still does not quite constitute reciprocal conventional battle as we have know it: the asymmetrical wars between large westernized militaries and poorer, less-organized terrorists, insurgents, and piratical forces. The list of such "half battle" theaters where conventional forces have battled unconventional guerrillas is almost endless—Afghanistan, Grozny, Iraq, Kashmir, Mogadishu, and the Somali coast, to name a few. Yet they all share one trait: No indigenous force dares to come out in the open, marshal its resources, and test head-on the firepower and discipline of a westernized force. History's record on that account—from Tenochtitlán to Omdurman—is not encouraging for those who might try.

True, insurgent groups sometimes fight one another, such as the Shiite-Kurdish-Sunni sectarian violence in Iraq, or the Tutsi-Hutu killing spree in Rwanda. But in those instances—while the ongoing, relentless violence in the aggregate can be every bit as lethal as a the one-day toll of an Austerlitz or Gettysburg—neither side has the resource, logistics, or organization to commit to or sustain a set battle.

On very rare occasions a weak state has either foolishly challenged in conventional fashion the United States or its allies or has been the subject of a surprise invasion. And while there has often loomed the specter of an old-fashion collision of arms, the obvious imbalance in conventional resources ensured that the result was relatively brief, one-sided, and mostly a rout—as we saw in the "Mother of All Battles" in January

1991, the NATO air assault against Slobodan Milošević (1999), the bombing of Tripoli (1986), the earlier British-Argentine showdown at Goose Green, Falklands Islands (1982), and the American invasions of Grenada (1983) and Panama (1989).

Those who have successfully attacked the United States—in Lebanon (1983), at the Khobar Towers, Saudi Arabia (1996), the American East African embassies (1999), the U.S.S. *Cole* (2000), and on September 11, 2001—did so as terrorists. And if nation-states other than Afghanistan sponsored such radical Islamist groups, they were careful to offer a deniability of culpability, preventing an all-out conventional war with the United States that they would inevitably lose.

Just as important as the nature of the combatants and the world political landscape in explaining the decline of conventional battles are other factors such as technology and the globalized communications of the twenty-first century. The conventional battlefield can now be seen and mapped to the smallest pebble. Aerial photography and second-by-second updated video-carrying drones ensure that surprise is rare. Potential combatants know far better the odds in advance. They can download minute information about their potential adversary from the Internet. Generals can see streaming videos of his pre-battle preparations and calculate to some degree the subsequent cost.

Uncertainty and the unknown were often essential to the course of decisive battle, since each opposing force usually felt it had some chance of operational success. If the British had satellite reconnaissance about the German lines in the days before and during the Somme, they might have curtailed their suicidal assaults. If the Americans had live streaming video of Japanese forces fortifying bunkers on Okinawa, they might not have chosen to assault frontally the Shuri Line. Pickett's Charge up Cemetery Ridge at Gettysburg was predicated on an erroneous assumption that there was an especially weak spot in the Union army's line—a conjecture that would have been easily disproved if General Robert E. Lee had a Predator drone at his disposal. We live in an age of successful surveillance when the counterresponse—jamming video feeds, destroying satellites, or short-circuiting electronic devices on a massive scale—has not yet caught up.

Weaponry likewise is not static. It also resides within a constant challenge-and-response cycle between offense and defense, armor and arms, surveillance and the maintenance of secrecy—a tension in which one periodically but temporarily trumps the other. Body armor may soon advance to the point of offering, if for a brief period only, protection against the bullet, which centuries ago rendered chain and plate mail useless. The satellite may become nonoperational by the satellite killer. The aerial drone soon may be forced down by more sophisticated electronic jamming.

Yet for now the arts of information gathering about an enemy trump his ability to maintain secrecy—and that too lessens the chance that thousands of soldiers will be willing to ride out to horrific battle, especially if they know they are being watched continuously on video by their adversaries. The conditions to enter decisive battle involve risk, delusions of grandeur, megalomania even—it's the irrational who thrive on ignorance and misinformation.

Just as important are the controversies concerning lethality and cost of the new munitions. To wage a single decisive battle between tens of thousands of combatants along the lines of a Gaugamela or a Verdun would cost hundreds of billions of dollars and is beyond the resources of most belligerents. A single B-2 bomber on patrol overhead represents nearly a one-billion-dollar investment. Abrams tanks cost more than four million dollars. Single cruise missiles are at least a million dollars. One GPS-guided artillery shell may cost one hundred and fifty thousand dollars; an artillery platform could expend over ten million dollars in ordnance in a few hours. Even a solder's M-4 assault rifle runs well over a thousand dollars. The result is that very few states can afford to outfit an army of, say, one hundred thousand infantry, supported by high-tech air, naval, and artillery fire—much less to keep it well supplied for the duration of battle. There is less likelihood, then, that Colombia or Venezuela would have the capital to deploy for very long two hundred thousand infantry soldiers in a vast collision of sophisticated arms.

Even in the smaller decisive battles of the 1973 Yom Kippur war, when armies were not huge and the weapons were cheap in comparison with today's models, both Israel and Egypt had to have the Soviet Union and the United States send in massive amounts of new weaponry shortly after the commencement of fighting. Arab and Israeli arsenals were near depletion within hours. Neither side had the resources to buy and transport replacement munitions without wealthier patrons—who themselves soon complained of the cost and difficulty of such resupply.

We have not seen a repeat of the Sinai battles of 1973 for various reasons—growing common regional interests between Israel and Egypt, satellite surveillance, the absence of an Arab nuclear patron to provide backup should an Egyptian gambit fail. But prominent among them is the cost of any such engagement, and the difficulty of finding an industrial big brother willing and able to budget billions for such efforts. Take away Iranian money, and terrorist organizations like Hezbollah and Hamas might have no missiles at their disposal.

In some cases, one belligerent may have the resources to offer a challenge to decisive battle, but it's unlikely that an enemy could be found with a similar hope to win through a head-on confrontation. Again, the frontline Arab states have for more than thirty years given up such a dream, as has Iran in its various aggressions against U.S. allies in Iraq and Lebanon.

The current ascendant anthropological notion in the West that war may well be unnatural, preventable, and the result of rational grievances—that can, with proper training and education, be eliminated or at least curtailed—perhaps has also made battle less tenable among the general public. To the millions of teachers, social workers, academics, medical professionals, and politicians in the West who are invested in such laudable notions, battle is seen as retrograde, a Neanderthal rejection of the entire promise of higher education itself. And so a sizable population of influential professionals in Europe and the United States actively opposes military action of any sort—and especially the prospect of a traditional slugfest in which repellently high casualties on one side would be inevitable. Such makers of public and often government opinion may likewise have played an indirect role in temporarily discouraging even the semblance of major conventional military confrontations.

The bombing of fleeing Iraqi bandit brigades from Kuwait on the so-called Highway of Death in the first Gulf War (1991) was halted by popular outrage because of the televised carnage. The argument that such enemies who had just committed pillage and rapine in Kuwait should be punished or preempted, given that they were likely to regroup back in Iraq to slaughter Kurdish and Shiite innocents, could hardly trump the Western abhorrence at the images of death on millions of television screens. Russia's shelling and destruction of Grozny escaped world condemnation only because a news blackout ensured Westerners would see little of mass death—and nuclear, oil-rich, and unpredictable strongman Vladimir Putin would have cared little if they had.

To suggest that Hezbollah and Israel, Hamas and Israel, or Syria and Israel, when the next Middle East war breaks out, be allowed to fight each other until one side wins and the other loses, and thus the source of their conflict be adjudicated by the verdict of the battlefield, is now seen not only as passé but also as amoral altogether. Who would wish a no-holds-barred showdown? And would not the loser simply try to reconstitute his forces for a second round?

We should remember that both victory and clear-cut defeat often put an end to a power's struggles in a way armistices and time-outs do not. Nazis, Fascists, and most Baathists have presently disappeared from the governments of the world. Military defeat ended not only their power but also discredited their ideologies to the extent that they have not resurfaced in any real strength in Germany, Italy, or Iraq.

A decisive end to war does not necessarily mean greater violence and human losses than what totalitarian governments are capable of in times of peace. Far more perished during Stalin's collectivization, the Holocaust, and the murdering and starvation brought about by Mao's various revolutions—mass genocides outside of formal military engagements—than in all the decisive battles of the twentieth century, which suggests that, at least in Hitler's case, they should have been stopped through force before they were allowed to kill millions more.

Again, modern scientific pacifism that tries to "prove" that bloody war is unnatural and has no utility in solving conflicts also tends to discourage the reappearance of decisive battle by inculcating such ideas among influential elements of the population. We certainly have no more Homers who sing of the *aristeia* of battling heroes, or Tennysons eager to write of another gloriously foolhardy charge by the Light Brigade. To read of gargantuan clashes of arms, replete with nobility in pursuit of exalted aims, is today to read fantasy—Tolkien's grand battle between orcs and men before the gates of Gondor.

Finally, globalization, through instant cell-phoning and text-messaging, use of the Internet, access to DVDs and satellite television, has created a world culture that depends on uninterrupted communications. It expects convenient airline flights, international banking, and easy access to imported consumer goods. The result is not quite a new worldwide pacifism or exalted humanity—one need only examine the membership of the United Nations Commission on Human Rights to see that there is no such thing as an evolving transnational morality outside the West.

Instead, electronic togetherness hinges on our shared appetites—and a growing communal comfort factor. After it invaded Georgia,

Russia's oil buyers became upset. As did its own aristocratic grandees, who saw international capital flee Moscow.

European states worry about oil shortages should the U.S. bomb Iran; China worries about its vital American export market should it invade Taiwan. We need not assume that "soft power" and the potential loss of easy twenty-first-century consumerism will always prevent set battles. After all, in the past, such a belief that global interreliance would prevent ruinous battle was clearly erroneous. Norman Angells's *The Great Illusion* (1909) argued that pre–First World War Europe simply had achieved too great an interdependence of financial credit, economic integration, and prosperity to throw it away on nihilistic warmaking. The Somme, Passchendale, and Verdun shortly followed.

Yet in a world in which an American can call his brother in the morning in Kenya, check his European 401(k) stocks over coffee, watch Japanese wrestling in the afternoon, and chat with Chinese Facebook friends in the evening, it is more difficult for a particular nation to marshal conventional forces, systematically seek out the enemy, encounter a like rival with similar hopes of success, and unleash a terrible fury of munitions—all under the instantaneous gaze of six billion. In the future, economic and cultural globalization increasingly may emulate old Roman imperium, becoming a superstructure that turns Africans, Asians, Americans, Europeans, and Latin Americans into a one-world province.

We are not yet facing the "end of history," with a final and total elimination of decisive set battles—and a united and harmonious world agreeing on the general protocols of globalized capitalism and consensual government. Armed struggles that at times result in horrific collisions of forces are as old as civilization itself, and a collective reflection of the constant and unchanging deep-seated elements in the human psyche. Tribalism, affinity for like kind, desire for honor, reckless exuberance—these expressions of our reptilian brains stay embedded within peoples.

The Return of Battle?

FOR THE FORESEEABLE future, we will remain in an age
without decisive battle, in which bloody war is unlikely to be played
out with swarms of Abrams tanks, rows of artillery pieces, a storm of
F-22s and B-1s overhead, and hundreds of thousands of infantry soldiers advancing to mass carnage against a like-minded enemy. Yet will
big battles haunt us once more?

Should the European Union dissolve and return to a twentieth-
century landscape of rival proud nations, should the former Soviet republics form a collective resistance to an aggrandizing Russia similar to
that in the nineteenth century, should the North Koreans, Pakistanis,
or Chinese choose to gamble on an agenda of sudden aggression in the
belief that a political objective could be obtained at a tolerable cost,
then we may well see a return of decisive battles.

New Waterloos or Verduns may revisit us, especially if constant
military innovation reduces the cost of war or relegates battle to the domain of massed waves of robotics and drones, or sees a sudden technological shift back to the defensive that would nullify the tyranny of
present-day horrifically lethal munitions. New technology may make all
sorts of deadly arms as accessible as iPods and more lethal than M-16s,
while creating uniforms impervious to small-arms fire—and therefore making battle itself cheap, unpredictable, and thus once more to
be tried.

Scenarios for battle's return are endless. Should a few reckless states
feel that nuclear war in an age of antiballistic missiles might be winnable,
or that the consequences of mass death might be offset in perpetuity in a
glorious collective paradise—an apocalyptic vision that sometimes seems
almost welcome in theocratic Iran—and therefore worth risk of a launch-
ing of ballistic missiles, then even the once unimaginable nuclear showdown becomes imaginable.

When the conducive political, economic, and cultural requisites for set battles realign, as they have periodically over the centuries, we will see our own modernist return of a Cannae or a Shiloh. And these collisions will be frightening as never before. In the words of Matthew Arnold,

> We are here as on a darkling plain
> Swept with confused alarms of struggles and flight
> Where ignorant armies clash by night.

CHAPTER 9

"Men Make a City, Not Walls or Ships Empty of Men"

*When high-tech is not always so high**

Cycles of Military Innovation

I F THE PRINCIPLES of war stay the same across the centuries, one reason that we of the present age sometimes doubt such continuity is the recent radical change in military technology, especially given the twenty-first-century advances in informational science and its applications. We forget sometimes that transformation in arms has always been a hallmark of warfare, even if not as radical as what we have witnessed in the past half century. As a rule, militaries usually begin wars

---

* The quote is from Thucydides' *History of the Peloponnesian War* (7.77.7). Parts of this essay, incorporate a review of Frederick W. Kagan's *Finding the Target: The Transformation of American Military Policy* (New York: Encounter, 2006) and Max Boot's *War Made New: Technology, Warfare, and the Course of History, 1500 to Today* (New York: Gotham, 2006), from the December 2006 *Commentary* magazine—as well as some material from the January–February 2008 *American*.

confident in their existing weapons and technology. But if they are to finish them successfully, it is often only by radically changing designs or finding entirely new ones. The Union military started the Civil War with muskets and cannonballs but ended it using bullet-firing repeating rifles and explosive artillery charges that were superior to those employed by the Confederacy. Ironclads, observation balloons, rubberized ponchos, canned meats, and elaborate telegraphic communications were birthed during the war—many of these inventions enriching peacetime America for decades.

In 1940 the five-year-old, continually improved B-17 Flying Fortress bomber was considered an indestructible aerial behemoth, the most radically innovative warplane in the history of aviation. By the end of 1945 even its huge replacement, the recently introduced B-29 Superfortress, was facing near obsolescence in the new era of rocket-armed jet fighters. Germany invaded Poland with armored columns spearheaded by Panzer Mark III tanks equipped with a 37mm gun. But by war's end even beefed-up high-velocity 75mm and 76mm tank guns were overshadowed by 88mm cannon—and finally by even larger 122mm models.

During the five-year course of the Second World War, sonar, radar, ballistic missiles, and atomic bombs evolved from speculation to battlefield-proven, deadly reality. We entered the Vietnam War with the Second World War and Korean-era "dumb" bombs, and ended it with laser-guided aerial and antitank munitions.

Things have not been much different in the recent Iraq war. In March 2003 the United States attacked Saddam's Iraq, confident in our superior Abrams tanks, GPS- and laser-guided aerial munitions, and fast-moving mechanized columns powered by Humvees and Bradley armored vehicles. Seven years later the U.S. military's prewar land arsenal has been radically altered in reaction to Iraqi terrorists and insurgents.

As in all our prior wars, two kindred developments occurred. First, what was once considered adequate quickly proved ineffective. In a new war without identifiable fronts, light-skinned, troop-carrying Humvees were soon shredded by ever-larger roadside improvised explosive devices (IEDs). Subsequent up-armored kits, with expensive electronic jamming devices, resulted in only marginally safer vehicles. The military then rushed in even more heavily armored Humvees. It was soon sending over Stryker and mine resistant, ambush protected (MRAP) vehicles, which use new defensive mechanisms such as deflector shields to thwart land mines—even as new Iranian-made shaped charges, with liquefying copper heads, show an ability to penetrate these vehicles.

Second, entirely new weapons systems appeared. We had experimented with drones for much of the 1990s, though they were never considered critical components of the military's battlefield arsenal. But in Iraq—with its vast expanses, clear skies, open borders, nocturnal terrorists, and constant enemy mining of thousands of miles of roads—Predator and Predator B aerial drones, along with a variety of other pilotless airborne surveillance craft, suddenly became vital to monitor and kill once inaccessible terrorists.

The sheer excellence of large conventional American weapons systems—planes, ships, tanks—means few enemies now challenge them directly. Instead, the rope-a-dope insurgent tactic is to kill individuals in urban environments, often in an asymmetrical equation of investing many terrorist lives and little money to take out just a few Americans and millions of dollars of their supporting infrastructure. A ten-dollar IED might blow up a five-hundred-thousand-dollar robot, in the same fashion that a lone suicide bomber might blow up both himself and an affluent American who has hundreds of thousands of dollars invested in his training, equipment, and education. So far American planners have not figured out a means of producing cheaper weapons that allow fewer casualties on the ground. In the present we are substituting money for lives, our enemies in contrast using lives in lieu of money.

General weapons parity—in rockets, small arms, body armor, computers, weapons manuals, and tactics—is easily obtained by private purchase from mail-order weapons outlets, just as instructions for making bombs and mines are freely downloaded off the Internet. The lethality of off-the-shelf modern weapons is enhanced in the protective landscape of urban warfare. An insurgent's three-thousand-dollar Russian-made rocket-propelled grenade launcher (RPG-7) need not match the sophistication of a superior model employed by a U.S. Marine to take down a twenty-million-dollar Apache helicopter hovering over an Iraqi apartment building—thereby allowing each dollar of jihadist military hardware to nullify $6,660 of American investment.

For now, this disturbing challenge from the Iraq War has no answer: In a globalized world of instant communications and easy commerce, how do we prevent ever-increasing enemies from acquiring sophisticated-enough weapons and tactical manuals at little cost to nullify our far larger investments quickly and cheaply? Western businesses—as they compete with manufacturers abroad that have lower costs, far fewer regulations, and far less concern about the morality and ecology of how they operate—may think they are immune from this existential military lesson. But the Iraq War also shows us why and how—with parasitic technologies, without care for international law, and with little regard for human life—our rivals are making weapons off the battlefield far more quickly and cheaply than we can respond to them.

So the question remains: Is there something about twenty-first-century military technology, both its lethality and its mass dissemination, that has altered the face of war altogether, that has posed challenges of a nature and an extent unseen before in the history of arms?

The Revolution in Military Affairs—and Its Discontents

IN RECENT YEARS, the phrase "revolution in military affairs" (RMA) has come to be applied to the vast changes that computerized intelligence and globalization have brought to the conduct of war. This catchy sobriquet, however, is only a new name for something very old. In fact, radical transformations in military practice have marked Western history at least since Sparta and Athens squared off in the Peloponnesian War in the fifth century B.C, and the Greek world soon saw strange new flamethrowers belching compressed gases and ever more sophisticated use of stone ramparts.

Such RMAs are also the focus of recent books by two of our most accomplished commentators on military affairs: Frederick W. Kagan in *Finding the Target: The Transformation of American Military Policy* and Max Boot in *War Made New: Technology, Warfare, and the Course of History, 1500 to Today*. I should note at the outset that both of these scholars are wise enough not to be taken in by the notion that today's technological breakthroughs in satellite communications, computers, and miniaturization have altered the nature of war itself rather than merely the present face of battle, much less that they can by themselves win wars outright. Both also share a keen interest in the contemporary "war against terrorism"—and in their articles (Kagan) and columns (Boot) have responded in similar ways to America's purportedly erratic progress in the Iraq War.

Early and vocal supporters of the invasion of Iraq, Kagan and Boot each became harshly critical of our postwar efforts at counterterrorism; each, furthermore, has at various times called for the resignation of Secretary of Defense Donald Rumsfeld and other high-ranking generals in Baghdad. Such zeal is periodic in Boot's work, more overt and constant in Kagan's, but it informs their shared concern over a Pentagon leadership that has supposedly put too much reliance on high-tech weaponry and organizational principles borrowed from business, and thereby contributed to the growing fragility of America's current position of military superiority.

Kagan's book, more contemporary in its frame of reference than Boot's, centers on three revolutions in the American military since the Vietnam War: the rise of the volunteer army with its high-tech equipment and weaponry, the appearance in the 1980s of precision-guided munitions, and the adoption of information technology. To Kagan's mind, these are often welcome developments, and yet their consequences in policy have gone hand in hand with a decidedly unwelcome failure of American military and strategic thinking.

No country, he writes, has a more diverse and effective arsenal than America. At the same time, however, no nation is so bogged down fighting wars in a manner it would prefer not to. His bipartisan indictment fingers two recent culprits: Bill Clinton, who dismantled crucial elements of the Cold War military establishment, and George W. Bush, who, not understanding the larger political purposes of war, lacked the necessary vision to reap the advantage of the vast conventional power that was reconstituted under his leadership.

Kagan is scornful of faddish concepts like "network-centric warfare" and of the idea that the American military needs to embrace the spirit and the tactics of successful American corporations—downsizing, seeking greater efficiencies through new technologies and on-demand supply trains, and overwhelming rivals with pyrotechnics. In his view, all such cookie-cutter notions miss the point of how best to defeat multifarious enemies. Old-fashioned armored divisions with tanks and massive artillery, and their expensive manpower costs, may not achieve as much bang for the buck. But such men and materiel are often better suited to war's proper aim: bringing about long-term political settlements favorable to the United States. In this case, "War is not just about killing people and blowing things up," he writes. "It is purposeful violence to achieve a political goal."

Of course, Afghanistan and Iraq are his object lessons. In both places, having put the military cart before the strategic horse, the United States easily toppled oppressive regimes only to find itself hard-pressed to replace them with something both lasting and better. To what advantage is all our high-tech weaponry, Kagan asks, if, after lightning-quick victories over the Taliban and Saddam Hussein, our soldiers are still, years later, falling prey to crude improvised explosive devices and primitive suicide bombers? What is the purpose of having high-tech weaponry replace soldiers on the ground, if men, not machines, are necessary to enforce postwar order?

Kagan's advice is that the U.S. military should undergo something of a counterrevolution. We need, he insists, not more gadgets but more human know-how. In practical terms, this means providing military officers with the resources and training—especially in cultural awareness and languages—that they need in order to serve as proconsuls in postwar landscapes. The victories of the future will be won and will endure, he argues, only when we have sufficient boots on the ground, filled by soldiers sophisticated in the ways of diverse enemies.

Max Boot's *War Made New* is a rather different creature, both in its temporal scope and in its methodology. A universal history of military transformation since 1500, the book deals with four quite different upheavals: the gunpowder revolution that began in the late sixteenth century; the first industrial revolution in the late nineteenth century, which brought rapid communications, large-scale transportation, and the internal-combustion engine; the second and more radical industrial revolution in the early- and mid-twentieth century, which led to the mass production of sophisticated ships, planes, and tanks; and, finally, our own information revolution of satellites, computers, and instant wireless communications.

For each of his four eras, Boot provides graphic accounts of three representative battles and a chapter on "consequences." His section on the second industrial revolution, for instance, opens with the 1940 Nazi blitzkrieg in France before moving on to the Japanese attack at Pearl Harbor and then the firebombing of Tokyo in March 1945. Throughout, Boot provides a vivid and engaging mix of historical narrative and analysis, showing the bloody real-world results of abstract decision making about the nature and degree of a country's military preparedness. His twelve case studies, stretching from the defeat of the Spanish

Armada to the current situation in Iraq, point to a variety of disparate lessons, but, once again, also some themes that are surprisingly constant over time and space.

The most important of these is an old reminder that sheer numbers do not always ensure victory. In the Sudan in 1898, Kitchener's redcoats defeated a Mahdi army that enjoyed as much as a three-to-one advantage in manpower over the English. As Boot argues, modern military success has depended less on bulk (or even firepower) than on the broader capacities possessed by nations that are "intellectually curious and technologically innovative." The key to success is not just advanced weaponry that replaces manpower, but knowledge that utilizes sophisticated weapons in the proper strategic context.

The dynamism of imperial Britain gave Kitchener the expertise, organization, and capital to build a railroad across a bend in the Nile, thus enabling his expeditionary force to arrive near Khartoum intact, with plenty of artillery and machine guns and better supplied than its native adversaries. A similar intellectual dynamism, illustrated in another of Boot's accounts, enabled the innovative Japanese navy to achieve its astonishing victory over the Russian fleet in 1905 in the battle of Tsushima. By the twentieth century, modern-looking regimes, often statist like Japan, were ostensibly best positioned to harness the natural resources and industrial labor demanded by modern warfare. They also appeared most adept at raising the mass-conscript armies that would distinguish the two world wars to come.

But, as Boot demonstrates, their seeming advantages proved transitory. In the Second World War, the American bomber plant at Willow Run, Michigan—a mammoth 3.5-million-square-foot structure that, by August 1944, was producing one B-24 every hour—ultimately counted much more heavily toward the outcome of the conflict than the innovation and craftsmanship that had given the Nazis V-2 missiles and a few hundred advanced ME-262 jet fighters. The initial battlefield successes of the Axis powers were made possible by surprise and a head start in rearming; but this was eventually reversed by the wartime defense bureaucracies of the Soviet Union, Britain, and the United States, all three of which, in their various ways, proved better at mastering the principles of interchangeable parts, the assembly line, and the fielding of millions of conscripts. The key again was not just whether a nation could produce sophisticated weapons, but whether it could do so in large numbers that were readily accessible and easily used by soldiers in the field—and in a manner that might ensure tactical victory in accordance with strategic goals.

Concluding his survey with the present revolution in information systems, Boot sketches the ironies inherent in our own recent experience. Today's battlefield, in the Middle East as elsewhere, tends to favor decentralized and unconventional forces. In a globalized and interconnected world, terrorists underwritten by the petrodollars of despots can buy weaponry off the shelf and have it FedExed to Beirut or Damascus, giving them near parity in this respect with Western militaries that, for a variety of practical and ethical reasons, appear restrained from bringing their full array of advantages to the conflict.

For our part, as ever more American dollars have been invested in ever fewer high-end military "platforms"—that is, advanced computerized ships and planes—we have seen our attenuated forces in the field becoming increasingly vulnerable and risk-averse. Who would want to send even a single B-2 bomber over terrorist enclaves when a cheap shoulder-fired anti-aircraft missile might take out a near-billion-dollar investment?

Still, Boot warns against too single-minded a focus on asymmetrical warfare and its vulnerabilities. When it comes to blasting away at terrorists a few feet from American troops in the Hindu Kush, the cannons of an old A-10 Warthog will indeed do a better job than the new F-22 Raptor, which is by far the most expensive and sophisticated jet in the world. But should the Chinese decide to storm Taiwan—hardly a fanciful possibility—it would be better to have that F-22 in the skies to ensure our strategic air superiority.

What this flexibility suggests is the need to avoid complacency—of any kind. In this fine book, Boot sees the five-hundred-year history he reviews as a warning. The rise and fall of past militaries remind us that the United States is not foreordained to maintain its present edge. Therefore, we must recognize and replenish the font of our power by continuing to incorporate unconventional ideas and approaches into our military operations—remaining aware all the while that the category of the newly "unconventional" can still include some old-fashioned and allegedly outmoded ideas.

Eternal Challenge and Response

THERE HAVE ALWAYS been unexpected and abrupt changes in the way men fight—even in preindustrial times. Military practice is most often turned upside down during wars of great savagery, in which states in breakneck fashion invest their human and material capital in trying to stave off annihilation. During most of the early fifth century B.C., the Hellenic city-states preferred to settle their border disputes by means of conventional collisions between phalanxes of hoplites.

But during the almost-three-decades-long cauldron of the Peloponnesian War (431–404), such traditional warfare fell by the wayside. Both conservative, landlocked Sparta and imperial, maritime Athens turned to other avenues and methods—triremes rowed by mercenary and slave oarsmen, innovative techniques in siege-craft, the use of light cavalry, even terrorism. These set off a cycle of challenge and response like nothing seen before in Greek history.

By the time of Athens's defeat in 404 B.C., this early RMA had changed Western warfare seemingly for good. Just as states could no longer envision armed conflict as a series of pitched battles among ranks of hoplites, so the old social classifications of the battlefield—with the wealthy on ponies, small property-owners in the phalanx, and the landless poor as skirmishers and rowers—no longer prescribed how and where men would fight. Moral philosophers and conservative generals decried these changes. These reactionaries complained that the rabble, war machines, and money were now the decisive factors in war—but to no avail.

This seeming break with the past, however, was hardly the end of the matter. In ancient Greece, exactly as today, sudden innovation did not completely overturn the old order. And those who believed otherwise would often come to regret it. Despite the obsolescence of hoplite phalanxes, the general idea of spearmen in close order—eventually modified to become mercenary soldiers with pikes—persisted for centuries after the Peloponnesian War. Generals from Epaminondas to Alexander the Great learned that phalanxes were still integral to armies—provided they were given ample support by siege-craft, artillery, and horsemen—and were especially useful for shattering enemy infantry and cavalry.

In much the same way—and despite the introduction of satellites, computers, and radically new metals and munitions—tanks not so different in appearance from those of the 1920s remain invaluable in modern warfare. They still fulfill the age-old need for a powerful mobile artillery providing protection for foot soldiers. Even horses have not been entirely displaced—as we saw in the famous photos of mounted Special Forces soldiers typing GPS coordinates into their laptops in the wilds of Afghanistan. It is instructive that today's sophisticated ceramic body armor makes modern soldiers look like nothing so much as medieval knights or indeed Greek hoplites, reminding us that the tension between offense and defense is eternal.

Certain laws of war—the need for unity of command, for integrating tactics with strategy, for devising strategy with political objectives in mind—have been immune to technological revolution. This is no surprise: War remains an irreducibly human phenomenon, and human nature itself has not changed over the ages. Thus, although the 1991 Gulf War was a memorably high-tech conflict, and although American M-1 Abrams tanks almost always destroyed their Iraqi counterparts in a first computer-guided shot, this by itself did not deliver lasting strategic advantage.

The reason was that American planners were unsure of their ultimate goal: Was it to defeat the Iraqi army in Kuwait while maintaining the unity of the wartime coalition, or to bring down the regime in Baghdad that was fielding that army? In contrast, an outclassed Saddam Hussein understood that the survival of his regime, and his continued control of Iraq's oil wealth, might mean a victory of sorts after the end of the Kuwaiti war, in the sense that unless there was a constant American military presence to monitor his behavior (in his view eventually a dubious proposition), he would be free to resume regional aggression and the subsidy of terrorism.

Military preeminence is often transitory. By the end of the Peloponnesian War, Sparta had fashioned the best hoplite army in the world; yet between 371 and 369 B.C., the Thebans proved it tactically and strategically obsolete. Thirty years later, Philip of Macedon and his son Alexander showed that even the once-innovative Thebans were no match for pike-bearing, mercenary phalangites supported by heavy cavalry with *sarissas*. Yet by the second century B.C., Hellenistic pikemen had ossified, and their dinosaur-like phalanxes fell easy prey to far more mobile and articulated Roman legions. Victors that rest on their laurels, whether today's or yesterday's, often have to play catch-up when the fighting starts, and can stumble badly.

We should note that almost every technological transformation of consequence has taken place under Western auspices—if not Western in the strict geographical sense, then Western in the notion of a cultural landscape shaped by free thought and the chance for profit. Even non-Western innovations, like stirrups and gunpowder, have been quickly modified and improved by Western militaries. Jet fighters, GPS-guided bombs, and laser-guided munitions are all products of Western expertise. Even the jihadists' most innovative and lethal weapons—improvised explosive devices and suicide belts—are cobbled together from Western-designed explosives and electronics.

But, as we have seen, this too is no cause for complacency. Precisely because such novel weaponry is a Western domain, there is always the danger that Westerners will underestimate the capacities of others. Crazy Horse at Little Big Horn, the Zulus at Isandlwana, Abu Musab al-Zarqawi in the Sunni Triangle—all have been able to import and use sophisticated weapons that they can neither make nor easily repair to kill Westerners with ease.

Where does that leave us? With reason for caution and circumspection, but also with clear advantages that are sometimes scanted by analysts fixated on our errors and missteps. True, our enemies may be able to exploit some of our advances, but unless they wish to alter their very culture, they will never match our intellectual dynamism. No society in the present age is so self-critical, so ready to embrace foreign ideas, or so transparent and merit-based as the United States. Far more lethal to the U.S. military than a new form of IED would be censorship of ideas back home in the United States, or religious restrictions on research, or politically guided rules of investigation and publication, or government-run monopolies on labor, management, and production. Innovative military technology, then, is not so much a catalyst of change as much as a symptom of a dynamic military that understands that new weapons still operate within the eternal laws of conflict.

Indeed, future historians may well attribute our recent successes— toppling the two worst regimes in the Middle East, presiding over the birth of consensual governments in their places, and losing fewer soldiers in the effort than during many individual campaigns of the Second World War or Korea—to an ever-innovative American military that learned quickly from mistakes of the kind described in *Finding the Target* and *War Made New*. The sometimes dour work of Frederick W. Kagan and Max Boot is itself emblematic of one of our society's greatest strengths: the capacity to adjust to changing events with the help of thinkers who rely on a more deeply informed sense of historical reality than is conveyed in the panicked conclusions of the twenty-four-hour news cycle.

Yet even recognizing our shortcomings, and even our strengths, is not enough. Military revolutions are missed not only because of military sloth, delusional leadership, or a reactionary romance with the past; they are also missed because of a failure at the elite levels of society either to perceive real threats posed by real external enemies or to countenance the sacrifices necessary to meet those threats. Notable examples include ancient Athens and Rome, turn-of-the-twentieth-century Russia, and France in the 1930s, which in varying degrees felt somehow that their long-entrenched habits, economic exceptionalism, or particular worldview ensured that they were immune from how war has operated over the centuries. In that sense, the principal challenge today is not only to hone our military in the face of constantly evolving challenges, but also to convince an affluent, leisured, and often cynical American public that that we should even try to do so.

CHAPTER 10

The American Way of War— Past, Present, and Future

Why does America fight the way it does?[*]

Culture!

WAR REFLECTS CULTURE. Weaponry, tactics, notions of discipline, command, logistics—all such elements of battle arise not just from the constraints of terrain, climate, and geography, but also from the nature of a society's economy, politics, and sociology. This is as true for the American military today as it was in ancient and medieval times, and as valid for non-Western as for Western civilizations.

For example, the files of the ancient Greek phalanx and the preference of its heavy-armored hoplites for quick, decisive shock battles over farmland grew out of a society of freeholding agrarian hoplites who

---

[*] This article is derived in spirit from an essay that appeared in the Spring 2003 *New Atlantis*.

purchased their own armor, worked farms of roughly equal size, and voted in land-owning assemblies on the condition of their own military service. Compare this with the rapid mounted onslaughts of nomadic horse-peoples of the steppes, or the huge imperial, multiethnic, and bureaucratic armies of autocratic and palatial Egypt and Persia. The infantry-minded Greeks of the city-state, it is true, lacked the large plains of Thessaly to the north that nurtured a horse-rearing culture of aristocratic grandees, but they also preferred panoplies of some fifty pounds that otherwise made no sense in a hot, dry Mediterranean climate. In the scorching heat of the Attic summer, Athenians in loin clothes might have been seen as more logical warriors.

Geography and climate influence the brand of war, but in themselves are not determinant. The small inland valleys of Persian Anatolia, for example, were not all that much different from those found in Greece; but the culture of farmers who worked the soil there most certainly was. The armies of Mycenaean Greece were far different from what followed in the age of the Greek city-state, even though the weather, the landscape, and the agriculture of Greece were roughly constant from 3000 B.C. to 338 B.C. In other words, culture changed the way these very different Greek-speaking peoples of these two diverse eras fought—not climate or geography, which remained largely constant.

Western warfare in general over two and a half millennia has shown a dynamism in its exercise of military power abroad that is not explained by the rather small population and territory of Europe, much less its natural resources. Why is this so?

To generalize broadly: Reliance on group discipline, confidence in a greater degree of personal freedom and individualism, a faith in rationalism more likely to be divorced from cultural or religious stricture, open markets, civic militarism arising out of consensual government, and civic audit of military operations—sometimes in piecemeal—filtered down to the battlefield, embodying both the contradictions and unique achievements of Western civilization. Such advantages—sometimes nearly lost or vastly altered over 2,500 years—allowed Western armies, from Alexander the Great and the Crusaders to colonialists and present-day European and American militaries, to trump the usual criteria that explained tactical victory or defeat: weather, geography, numbers, location, individual genius and bravery, and simple chance. Once Xenophon's Ten Thousand were trapped in Asia, the army became a veritable itinerant polis, as committees and assemblies delegated responsibilities and elected new leaders, and individuals sought to craft novel strategies and adopt weaponry to radically different challenges. In contrast, after Xerxes' defeat at Salamis, he sailed back home, abandoning the fight, and entrusting his huge army to Mardonius, who was later defeated and killed at Plataea, and the survivors left to retreat home under Artabazus.

A key component to the rise of Western military influence has been the role of military technology. Again, Westerners did not invent triremes, stirrups, or gunpowder. But their greater propensity to encourage unfettered research and profit through free exchange and markets ensured that Europeans soon improved on such inventions in a way impossible elsewhere. European navies and armies went to Tenochtitlán, Zululand, and China rather than vice versa because of singular oceangoing ships, superior guns, and better supply—not out of some singular savagery or monopoly on imperial grandeur. It is not that the West did not suffer occasional battle defeats, or learn from other illustrious military traditions, or steal military inventions from abroad. But rather Westerners were able to fashion a flexible military culture that could overcome setbacks and spread influence well beyond the shores of an often divided and warring Europe.

While American military practice is inexplicable apart from this larger Western tradition, the American character and the peculiar history of the United States make its military force exceptional in ways that transcend the nation's large territory, plentiful resources, and population. This military power by the mid-twentieth century became unmatched by contemporary Europe—a fact that suggests, as many have written, that America and Europe may be heading in different cultural directions. This exceptionalism has much to do with both America's origins and recent past—both our democratic culture and frontier history—but also our unique role in the Second World War and the Cold War that followed, when leaders were determined after two global conflagrations to intervene permanently in world affairs and craft some sort of stable economic and political system contingent on U.S. security guarantees.

In particular, the United States has taken preexisting Western notions of political and economic freedom, the culture of individualism, and the commitment to constant self-critique and change, and advanced these practices nearly to their theoretical limits—certainly in a manner unlike what is found in contemporary Britain, France, or Germany. While there is much to say about the divide between America's military and civilian cultures, the shared dynamism of both is far more significant for understanding the future of American military power.

Why We Fight as We Do

WHAT, THEN, IS the American way of war? Without a national religion or a common race or ethnic culture, Americans are united first by shared ideas and commitments, such as the ideals of equal opportunity and individual merit, as well as the history and legends that give these ideas concrete meaning. Our military functions more as a reflection of our national meritocracy, where wealth and breeding, or tribal affiliations and favoritism, do not necessarily guarantee rank, privilege, and promotion.

In theory, this allowed that a gifted but shabby-looking general like Ulysses S. Grant—a failure in both earlier civilian and military life—could more successfully lead the Army of the Potomac than the aristocratic ex-railroad president George McClellan. We admire the uncouth George Patton for his often crude genius, despite, not because of, his aristocratic roots—in the same manner that the plebian background of Omar Bradley and Dwight Eisenhower often seemed to work to their advantage by suggesting both were self-made men who had advanced without wealth or social connections, and they therefore easily resonated with the American public and press. This reliance on presumed merit rather than class has sometimes given American armies singular commanders who were swashbuckling and unseemly—an unlettered Nathan Bedford Forrest, a shabbily dressed William Tecumseh Sherman, a cigar-chomping Curtis LeMay—and who might otherwise have found little opportunity in more aristocratic or tribal militaries.

Second, the frontier experience on such a vast continent made Americans by needs conquer time and space, explaining why European inventions in transportation and communication came into their own in America on a scale undreamed of elsewhere—railroads, steam engines, the telegraph and telephone, and electric power. America's role as a "receptacle of the unwanted"—an arena where audacious individuals, fleeing from poverty or discrimination, were in a hurry to start over and succeed rapidly—only added to the restless fascination with machines that were so disruptive of the traditions and tranquility of the past. Mechanization was equated with a culture of youth, restless and eager to go places, the more distant and more quickly, the better.

To meet General John Pershing's promise of getting "a million men" to France before the end of the war—in truth, forty-eight divisions of 28,000 men made it to Europe by the 1918 armistice, or over 1,200,000 combat troops—Americans overnight reorganized their rail systems, built and commandeered hundreds of ships (building more tonnage in April 1918 than America had in all at 1914), and managed to implement a draft that sent hundreds of thousands from farms in the heartland to France without losing a single recruit to German submarines or surface raiders on the routes over. The Army of the Potomac and the Union navy started off with flintlocks and wooden sailing ships and fought a mere four years later with dreadful new weapons, such as repeating rifles (lever-action Spencers spitting seven shots in twelve seconds), Gatling guns (two hundred shots per minute), and ironclad warships with eleven-inch guns. There was rarely an American version of a Spartan king, a Chinese mandarin, or an aristocratic knight to deplore the unchivalrousness and egalitarianism of such new tools of mass killing.

A sort of breakneck quality to American life arose where immigrants sought to find immediate status and economic security—often through an embrace of modernism and a rejection of tradition and custom. In reaction, American militaries in the technological sense have always reflected just that emphasis on impatient mobility and mass production—made easier because our youths are intimately acquainted with equipment of all sorts, from Model Ts to video games. By the mid-twentieth century, American sixteen-year-olds drove, owned, fixed, and customized cars. We entrust them at an early age with expensive and sometimes dangerous machines, whether pickup trucks, tractors, or fork-lifts, perhaps explaining why twenty-year-olds drive seventy-ton Abrams tanks and wave fifty-million-dollar jets onto the decks of five-billion-dollar carriers.

Those who "rolled with Patton" across France were at home with tank, truck, and jeep engines; they were eager and able to fix broken equipment that was analogous to what they had grown up with in both farm and town. Unlike that of modern Arab armies, Patton's problem was not an inability to keep his motorized fleet in good repair, but rather the shortage of gasoline and the ensuing boredom—and danger—when thousands of restless G.I.s ground to a halt in September 1944. It was no accident that American divisions in the Second World War were the most mechanized of all those in the conflict—with almost four thousand vehicles in each division, allowing sixteen thousand men to move at almost fifty miles per day across poor roads. The great American contribution to the Red Army was not just food stocks and strategic materials but nearly four hundred thousand heavy transport trucks, which eventually allowed Stalin a mobility and rapidity lacking among his Nazi enemies on the eastern front.

In contrast, the supposedly modern Wehrmacht largely was fed and fueled by horse-drawn transport. In 1991 and 2003, Americans moved hundreds of thousands of troops to new Persian Gulf quarters in the same way they built housing tracts here at home—rapidly, en masse, and with an eye to the next project even before the present job was done.

Unlike Hitler with his finely crafted and calibrated Panther and Tiger tanks, which were qualitatively superior in terms of firepower and protection but harder to maintain and not so easily mass produced, Americans sought to turn out almost limitless supplies of easily accessible weaponry—Sherman tanks, B-24 bombers, and M1 assault rifles—to achieve quantitative advantage. True, a ponderous fifty-six-ton German Tiger tank could blow apart dozens of Shermans. But there was no guarantee that it would be running when hordes of the latter swarmed German rifle brigades. In general the mass-produced, standardized Sherman tank required far fewer hours of maintenance per hours driven—and was far more easily serviced by those who manned it than any of its better armored, better armed, and more lethal German counterparts.

By late 1942 and early 1943, U.S. industry was already turning out more warplanes annually than Germany, Japan, and Britain combined, despite America's virtual disarmament until the late 1930s. While German technical and engineering genius at war's end produced the world's first guided missile (the V-2), the first jet fighter (the Me-262), and the first surface-to-air missile (the Waterfall), it was the American propensity for mass production, coupled with constant debate about the mission and nature of such weapons, that made their successors appear in such great numbers in the Cold War arsenal of the United States.

Despite the wizardry involved in crafting guided missiles and jet fighters, we should remember that neither weapon in the Second World War did a fraction of the damage done by thousands of more-pedestrian and more-practical B-17 bombers and P-51 fighters, which were mass-produced, reliable, easily piloted, and constantly improved. Hitler's madcap directives for V-2 production—without American-style audit and consensus—cost as much money as the Manhattan Project, but one atomic bomb had more concentrated firepower than all the German V-2s put together.

Alternatively, had Hitler invested in something akin to the B-17 or B-29 (which also cost more than the Manhattan Project), rather than in the more expensive research and development involved in guided missiles, he might well have been able to bring untold damage to Great Britain even in the latter months of the war. American pragmatism—in the tradition of a Henry Ford or Henry J. Kaiser—of delivering x-amount of explosive ordnance to the target at y-cost in men and materiel ultimately was at the foundation of most debates over military investment.

In addition, unlike the Soviet experience or even modern European practice, Americans tend to distrust central government and state-run industries. A nation of citizens with the constitutional right to bear firearms has kept most of the American arms industry outside state arsenals, or at least in the hands of private subcontractors with government licenses. Such companies usually operate more on free market principles, for the most part guaranteeing a greater propensity to produce cheaper and more plentiful weaponry. It is hard to think of other militaries that have produced better or more numerous carriers, jet fighters, or tanks since 1945. For nearly thirty years, the Soviets achieved theoretical military superiority in central Europe, but the Warsaw Pact's advantages in the numbers of tanks and artillery were explained by its favorable location and Russia's spending 30 to 40 percent of its GNP on defense versus the 6 percent allotted by the United States. In the end, as we learned, this "superiority" was unsustainable.

In short, the culture of the United States—characterized by an emphasis on youth, individualism, and practicality—is evident in our manner of making war. The controversial practice of widespread gun ownership in the United States has meant that a large segment of American youths does not grow up afraid of, or inexperienced with, firearms. Young people with guns—other than those in inner-city gangs—do not arouse the suspicions of the state police or incur social ostracism. From the pensions of the Grand Army of the Republic to the G.I. Bill and the Veterans' Hospitals, the American military has been closely integrated with American society, whether as a source of income in old age or of subsidies for continuing education. The result is that military service and the idea of using weapons are not seen as strange or antithetical to our society at large—as has become true in contemporary Europe. For millions of Americans, military service provides access to education, health care, and retirement benefits—as well as generally recognized prestige and public thanks.

Shooting guns in uniform is accepted not only as central to the defense of our country but also as a legitimate avenue for career advancement—all paradoxically in a democratic climate deeply suspicious of militarism. American ideas of muscular independence are deeply embedded in our frontier experience, when guns and the willingness to use them were a means to feed one's family, enforce justice when the "law" was a three-day-ride away, and form ad hoc militias to hunt down organized intruders, rather than serving in a centralized and permanent army.

Rising Expectations and Modern War

AMERICAN THINKING ABOUT military strategy reflects these larger restless imperatives. The public puts a premium on employing overwhelming firepower to end wars quickly—as in Grant's unthinking bloody hammer blows at the Wilderness and Cold Harbor, Pershing's insistence on keeping a cohesive American army for massive assaults on German lines, and the Overlord strategy of simply blasting a path in a "broad thrust" through Normandy across the Rhine. Even our most skilled and successful commanders, such as William Tecumseh Sherman and George Patton, who sought to avoid casualties by employing flank attacks or deep sweeping penetrations into the enemy heartland, always labored against the charge that they were afraid of head-on assaults that might more quickly batter the enemy and end the war.

With such vast reservoirs of men and materiel, and a democratic population far removed from Asian and European squabbling, wouldn't conventional American doctrine suggest using our forces to win quickly and bluntly, and then go back home? Indeed the purportedly uncouth language of a maverick Sherman or Patton may have simply been a necessary convention to ensure the public of their wartime ferocity. In fact, both were cerebral generals who sought a more mobile and flanking sort of indirect approach that might reduce American battle causalities and cause the collapse of enemy formation without costly frontal assaults.

Aircraft carriers are perhaps the best symbols of the contradictory American desire to be mobile, independent, and yet overwhelmingly powerful enough to annihilate an enemy through direct massive blows. They have now evolved into a virtual American institution. France has one, England three—all four together possess less offensive power than any one of our current eleven fleet counterparts.

Indeed, an American carrier's flight deck of almost five acres possesses more lethal planes than the entire air force of most other nations. These hundred-thousand-plus-ton homes to five thousand men and women appear to the untrained eye as clumsy behemoths, but they can cruise well over six hundred miles in a day, at a clip of thirty-five knots, without seeking the permission of nearby countries or granting concessions to hosts for landing rights. The initial cost to build, man, and deploy an entire American carrier group can easily exceed twenty billion dollars.

American restlessness and mobility have also meant that political pressure can quickly mount against wars that get bogged down with high casualties and little progress. By spring 1951 the United States had essentially stopped North Korean and Chinese aggression, and was poised to retake the north. Yet public opinion was already tired with a conflict that did not seem to ensure decisive and immediate victory, had cost tens of thousands of American dead and wounded, and raised the specter of nuclear escalation. So Americans settled for stalemate and saw it as a victory that at least South Korea was saved. Yet over a half century later the United States was still talking of North Korea as "evil," as the regime threatened to send ballistic missiles toward Hawaii.

Despite the establishment of a viable South Vietnamese government by 1973, the American public, after nearly a decade of fighting, was in no mood to continue bombing to repel the Communist invasions of late 1974 and 1975 that violated the armistice. And so the United States lost the peace negotiated at the Paris peace talks, not the shooting war against invading North Vietnam forces. It is controversial to what degree an American president can maintain support for a distant war of high casualties; what is not in dispute is that the American public will turn quickly on any commander in chief who cannot assure them that American armies are mobile, are on the offensive, and will bring home victory rather than become mired in stalemate, pitted against terrorists and insurgents, and subject to a negotiated armistice.

American culture and military technology have also shaped our approach to multilateralism, or the desirability of using force only under the auspices of international authorities. In fact, America's deep-rooted individualism, coupled with our distance from Europe and Asia, has never made us very comfortable with fighting in coalitions, despite protestations to the contrary. For the first 130 years of our history, we conducted no major wars outside our own continent; and while the United States intervened constantly in South America, Asia, and North Africa, nineteenth-century American marines and gunboats usually did so solely under the direction of the president.

We came into both the First World War and the Second World War late, and were always somewhat uneasy with our allies, preferring to work mostly alone in the Pacific war from 1942 to 1945. The story of the European theater of the Second World War is a narrative of acrimony between General Dwight D. Eisenhower and General Bernard Montgomery, and their legions of lieutenants who bickered constantly over everything from adaptations in American-supplied equipment to the strategy of a narrow- or broad-front advance into Germany. To read the memoirs of General John J. Pershing is to learn of daily strife with his French and British counterparts who wished to incorporate American troops under their own command aegis. The United Nations participation in the Korean War was a fluke, due to a temporary Soviet boycott of the Security Council that facilitated international sanction and support to what began and remained, in terms of aggregate troop strength on the ground, largely an American effort. Most nations agreed to send troops only when it seemed that, after Incheon, American forces were quickly going to reach the Yalu and unify the peninsula—and then became horrified that their battalions were instead facing hundreds of thousands of advancing Chinese.

NATO was not involved in Vietnam, a war that remained, for good or evil, mostly an American unilateral affair. And looking back to the first Gulf War, the chief criticism of the first Bush administration was the failure to invade Baghdad and remove Saddam Hussein. This controversial decision is usually attributed to the fear of losing Arab support and dividing our U.N.-mandated coalition—a restraining multilateralism not repeated against Milošević or in the subsequent campaign against Saddam Hussein, despite the presence of allies in both later conflicts. It mattered little to the reluctant Europeans—who had no desire to send sizable combat contingents to Afghanistan to bulk up NATO expeditionary forces—whether George W. Bush or Barack Obama was the American commander in chief begging them to participate in more bellicose fashion along the Pakistani border.

For all the depression over the long war in Iraq, the worry about the global financial crisis, and calls for far more American consultation with allies, this spirit of American military independence nevertheless has grown with our increasing confidence in the unrivaled capability of our military power, as well as our vague sense of being the only force on the world scene capable of ensuring order in the post–Cold War, post–September 11 world. America's long commitment to a blue-water navy, multistage guided missiles, long-range bombers, antiballistic missile systems, Mach 2 interceptors, Star Wars, and airborne divisions reflects this desire to project military power abroad, with minimum reliance on other nations, while keeping the battlefield away from the continental United States.

When we talk of properly acting in concert with either Western or democratic allies, we really mean the desire to obtain global legitimacy, additional financing, the assistance of "soft power" allied boycotts and embargoes of rogue nations, or bases proximate to the front. Allied support does not usually entail an additional Indian aircraft carrier, German air wing, French armored division, or Dutch Special Forces brigade.

The Future of American Warfare

WHAT IS THE future of American military practice, both technological and strategic? Will it conform to these general cultural traits so deeply embedded in our past? Technologically, the

United States will continue to seek ways of conducting small-scale wars rapidly with few casualties—along the lines of employing current GPS-guided bombs and cruise missiles that can be accurately controlled by a few highly trained ground operatives with laptops, cell phones, and radios.

That said, our enemies know better. The way to check American power by nonstate belligerents such as terrorists and insurgents is to draw Americans into urban warfare or operations on difficult terrain, with plenty of civilian bystanders who, in the enemy's mind, can conveniently become collateral damage, protest on global television, or serve as human shields for the terrorists among them. Only that way can American technological superiority be nullified, and American soldiers killed by the dozen, photographed, and broadcast instantly around the globe.

The best path for a Hezbollah terrorist or Iranian Revolutionary Guardsman to kill Americans is not to be exposed in open terrain like the Serbians of 1998 or Saddam's Baathists in 1991. The more American officers emphasize counterinsurgency, the obvious need for a greater mastery of foreign languages, closer affinity with diverse cultures, and more subtlety in winning hearts and minds, the less likely the public will wish to deploy their "special operations" contingents that cannot promise either traditional victory or a short and clearly-defined war. In contrast, the American character has always been more at ease with instantaneous bombing, shelling, and sweeping across open terrain in firing tanks—not nation-building, counterinsurgency, and theaterless battlefields where victory takes years and progress is not measured in the number of enemy dead or miles of enemy territory gained. Indeed, postmodern Americans are on the horns of a dilemma, in a variety of contexts.

We concede that American success in fostering democracy in postwar Germany, Italy, and Japan was predicated by age-old, rather dark assumptions that the Nazis, Fascists, and Japanese militarists had to be defeated, humiliated, and only then helped—and in that order. But whereas we now welcome the latter step of aiding a former enemy in the building of democracy, we loathe the first two requisites of inflicting a level of damage to ensure its success.

In terms of the tools of war for larger, more conventional theater conflicts, we may return to the past practice of "more, not just better," as the costs of high-tech weaponry and training reach astronomic levels. In the Second World War, America produced tens of thousands of durably built and simply operated fighters and bombers. We may see a similar reliance on mass-produced and inexpensive weapons in wars to come. The exorbitant expense of individual aircraft—B-2 bombers, for example, cost $1 billion each, older B-1 bombers cost $250 million—coupled with the idea of the inviolability of our pilots' lives, is already turning our attention to the mass production of drones. Sending a fleet of one hundred Predator drones with Hellfire missiles against a target might be as cheap and effective as two Air Force F-22 strike fighters—together costing $300 million, apart from their multimillion-dollar arsenals.

In short, we sense that the Pentagon is spending too much money on too few weapons, thus raising constant worries over the catastrophic financial consequences of losing a B-2 or F-17—even as we see spectacular one-sided punitive air victories precisely because of the qualitative superiority of assets like these.

The entrepreneurial genius of Silicon Valley and its epigones, coupled with the engineering and technological savvy of our universities, has ensured space-age weaponry far in advance of anything seen abroad. But the very temptation to constantly evolve and improve this technology has meant that we are now caught in the position of having ever fewer near-perfect arms rather than a plethora of very good weapons that will do. Given the horrors of 1941-43, when prewar disarmament ensured that thousands of American soldiers were killed in substandard tanks and planes, and given American chauvinism that we must be "best" in the world in terms of our weaponry's performance, it is ever harder for war planners to adopt a "good enough" attitude that would accept munitions far better than those available to our enemies, but not as good as the United States in theory could design and produce, albeit in smaller numbers.

Americans apparently cannot fathom the idea that a ragtag bearded jihadist, without formal education and burdened by seventh-century cultural prejudices, is often in fact an adroit strategic thinker, with an uncanny understanding of American national character, both our strengths and fallibilities. He rightly senses that a roadside bomb and a propane tank can not only take out a four-million-dollar tank but also, more important, cause a level of frustration and demoralization even greater than the material loss. To resolve this paradox of cost and protection, planners will have to find a way to make more weapons more cheaply, while at the same time reducing the requirement for more manpower—and the concurrent rising risk of greater exposure to death and dismemberment. And yet, as we have seen in prior chapters, there is no substitute for manpower on the ground, despite the killing power of new high-tech weaponry.

Consequently, emphasis on defense—from body armor to antiballistic missile systems—will become an ever-higher priority, as ever more affluent Americans, like Greek hoplites or medieval lords of old, grow increasingly sensitive to the casualties of war. The current weight of fifty to eighty pounds of gear that so burdens individual soldiers is not so much to provide them with additional offensive power as to achieve better communications, body protection, and survivability. This effort to ensure the absolute minimum of casualties may ultimately lead to the removal of the human agent whenever possible. After all, there is no strategic reason why the robots we now see in the sky will not soon descend to the battlefield itself—the cheaper and more numerous, the better.

At the same time, America's latent suspicion of the costs of military service abroad will reassert itself in the century to come. With the demise of the Soviet Union and disappointments with our allies in the present conflicts, we may see a gradual tendency to return to pre–Cold War characteristics of muscular independence, including the development of new technologies that explicitly serve this purpose. The United States is often criticized as interventionist, but in fact America's traditional propensity has been more isolationist—willing to act forcefully in the world when absolutely necessary, but preferring to be unencumbered. That urge is long-standing and bipartisan, and perhaps will be accelerated under more liberal administrations: When conservatives question the expense of the Atlantic Alliance, they are sometimes portrayed as gratuitously punitive of Europe. When liberals wish to pull back in the same manner, it is more palatably seen as an overdo effort to bolster multilateralism and transnational institutions by allowing Europe some breathing space, and encouragement to develop their own forces as partners rather than subordinates.

Either way, over time, Americans may look for ways—strategic and technological—to keep the global peace without involving ourselves in the political and cultural quagmires abroad that we usually associate with traditional alliances and bases. Sadr City and Mogadishu are precisely landscapes that the U.S. military wishes to avoid, but fears will most likely be our next theaters of confrontation. As a result, the Pentagon is desperately looking for technologies and radical changes in tactics that might ensure that any future interventions into such classic traps are far lass lethal and humiliating.

American planners will probably seek not merely alternate bases in Eastern Europe but also a greater reliance on lightly manned military depots, multifaceted sea- and land-based antiballistic missile systems, renewed commitment to carrier forces, and novel technologies that might provide floating logistical caches, mobile airfields, rapid ship transport, and increased airlift capacity. America's tendency toward isolationism will never really disappear, even as our global responsibilities increase. We will seek new technologies that will allow Americans to serve abroad in ways that require the least amount of political concessions and obligations to foreign hosts while preserving an ever wider range of military options.

For example, if we believe that a nuclear North Korea means to blackmail the United States by holding Hawaii hostage or threatening to shell our South Korean allies or our troops in the demilitarized zone, the way of facing such a crisis will not just be to rally a tentative Seoul or a worried Tokyo around a conventional coalition of ground troops. Instead, we might prefer to encircle the peninsula quickly and unilaterally with stealthy submarine-based antiballistic missile systems that could hit Pyongyang's nukes in their nascent trajectory, keep our forces at sea ready for blockades and embargos, but uncommitted, and then let the concerned powers ask us for advice and support, rather than the reverse. A small air base, with fortified and subterranean hangars in little-populated areas far to the south in Korea, might be more advantageous to our national interest than exposing conventional forces right on the demilitarized zone, where they would be held hostage, in a sense, by enemy Koreans to the north and serve as catalysts for political disparagement from allies in the south.

"The Human Thing"

IT IS, OF course, always a fool's errand to predict too far into the future. The most dangerous tendency of military planners is the arrogant belief that all of war's age-old rules and characteristics are rendered obsolete under the mind-boggling technological advances or social revolutions of the present. Tactics alter, and the respective roles of defense and offense each enter long periods of superiority vis-à-vis each other. The acceptance of casualties is predicated on domestic levels of affluence and leisure, fueled by the degree of instantaneous communications with the front.

But ultimately the rules of war and culture stay the same—even as their forms change. Efficient modern pumps throw out far more water than their predecessors, but the essence of water remains unchanged. If robotics removes more and more humans from the battlefield, it is still likely that the people who pilot, direct, and make such machines will become targets—however far away they are ensconced from the frontline killing. The body-armor-piercing bullet is already near production, as is the body-armor-piercing bulletproof vest. What remains the same is the age-old calculation of how to use and protect precious infantry for tasks that even the most sophisticated technology cannot quite absorb. As long as war involves what Thucydides called "the human thing," even in our brave new world of war to come, there will be a need for real live soldiers walking amid the robots to win hearts and minds, or to survey and assess the carnage of the battlefield, or to dispense wisdom among the civilian population.

If, in our growing moral repugnance for war, we develop more discriminating weapons that stun rather than kill our adversaries, we may be confronted with the dilemma of letting those with evil pasts and bloody hands escape, only to inflict more deadly misery on the innocent. At least some wars are matters of trying to stop killers from killing the innocent—killers who could not be stopped by anything short of lethal force. General Curtis LeMay may have been uncouth, but he was not necessarily wrong when he suggested that ultimately wars are won when large numbers of enemy combatants are killed—inasmuch as each represents a potential to do great harm to one's own cause.

The paradoxes of contemporary war will not stop with LeMay's observation. The American controversy over terrorists incarcerated in Guantánamo Bay, Cuba, reveals the dilemma, indeed the contradiction, that a postmodern, lawful society is confronted with when it tries to detain lawless jihadists and treat warriors in detention as civilian criminal suspects.

At present, much of the Western legal world deems the American detention at Guantánamo of terrorists caught on the battlefield, and the interrogation techniques used to extract information from them, as inhuman and out-of-bounds. But apparently they do not object as strenuously to the simultaneous judge-jury-and-executioner practices of incinerating their suspected counterparts, along with family and friends, in Waziristan by Predator drone missiles, or blowing apart the heads of Somali pirate hostage-takers by sniper fire as they negotiate over ransom. In the former, widely condemned case, one is trying to get information from a handful of suspected terrorists to save civilian lives; in the latter, more correct instances, one decides such nonuniformed terrorists are already guilty and deserving of execution.

Apparently, the United States took great efforts to ensure that former Guantánamo detainees were sent to Bermuda, and photographed strolling the beaches, and that suspected terrorists in Pakistan were vaporized and their ashes scattered to the winds. Who can sort out the comparative morality? One might argue that there is far more precision and care taken in categorizing the range of prisoners at Guantánamo than in obliterating a house full of people in the Hindu Kush on the knowledge that a Taliban terrorist of some sort is inside.

As technology and purported morality evolves, the old politically incorrect notion that cruel enemies stop their mayhem only when their troops and leaders face death as a consequence of their aggression may be replaced by the promise that instead they will be merely stunned on the battlefield, detained in bases, tried in courts, and rehabilitated in long-term detention areas. Future generations will learn whether human nature has remained constant—and thus enemies who face only a temporary loss of freedom will prove more, not less, bloodthirsty against both soldier and civilian.

Americans will always remain deeply ambivalent about, but very good at, fighting wars abroad. As in the past, they will be increasingly restless, impatient, and intolerant of delays and losses, as planners continue to seek ways to win quickly through overwhelming firepower without incurring fatalities—in accordance with the perceived pulse of public opinion. Our weapons and strategies will continue to reflect just those unchanging realities, as we face a future in which American troops not only are not supposed to die in war but also, in the thickening fog of battle, perhaps not supposed to kill either.

PART IV

How Western Wars
Are Lost—and Won

CHAPTER 11

Your Defeat, My Victory

*The Nature of Past and Present Military Error**

A Little Humility?

A s w e h a v e seen, lacking familiarity with our military past, we suffer from the affliction of "presentism." That is the notion that our current generation at war is mostly unique, in both its accomplishments and its pain and suffering. We claim technological advances as our own—themselves based on the steady, incremental research and contributions of those of the past—and then compound such egotism by confusing material improvement with cultural or even moral progress.

That conflation in turn prompts us—the most affluent and leisured in civilization's history—to convince ourselves that we are a kinder

---

* Parts of this essay originally appeared in the winter 2007 *Claremont Review*.

and more reflective generation than those before us, who faced a far more brutal and unforgiving world, and that for some reason we are exempt from the rules that accompany human nature and its expression during conflict. This infatuation with the present self, again coupled with ignorance of history, convinces us that the mess of a Vietnam, a Mogadishu, or an Iraq is unlike anything in the past. The result is that we are deluded into thinking that our near mastery of the physical world through technology should likewise make conflict equally domesticated—that the uncertain events of war must never be uncertain at all. Yet conflict is not as controllable and predictable as talking across the globe on our cell phones or calling up a Web address on the Internet.

"Iraq," said former vice president Al Gore, "was the single worst strategic mistake in American history." Senate majority leader Harry Reid agreed that the war he voted to authorize became "the worst foreign policy mistake in U.S. history," and indeed was already "lost."

Many of such historically minded politicians and commanders weighed in with similar "—est" and "most" superlatives. Retired General William Odom called Iraq "the greatest strategic disaster in United States history." Senator Chuck Hagel, who voted for the war, was somewhat more cautious, calling Iraq "the most dangerous foreign policy blunder in this country since Vietnam." Jimmy Carter took the loftiest view: The Iraq War, and Great Britain's acquiescence in it, he said, constituted "a major tragedy for the world" and proved that the Bush administration "has been the worst in history."

Certainly there were legitimate questions about Iraq, as there have been about all wars. Why, for example, did Tommy Franks, the Centcom commander who led American forces in a brilliant three-week victory over Saddam Hussein, abruptly announce his retirement in late May 2003—prompting a disruption in command just as the successful conventional war ended and an unexpected insurgency in Iraq gathered steam? Would General George Patton have declared victory and then resigned when Third Army crossed the Rhine River?

Why were looters allowed to ransack much of Baghdad's infrastructure following the defeat of the Baathist army? Would the conquered Japanese in August 1945 have been allowed to strip what was left of Tokyo's power grid?

Why "disband" the Iraqi military and not reconstitute its officer corps of Baathists at precisely the time that law and order—not tens of thousands of unemployed youths—were needed?

And weren't there too few occupying troops in the war's aftermath, along with too restrictive rules of engagement—but too prominent a profile for the American proconsuls busily dictating to the Iraqis? What can be worse than the foreign infidels who both bother you and yet cannot keep you safe?

The queries don't stop there, alas. Why in advance weren't there sufficient new-model body armor and armored Humvees to protect American troops? Why did we begin to assault Fallujah in April 2004, only to pull back for six months and then have to retake the city after the American election in November? Why were the country's borders left open to infiltrators, and its ubiquitous ammunition dumps kept accessible to terrorists who ransacked them for future explosive devices that would kill thousands of Americans? Did we really think that neighboring Jordan, Kuwait, and Saudi Arabia were going to play supportive roles when democracy in Iraq might result in a Shiite-dominated government that threatened their own Sunni-dominated autocracies?

The catalog of military error and postbellum naïveté could be multiplied ad nauseam. Then there are also the inevitable strategic conundrums over the need to attack Saddam's regime in the first place, given the nature of the terrorist threat, the ascendant Iranian theocracy next door, and the colossal intelligence failures concerning imagined vast depots of chemical and biological weapons.

But what was missing from the almost ritual national denunciation of the "worst" war in our history was much appreciation of past

American military errors—political, strategic, technological, intelligence, tactical—that once nearly cost us victory in far more important conflicts. Nor do we accept the savage irony of war—that only through errors, tragic though they may be, do successful armies adjust in time to discover winning strategies, tactics, and generals. We completely miss the paradoxes of war through which events that were never imagined during a war's planning transpire, and often prove providential. And we forget that sometimes one can still win a poorly conceived war—and that to do so may be better than losing it.

Preoccupied with the daily news from Baghdad, we seemed to think that our generation in the twenty-first century was unique in experiencing the heartbreak of an error-plagued war. We forgot that victory in every war goes to the side that commits fewer mistakes—and learns more from them in less time—not to the side that makes no mistakes at all. A perfect military in a flawless war has never existed—though after Grenada and the air war over the Balkans, Americans apparently thought otherwise. Rather than sink into unending recrimination over Iraq and Afghanistan, we should reflect about comparable errors in America's past wars and how they were corrected.

Intelligence Failures

TAKE ONE OF the Iraq War's most controversial and enduring issues: intelligence failures. Supposedly we went to war in 2003 with little accurate information about either Iraq's weapons of mass destruction (WMD) or its endemic religious factionalism. As a result the U.S. government lost credibility and goodwill at home and abroad, and was soon plagued by enormous political and military problems in trying to stabilize a constitutional government in Iraq. This may prove to be true in large part, but is it unusual? And have lapses of this magnitude been infrequent in past wars?

Not at all, in either a strategic or a tactical context. American intelligence officers missed the almost self-evident Pearl Harbor attack, as an entire Japanese carrier group steamed unnoticed to within a few hundred miles of Hawaii. After fighting for four long years, we were completely surprised by the Soviets' efforts to absorb Eastern Europe, and their rejection of almost all wartime assurances of elections to come. Almost no one had a clue about the Communist invasion of South Korea in June 1950—or the subsequent Chinese entrance en masse into North Korea months later in October and November. Americans were as surprised as Israelis by the sudden 1973 joint Arab attack on Israel. Neither the CIA nor the State Department had much inkling that Saddam Hussein would really gobble up Kuwait in August 1990, or that Pakistan was about to detonate a nuclear weapon in 1998.

We should remember that long before the WMD controversy, the triggers for American wars have usually been odd affairs, characterized by poor intelligence gathering, inept diplomacy, and plenty of duplicity—and thus endless controversy and conspiracy mongering. Consider, for example, the so-called Thornton affair that started the Mexican War; the murky circumstances surrounding the defense and shelling of Fort Sumter; the cry of "Remember the Maine!" that heralded the Spanish-American War; the disputed claims surrounding the 1915 sinking of the *Lusitania* that turned public opinion against the kaiser; the Pearl Harbor debacle; an offhand remark in January 1950 by Secretary of State Dean Acheson that South Korea was outside our "defense perimeter"; the Gulf of Tonkin Resolution; and an American diplomat's apparent signal of nonchalance to Saddam Hussein immediately before he invaded Kuwait. It is no overstatement that almost *every* American war involved some sort of honest intelligence failure or misinterpretation of an enemy's motives—or outright dissimulation.

At the battlefield level, America's past intelligence failures were even more shocking. On April 6, 1862, on a quiet early Sunday morning,

Union forces at Shiloh allowed a large, noisy Confederate army under General Albert Sidney Johnston to approach unnoticed (by superb generals Ulysses S. Grant and William Tecumseh Sherman) to within a few thousand yards of their front with disastrous results. Grant—still clueless as to the forces of nearly sixty thousand arrayed against him— compounded his error by sending an ambiguous message for reinforcements to General Lew Wallace, resulting in a critical delay of aid for several hours. Hundreds of Union soldiers died in the meantime. Following the battle, victorious Union generals knew even less concerning the whereabouts of the retreating, defeated Confederate forces and thus allowed them to escape in safety—and to reform into new units to kill more Northern soldiers. The hard-won Union victory became an object of blame-gaming for the remainder of the nineteenth century—as was true of Antietam, and as was true of Gettysburg.

Perhaps the two costliest intelligence lapses of the Second World War preceded the Battle of the Bulge and Okinawa—both toward the end of the war, *after* radical improvements in intelligence methods and technology and long experience with both German and Japanese modes of attack. Americans had no idea of the scope, timing, or aims of the massive German surprise attack through the Ardennes in December 1944, despite the battle-tested acumen of our two most respected generals, Dwight Eisenhower and Omar Bradley, and British and American intercepts of Wehrmacht messages. Days into the German offensive, there was no consensus about German aims or the proper way to push back the salient. Again, in such circumstances we are talking about errors costing the lives of tens of thousands of Americans in a matter of days, not four thousand Americans over several years in Iraq.

At Okinawa, American intelligence officers grievously underestimated the size, position, and nature of the Japanese deployment, and thus vastly overestimated the efficacy of their own pre-invasion bombing attacks. Army commanders—in near insane fashion—persisted in head-on attacks against the nearly impenetrable Shuri Line, without a clue how well prepared the Japanese were for just such an unimaginative strategy. Yet Okinawa was not our first experience with island-hopping. It unfolded as the last invasion assault in the Pacific theater of operations—supposedly after the collective wisdom gleaned from Guadalcanal, the Marianas, Peleliu, the Philippines, Tarawa, and Iwo Jima had been well digested. Yet this late in the war, still more than 140,000 Americans were killed, wounded, or missing in the Ardennes and on Okinawa.

Strategic and Tactical Lapses

A T THE GEOSTRATEGIC level, American diplomats have had to make devil's bargains far more morally suspect than going into Iraq. General George Patton and others lamented that the Second World War had broken out in 1939 over saving the free peoples of Eastern Europe from totalitarianism—only to end, through the broken 1945 Yalta accords, ensuring their enslavement by an erstwhile Soviet ally whose military we had supplied lavishly. In 1776, Americans, bent on establishing a free republic, looked to the soon-to-be-dethroned monarchy in France and its court aristocracy for help in a war against a more liberal parliamentary Great Britain.

Today we worry whether the United States should have armed some anti-Soviet jihadists in Afghanistan in the 1980s or whether it was moral to watch with unrestrained glee as the Ayatollah Khomeini's Iran and Saddam Hussein's Iraq nearly annihilated each other between 1980 and 1988—each in some small part occasionally helped by U.S. arms or intelligence. We forget that even worse choices than those have confronted us in the past—like sending billions of dollars of aid to Joseph Stalin to stop Adolf Hitler, just a few years after the former had slaughtered or starved to death twenty million Soviets, invaded hapless Finland, carved up Poland with Hitler, and sent strategic materials daily to the Third Reich as it firebombed London. America in the past has offered support for authoritarians such as General Somoza of Nicaragua and Ferdinand Marcos in the Philippines to prevent both countries from falling into the sphere of an even worse Soviet Union, apparently on the logic that a right-wing anti-Communist dictatorship could either evolve or be pressured to reform in a way that a Stalinist satellite could not.

The Carter administration by 1979 was confused over whether to support, abandon, or ignore the longtime allied, but increasingly beleaguered, shah of Iran—the object of hatred of thousands of Iranians (the Iranian left despised his repression and corruption, the Islamic right his efforts at modernization and secularization). In the end, the United States somehow simultaneously managed to lose a strategic ally in the Cold War, ensure the beginning of a three-decade-long aggression of Iranian-backed Islamic terrorists against American interests, and leave left-wing socialist reformers to be butchered by second-wave revolutionary Islamic fundamentalists. "The Great Satan" originally arose as a slur against Jimmy Carter's kinder and gentler United States—at the same time democratic allies from Europe to Asia condemned America as an equivocal and unreliable ally. Thousands of Iranians flocked in waves to the United States, furious—depending on their own circumstances and politics—that a naive Carter either had sold out a staunch American Cold War ally or had sold out principled and secular left-wing reformers.

In many of our wars, this country has committed strategic mistakes far greater in number and consequence than anything seen in Iraq. Perhaps the worst was to send thousands of American crewmen in daylight bombing raids over occupied Europe in 1942–44. To visit American cemeteries in Europe today is to walk among thousands of graves, marked with the shared information "8th Army Air Force" and the dates of those killed between 1942 and 1944. Prewar dogmas of the "bomber always gets through" blinded zealous proponents of strategic air power.

Ignoring its critics, ossified Army Air Force planners sent hundreds of highly trained crews to their deaths on slow, unescorted bombing runs in broad daylight, amid thousands of German flak batteries and Luftwaffe fighters—and achieved very little in return until early 1944. By August and September 1943 the Wehrmacht may have been shooting down B-24 Liberators and B-17s almost as quickly as replacement crews and planes arrived in England. Before the war ended, more than ten thousand American bombers and escort fighters were lost to enemy flak, aircraft, and accidents—in a strategic bombing campaign deemed a "success." Sending air crews over Europe in 1943 was analogous to British officers in the First World War ordering their men "over the top" to be slaughtered during the initial minutes of the Somme offensive of 1916. That said, where and how exactly was a previously unarmed, inexperienced, and unprepared United States supposed to attack Nazi Germany in 1942–43, if not largely through the air and on the periphery in North Africa and Sicily? Before we in hindsight damn the stupidity of our Army Air Force generals, remember that every flak gun transferred westward to shoot down B-17s, every German fighter redeployed over Europe, every factory bombed in Germany, meant that our allies on the eastern front had a greater chance to stop, defeat, and destroy the great majority of Wehrmacht infantrymen who fought in the Second World War.

Even more regrettable was Admiral Ernest King's initial decision in 1942 not to use American destroyers and destroyer escorts to shepherd merchant ships across the Atlantic to Great Britain. German U-boats had a field day, torpedoing slow-moving cargo vessels right off our east coast—which was lit up each night, almost as if to silhouette undefended American targets at sea and enhance submarine torpedo accuracy. King persisted despite ample evidence from the First World War that the convoy system had worked, and despite pleas from veteran British officers that their own two-year experience in the war had taught them the folly of sending unescorted merchant ships across the Atlantic.

We often read of the tragedy of the September 1944 Arnheim campaign. Impossible logistics, bad weather, lousy intelligence, tactical imbecility, and much more doomed operation Market Garden and led to the infamous "a bridge too far" catastrophe. Thousands of Anglo-American troops were needlessly killed or wounded—even after the Allies had recently crushed an entire German army group in the west (although they had tragically allowed one hundred thousand Wehrmacht troops to escape at the so-called Falaise Gap). The foolery of Market Garden, which sought to push tens of thousands of Allied troops over a sole, narrow road toward the Rhine, also ate up scarce resources, manpower, and gasoline at precisely the time the American Third Army was nearing the Rhine without much major opposition. Once the Allied armies stalled for want of supplies, they were unable to cross the border of the Reich for another half year—in which the majority of Americans lost on the Western European front died. The Germans used the breathing space after their victory in Holland to rush defenders to the so-called Siegfried Line, which had been theretofore mostly undefended, and to refit once-shattered Panzer divisions. No senior planners involved with the Operation Market Garden disaster were sacked, despite the fifteen thousand allied casualties.

Had General Douglas MacArthur in late 1950 listened to both superiors and subordinates, he would not have sent thousands of G.I.s with long vulnerable supply lines into the far reaches of mountainous, wintry North Korea—on his gut instinct that hundreds of thousands of Chinese "volunteers" would not cross the Yalu River and that his troops would be "home for Thanksgiving." When Mao ordered the massive People's Army to invade, the longest retreat in the history of U.S. forces ensued, with thousands of American casualties—and hysterical cries back home both that the war was now "lost" and that we had been stabbed in the back by Communist sympathizers. The real mystery was why and how any informed public could believe that a rather small American army could drive an enemy four hundred miles distant in frigid cold into the sanctuary of a hostile, eight-hundred-million-person Communist country—and not expect abject catastrophe to ensue.

Our tactical decisions have remained even more error-prone. Grant was still sending ranks of soldiers against entrenched Confederate positions for most of the horrific summer 1864, despite Sherman's angry protests against the folly of such assaults in a rapidly changing war of massed firepower. Had our greatest general of the age continued with another Cold Harbor–type assault, and had Sherman not taken Atlanta, Lincoln would have lost the autumn election of 1864, and the country might have been permanently divided. In the First World War, despite our assurances that our well-trained riflemen could broach enemy positions, seasoned British and French commanders warned novice American planners against mass attacks into the German rapid-firing artillery, machine guns, tanks, and poison gas. Americans died in droves before we got it right by early 1918.

For all its surprises and mistakes, D-Day was carefully planned and a brilliant success; its immediate aftermath was often a near disaster. Within a week of the landings, Allied army groups leaving Omaha Beach stalled in the hedgerows for over six weeks. We suffered tens of thousands of casualties while Americans were flummoxed by entrenched, camouflaged German positions amid the narrow lanes and thick hedges. Apparently no planner had thought much about the terrain or navigability of the *bocage*—although the area in Normandy beyond Omaha Beach was well-traveled and should have been familiar to American officers, many of them veterans of the fighting in France during the First World War. In the end, lower-echelon officers and enlisted men jerry-rigged spiked-battering rams on Sherman tanks to break through the underbrush. Finally exasperated generals called in B-17s to blast holes through enemy lines to break out of the confining landscape.

Outgunned

How about weapons parity? America has a reputation for technological prowess and machine mastery. The phone and electric lightbulb were singular American innovations; the Wright brothers invented the airplane; Richard Gatling the first modern successful machine gun. As we have seen, no other culture is so adept at marrying man and machine in war. Nevertheless, in nearly every one of our major wars, American troops initially entered combat with arms inferior to their more experienced enemies. In this regard, Vietnam, the 1991 Gulf War, and the present Middle East conflicts are exceptional; these were our first major land engagements in which American weaponry at the outset was superior in almost every category. Yet sophisticated American infantry battalions often found their initial complex models of M16 rifles far less dependable than the less complex, less accurate, and less lethal AK-47s used by the Viet Cong and regular North Vietnamese regiments.

We sent a million troops to Europe between 1917 and 1918 with weapons qualitatively inferior to both our German enemies and French and British allies. We had no tanks—and would never produce our own in any numbers until the war was well over. We relied for the most part on British- or French-designed machine guns and artillery. European airplanes were far better than American Dayton-Wright and Curtiss models. Only the American model M1903 Springfield rifle, and later the Browning automatic rifle (BAR), proved fit for the rapidly changing technological conditions of the western front.

Our initial ill-preparedness was in some sense still worse in both the Second World War and Korea. The United States went to battle in 1941 equipped with far fewer aircraft carriers in the Pacific theater than the Japanese. Wildcat frontline fighters were inferior to the Japanese Zero; obsolete Brewster F2A Buffalos were rightly known as "flying coffins." The Douglas TBD Devastator bomber was a death trap, its pilots essentially wiped out or rendered impotent at the Battle of Midway trying to drop often unreliable torpedoes into the wind at net speeds of not more than sixty miles per hour. American-designed Lee, Grant, and Stuart tanks—and even the much-heralded reliable Shermans ("Ronson Lighters")—were intrinsically inferior to most contemporary German models, which had far better armor and armament, as well as a lower profile. With the exception of the superb M1 rifle and heavy bombers like the B-17 and B-24, it is hard to rank any American weapons system as comparable to those used by the Wehrmacht, at least until 1944–45. We never developed guns quite comparable to the fast-firing, lethal German .88 artillery platform. Our antitank weapons of all calibers remained substandard. Most of our machine guns and mortars were reliable—but of First World War vintage.

The American military learned immediately in Korea that our first-generation jet fighters—F-80 Shooting Stars—could not match Russian MiG-15s. For much of the summer of 1950, North Korea enjoyed air superiority, as Communist pilots often flew jets against our own propeller-driven fighters. Even improved Sherman tanks and newer M24 Chaffee light tanks through much of 1950 were outclassed by the Second World War–vintage Russian T-34s and T-85s. Indeed, it was nearly inconceivable that the abjectly poor North Koreans would have had access to tanks in 1950 superior to those of the Americans, despite our reputation as the recent winners over sophisticated Japanese and Germans. The United States, despite the harsh lessons of the Second World War, would not produce the world's preeminent tank until the appearance of the Abrams in the early 1980s.

Poor Leadership

HAVE THERE EVER been lapses in military leadership like the ones that purportedly marred the Iraq effort? The "revolt of the generals" against Secretary of Defense Donald Rumsfeld—in which a number of retired generals publicly lambasted the Pentagon chief for not listening to their prewar warnings—was nothing compared to the "revolt of the admirals" which led to Secretary of Defense Louis Johnson's forced resignation in the midst of the bitter first year of the Korean War.

Johnson himself, remember, had come to office following the removal (or resignation), and then probable suicide, of Secretary James Forrestal, whose last note included a lengthy quotation from Sophocles' *Ajax*. Johnson's successor, the venerable General George Marshall, lasted less than a year—hounded out by Joseph McCarthy, and an object of furor in the wartime 1952 election that brought in Eisenhower (who did not defend his former superior from McCarthy's slanders). The result was that four different secretaries of defense—Forrestal, Johnson, Marshall, and Robert Lovett—served between 1949 and 1951, all with radically different agendas and ideas about how to reshape the military to confront an array of new global challenges. At one point Secretary Johnson advocated ending the Marine Corps altogether, with some initial encouragement from President Harry Truman.

Critics of the Iraq War wonder how the workmanlike Lieutenant General Ricardo Sanchez, on whose watch Abu Ghraib occurred and the insurgency grew, rose to command all coalition ground forces in the first place, or later why General George Casey persisted in tactics that were aimed more at downsizing our forces than going after the enemy and fighting a vigorous war of counterinsurgency. But surely these armchair critics can acknowledge that such controversies over personnel pale in comparison to past storms. Lincoln serially fired, ignored, or bypassed mediocrities like Generals Burnside, Halleck, Hooker, McClellan, McDowell, Meade, Pope, and Rosecrans before finding Grant, George Thomas, Sherman, and Philip Sheridan—all of whom at one time or another were under severe criticism and nearly dismissed. Before the Battle of Shiloh, Sherman was felt to have been crazy and unreliable;

after the victory, it was Grant's turn to be accused of everything from drunkenness to gross incompetence.

The Second World War was little better. By all accounts the sacrosanct General John C. H. Lee set up an enormous logistical fiefdom that indulged in perks and privilege while American armies at the front were short on manpower, materials, and fuel. To this day military historians cannot quite fathom how and why Major General Lloyd Fredendall was ever given an entire corps in the North Africa campaign, or why John Lucas was given command of the Anzio landings. The former's uninspired generalship led to the disaster at the Kasserine Pass and his own subsequent removal; the latter lost an opportunity to either take Rome or surround several German divisions in Italy. Thousands of dead and wounded paid the price for the lapses of each.

Lieutenant General Simon Bolivar Buckner, a competent officer, was bewildered by the unexpected Japanese resistance on Okinawa, and unimaginatively plowed head-on through fortified enemy positions—until killed in action on the island, the most senior-ranking officer to die by enemy fire in the Second World War. The plodding generalship of charismatic Mark Clark in Italy often proved disastrous—perhaps analogous to the slothful command of General Henry Halleck, who, after the victory at Shiloh, took de facto command from Grant of Union forces in the west, only to let the retreating defeated Confederate army escape annihilation.

The story of the U.S. Army at war is one of frequent sacking, sidetracking, or ostracizing of its highest and best-known commanders in the field—Grant after Shiloh, Douglas MacArthur in Korea, Patton in Sicily, and William Westmoreland in Vietnam—for both good and awful reasons, and not until thousands of Americans had first tragically died. Iraq and Afghanistan are peculiar in that there have been so few personnel changes, much less a general consensus about perceived military incompetence. In comparison to past conflicts, the wonder is not that a gifted officer like General David Petraeus came into real prominence relatively late in the present war, but that his unique talents were recognized quickly enough to allow him the supreme command and latitude to alter the entire tactical approach to the war in Iraq.

Live and Learn, Learn and Live

WHAT CAN WE learn from the wartime blunders and controversies that together cost hundreds of thousands of American lives but usually did not endanger eventual victories? Surely, we should not shrug, concede that "stuff happens," keep quiet, and simply support our troops, no matter what.

Instead, first, remember that such failings usually were aired in a long tradition of investigative, hard-hitting exposés and columns. Long before Seymour Hersh and Peter Arnett, Thomas Knox, Edward Crapsey, Ernie Pyle, Drew Pearson, and Walter Winchell wrote scathing critiques of American military performance. In reaction, the most vehement attack on the wartime press came not from Richard Nixon but from William Tecumseh Sherman. "If I had my choice I would kill every reporter in the world," he sighed, "but I am sure we would be getting reports from hell before breakfast." Yet until the defeat in Vietnam, there was a sort of tragic acceptance of military error of some sort as inherent in war. Senator Harry Truman won national attention only through his Truman Committee, which uncovered billions of dollars of military waste and fraud during the war years. True, he relieved General Douglas MacArthur in April 1951, but for interfering in politics, not the general's incompetence and laxity in being surprised by a Chinese invasion.

Ours was once a largely rural population, a harvest away from hunger and inured to hard physical labor, accustomed to natural disaster and resigned to human shortcoming, without instant communications or the contemporary unspoken faith that we may all die in our sleep. Though presidents Lincoln and Truman were both at times reviled, Americans still felt that ultimately the American system of transparency and self-criticism would correct wartime mistakes. Fault-finding and partisan grandstanding there were aplenty, but the common desire for victory usually overcame perpetual finger-pointing and despair. Pearl Harbor and its attendant conspiracy theories may have set the Greatest Generation back, but such losses, humiliation, and suspicion were hardly considered tantamount to American defeat.

So we plowed on, accepting that, in war, choices are only between the bad and worse. Yes, it was foolhardy not to escort convoys early in the Second World War, but Admiral King—always suspicious of British motives—erred because he believed that such a commitment would divert precious assets from the Pacific War, where the United States, largely alone, had to face the Japanese fleet, which was far larger and more formidable than Hitler's. Unescorted daylight bombing raids in 1942–43 were suicidal, but slowly the planners in the American Eighth Air Force learned from their errors, and by late 1944 improved B-17s, drop tanks, and long-range fighter escorts, refined tactics and ordnance, and far more skilled and experienced personnel led to the destruction of most of the key German urban and rail centers. The Sherman tank trapped and incinerated thousands of Americans when easily torched by Panthers and Tigers, but Patton himself saw that its dependability, speed, easy maintenance, and sheer numbers offered countervailing advantages in racing toward the Rhine.

By the same token, for every recognized blunder in Iraq, there was at least an understandable reason why such a lapse occurred in the context of human imperfection, emotion, and ignorance. Such considerations do not mitigate the enormity of military mistakes, but they should foster an understanding of how and why they occur. Such recognition might lend humility to criticism, and wisdom to the perpetrators—and prepare us to accept and deal with similar human fallibility in the future.

So shoot the Baghdad looters of April and May 2003—and CNN likely would have libeled the occupation forces as recycled Saddamites. Level Fallujah in April 2004—and Iraqis would have compared us to the Soviets in Grozny. Had we kept together the Republican Guard in 2003—if that were even possible—charges of perpetuating the agents of Saddam's genocidal regime would have followed, with unfavorable contrasts to our successful de-Nazification program after the Second World War. Granted, there were not enough American troops to close borders, monitor ammunition depots, and maintain order. But as a result, there were enough deployed elsewhere to discourage trouble in the Korean peninsula, reassure Europe and Japan of our material commitment to their security, fight the Taliban in Afghanistan, help keep order in the Balkans, and man dozens of bases worldwide.

When MiG-15s surprisingly proved superior to American F-80s, our Korean War planners took a pass on blaming one another and instead deployed with blinding speed the superb F-86 Sabre jet, which soon often surpassed its Russian counterparts. Once a General Hooker or Fredendall was found incompetent, Americans expected that someone like Grant or Patton would eventually step forward from a large officer pool of the formerly peacetime army. A general like Sherman or Petraeus doesn't emerge on the first day of war. Only the lethal experience during early high-level B-29 bombing missions from the Marianas led to appointment of General Curtis LeMay, who, in unorthodox fashion, turned a sophisticated, million-dollar precision bomber into a relatively low-level, low-tech night raider spewing napalm over Tokyo.

We are relieved that the recent emphasis on counterinsurgency under General Petraeus has brought radical improvement in Iraq in a way that previous counterterrorism tactics did not—but much of our current wisdom nevertheless accrued from the hard years of fighting between 2003 and 2006, when Americans severely weakened both al-Qaeda and the Sunni insurgents, and gained invaluable knowledge in the process about the tribal fissures and affinities within traditional Iraqi society. The notion that America was "surging," and not leaving, likewise had enormous psychological benefits to the struggling Iraqi security forces that grew and improved all through 2008 and 2009. Again, what loses wars is not necessarily the inevitable mistakes but the failure to correct them in time—and the degree to which defeatism and depression (because errors occurred at all) are allowed to erode morale.

The quagmire in the Normandy hedgerows in 1944 led to thousands of American deaths, but also to innovations and new tactics, whether specially equipped "Rhino" Sherman tanks or using B-17s to blow holes in the German lines (and by mischance kill hundreds of Americans in "friendly fire" blunders). Likewise, the United States may have started in Iraq with the naive belief that thin-skinned Humvees were simply updated Jeeps good enough to transport personnel behind the lines. But troops quickly learned that, in a war with no lines, the Humvees became underarmored coffins—prompting a challenge and response cycle between the enemy's improvised explosive devices and our armor.

Frenzied development efforts produced up-armored kits, factory-designed models with superior protection, and entirely new vehicles like the Strykers, MRAPs (mine resistant, ambush protected), and Rhinos. Technological improvements, along with experience gained in identifying the profiles of bomb-laying terrorists, meant that by late 2008 almost no Americans were dying from IED road mines, while those who planted them were often killed or captured.

Back at Home

AMERICANS ON THE home front once accepted that our adversaries faced the same obstacles and challenges of war.

Moreover Americans assumed that the enemy, usually being less intro-
spective and self-critical, was even more prone to military error than we
were—and less likely to innovate and correct. The lack of free-thinking
Nazi generals and general staff debate eventually would doom the
megalomaniac Hitler to commit strategic blunders; ossified standard
Soviet tank and infantry doctrine would ensure that North Korean
and Red Chinese invaders would finally fight in predictable fashion,
and not adapt to changing conditions on the ground as quickly as
their American counterparts. A mere three months after they trium-
phantly crossed the 38th parallel into South Korea in January 1951, the
Chinese in dejection were pushed back across it, suffering tens of thousands dead.

That wartime confidence of past generations, embedded within a
more general realistic view of human limitations, often ensured that the
public saw mistakes not just in absolute but also in relative terms. Yet
currently is there any serious discussion at home about the terrible effects of Predator drone attacks on bin Laden's terrorists in Waziristan,
the wear and tear on his minions living under constant aerial attack, or
the lopsided ratios of human losses that typically follow Taliban-NATO
firefights?

The First World War saw one million ill-equipped Doughboys deployed against the most experienced and deadly modern army the world
had yet seen. But the mass drafting of one million soldiers, equipped and
sent across the Atlantic in a mere year without losses to German U-boats,
was acknowledged on all sides as a feat even beyond the ability of the
kaiser's general staff. It was not the newcomer United States that found
itself in a hopeless two-front war in the First World War, but the sophisticated planners of Bismarck's new Germany.

In the Second World War, lapses in our convoy system were hardly
as damaging to us as Germany's repeated mistakes at sea were to the
Nazi cause—faulty German torpedoes, poor air support for submarine
operations, and abject security breaches that lent the Allies almost

instantaneous knowledge of the Kriegsmarine's operations. There is no need to document the stupendous Baathist strategic and tactical blunders that led to Saddam's ignominious defeats in both 1991 and 2003. But in his wake (and after his demise), the supposedly sophisticated jihadists have made just as many mistakes. In a self-proclaimed war of Islamic liberation that hinges on public support, al-Qaeda in Iraq has mutilated, butchered, and terrorized a once largely sympathetic population. As a result, the radical Islamists have nearly pulled off the impossible: A formerly receptive Sunni tribal community has turned against Sunni Muslim jihadists and joined with American infidels, sometimes alongside the troops of a Shiite-led government.

In past wars there was recognition of factors beyond human control—the weather; the fickleness of human nature; the role of chance; the irrational; and the inexplicable. All that lent a humility to our efforts and tolerance for unintended consequences. "Wars begin when you will," Machiavelli reminds us, "but they do not end when you please." The star-crossed and disastrous Dieppe raid of August 1942 did not mean that D-Day two years later had to fail. The unnecessary surrender of Wake Island in spring 1942 did not mean that Japanese amphibious forces were unstoppable.

Again, when in March 1945 maverick General Curtis LeMay sent high-altitude precision B-29 bombers carrying napalm in low over Tokyo, with little if any armament, the expected American bloodbath did not follow—thanks to a ferocious jet stream and dark, cloudy nights that meant the huge planes came in much faster and with better cover. In war not everything can be anticipated or planned for. "To a good general," wrote the Roman historian Livy, "luck is important." When presented with a list of generals for promotion, Napoleon purportedly sighed, "I want none of those. Go back and find me a lucky general."

By contrast, the American media went into near hysterics during the so-called pause in the 2003 three-week victory over Saddam, when an unforeseen sandstorm temporarily stalled our preordained successful advance. Only later was it revealed that air operations with precision weapons had continued all along to decimate Saddam's static forces. Few journalists seemed to grasp that sand and poor weather bothered both forces—but the side that had a history of better adaptation to the unforeseen might find such natural obstacles of some comparative advantage.

WMDs were not found in Iraq, it is true. Yet an earlier American generation might have consoled itself with the notion that at last we had proved (as previous intelligence had not) that Saddam no longer posed a threat, and ensured that Iraq would not again translate oil wealth into the deadly forces with which it had attacked four of its neighbors. They would have added that at least twenty of the original twenty-three congressional writs (Public Law 107–243) that authorized the war—ranging from genocide to prior violations of U.N. protocols and armistice agreements—remained valid reasons for his removal.

Our ancestors might have even sighed that the mishandling of the war had effectively raised our standard of proof from "You must prove that you don't have WMDs" to "We must prove that you do." In any case, Libya, for example, may well have had more WMDs in stock than Saddam did—and may well have given them up to avoid the latter's fate. Pakistan mysteriously put its national hero and world nuclear proliferator Dr. A. Q. Khan under house arrest—just weeks after the capture of Saddam Hussein in Iraq. Selling the Iraq War on the premise that displays of American resolve would force Mu'ammar Gadhafi to give up his illicit nuclear program would have been as ill-advised as in fact were promises that removing Saddam was essential to neutralizing a sizable Iraqi biological and chemical arsenal.

Has War Changed, or Have We?

VICTORY DOES NOT require achieving all of one's objectives, but achieving far more than an enemy does of his. Patient Northerners realized almost too late that victory required not merely warding off or defeating Confederate armies, but also invading and occupying an area as large as Western Europe in order to render an entire people incapable of waging war. That enormous effort required an "Anaconda" plan of blockading the eastern and southern coasts of the southeast quadrant of North America, controlling the entire length of the Mississippi River, invading from the northern Midwest, and sending thousands of troops into northern Virginia—simultaneously, and as part of a moral crusade to end slavery in the South, keep the border states in the Union, and maintain the western expansion and diplomatic relations overseas in the midst of a horrific Civil War. And twelve years of postwar Reconstruction had no more success in ensuring lasting racial equality in the South than did twelve years of no-fly zones of removing Saddam Hussein.

Blunders were seen as inevitable once an unarmed United States decided to fight Germany, Italy, and Japan all at once in a war to be conducted far away across wide oceans, against enemies that had a long head start in rearmament. We had disastrous intelligence failures in the Second World War, but we also broke most of the German and Japanese codes in a fashion our enemies could neither fathom nor emulate. Somehow this generation forgets that going into the heart of the ancient caliphate, taking out a dictator in three weeks, and then staying on to foster a constitutional republic amid a sea of enemies like Iran and Syria and duplicitous friends like Jordan and Saudi Arabia—and tragically losing four thousand Americans in the six-year enterprise—was beyond the ability of any of our friends or enemies, and perhaps past generations of Americans as well.

But perhaps the American public, not the timeless nature of war, has changed. Present generations of unprecedented leisure, affluence, and technology no longer so easily accept human imperfections. We seem to care less about correcting problems than assessing blame—in postmodern America it is defeat that has a thousand fathers, while the notion of victory is an orphan. We fail to realize that the enemy makes as many mistakes but probably addresses them less skillfully. We do not acknowledge the role of fate and chance in war, which sometimes upsets our best endeavors. Rarely are we fixed on victory as the only acceptable outcome.

What are the causes of this radically different attitude toward military culpability?

A sophisticated society takes for granted the ability to select from five hundred cable channels; so too, contemporary Americans, spurred on by "greeted as liberators" assurances by our naive leaders, almost expect Saddam instantly gone, Jeffersonian democracy up and running reliably, and the Iraqi economy growing like Dubai's in a few seasons. If not at all so, then someone must be blamed for ignorance, malfeasance, or inhumanity. If one believes that the administration was successful in downplaying real risks while assuring unrealistic and rosy prognoses, why were the public and media so open to such guarantees? It is as though we expect contemporary war to be waged in accordance with warranties, lawsuits, and product recalls, and adjudicated by judges and lawyers in stale courtrooms rather than won or lost by often emotional youths in the filth, confusion, and barbarity of the battlefield. Stopping lunatic regimes like those in Iran and North Korea from acquiring—and using—nuclear weapons is nearly impossible, and yet we blame both liberal and conservative administrations for either being too stern or too lax for allowing proliferation to continue.

Vietnam's legacy was to suggest that if American aims and conduct were less than perfect, then they could not be good at all, as if a Stalinist police state in the north of Vietnam were comparable—or superior—to a flawed quasi-democratic autocracy in the south, with the potential to evolve in the manner of a South Korea. The Vietnam War was not only the first modern American defeat; it was also the last, and so its evocation turns hysterical precisely because its outcome was so unusual. Yet later victories in Grenada, Panama, Gulf War I, and the Balkans persuaded Americans that war could be redefined, at the end of history, as something in which the use of force ends quickly, is welcomed by locals, costs little, and easily thwarts tyranny. When all that proved less than true in Somali, Haiti, Afghanistan, and Iraq, the public proved ill-equipped to accept that walkover victories like Grenada were military history's exceptions rather than its rule, and that temporary setbacks hardly equated to Vietnam-like quagmires.

We also live in an age of instant communications increasingly contingent on genre and ideology. The *New York Times*, CBS News, National Public Radio, and Reuters—the so-called mainstream media skeptical of the American military's morality and its ability to enact change abroad—instill national despair by conveying graphic scenes of destruction in Iraq without, however, providing much context or explaining how such information is gathered and selected for release.

In turn, Fox News, conservative bloggers, and talk radio hear from their own sources that we are not doing nearly so badly and try to offer real-time, wildly optimistic alternative narratives to the conventional newspapers and major networks. The result is that the war is fought and refought in twenty-four-hour news cycles among diverse genres with their own particular audiences, in which the common denominator is that sensationalism brings in ad revenue or enhances individual careers. Rarely is there any sober, reasoned analysis that examines American conduct over periods of six months or a year—not when the "shocking" stories about Jessica Lynch or Abu Ghraib or by fabulist Scott Beauchamp make and sell better copy.

Sensationalism was always the stuff of war reporting, but today it is with us in real time, 24-7, offered up by often anonymous sources, and filtered in a matter of hours or minutes by nameless editors and producers. Those relentless news alerts—tucked in between apparently more important exposés about Paris Hilton, Michael Jackson, and Anna Nicole Smith—ultimately impart a sense of confusion and bewilderment about what war has become. The result is a strange schizophrenia in which the American public is too insecure to believe that we can rectify our mistakes, but too arrogant to admit that our generation should make any in the first place.

What can be done about our impatience, historical amnesia, and utopian demands for perfection? American statesmen need to provide constant explanations to a public not well versed in history—not mere assertions—of what misfortunes to expect when and if they take the nation to war, and of both the costs and benefits of *not* striking at a known enemy. The more a president evokes history's tragic lessons, the better, reminding the public that our forefathers usually endured and overcame far worse against the British, Germans, Italians, Japanese, Russians, Chinese, and Koreans.

Americans should be told at the start of every conflict that the generals who begin the fighting may not finish it; that what is reported in the first twenty-four hours may not be true after a week's retrospection; and that the alternative to the bad choice is rarely the good one, but usually only the far worse. They should be apprised that our morale is as important as our material advantages—and that our will power is predicated on inevitable mistakes being learned from and rectified far more competently and quickly than the enemy will learn from his. What is remarkable about Pericles' prewar speeches, as recorded in the first and second books of Thucydides' history, is not his morale-boosting exhortations to fellow Athenians or demonization of the Spartan enemy, but rather his sober assessments of the dangers in fighting the Spartans—and Athenian countermeasures that would offer some hope of success.

If the United States is to fight future wars, our national wartime objective should be victory, a goal that brings with it the acceptance of tragic errors as well as the appreciation of heroic and brilliant conduct. Yet if as a nation we instead believe that we cannot abide error, or that we cannot win because of necessary military, moral, humanitarian, financial, or geopolitical constraints, then we should not ask our young soldiers to continue to try.

As in Vietnam, where we were obsessed with recriminations rather than learning from our shortcomings, we should simply accept defeat and with it the ensuing humiliating consequences. But it would be far preferable for Americans undertaking a necessary war to remember these words from Churchill, in his 1930 prewar memoir: "Never, never, never believe any war will be smooth and easy, or that anyone who embarks on the strange voyage can measure the tides and hurricanes he will encounter."

CHAPTER 12

The Odd Couple—War and Democracy

Why Democracies Fight, Win—and Lose—Wars.[*]

Distrusting the Military

IN PREVIOUS CHAPTERS we have seen the paradox of a nation that is a ferocious war maker, but yet has little confidence in its ability to wage modern wars, or harness its military to moral objectives. The somewhat ill-defined relationship between the military establishment and constitutional government is also a related subject that has made many Americans uncomfortable—especially in the modern era when the United States has assumed a leadership role in world affairs. American Cold War–era culture, after all, cautioned us about the intrinsic anti-democratic nature of top-ranking military officers. We all

---

[*] A portion of this essay is based on material from an article that appeared in the June 2007 *American Spectator*.

recall the cinematic portrayals like *Seven Days in May* or *Doctor Strangelove* or the very real politicking of retired generals like George McClellan, Douglas MacArthur, Curtis LeMay, or Edwin Walker.

In reaction to these Cold War–and Vietnam-era fears, scholars such as Samuel P. Huntington (*The Soldier and the State*) and, more recently, Eliot Cohen (*Supreme Command*) have written insightfully about the proper relationship between civilian and military authorities in a constitutional democracy like ours. The delicate balance was sometimes upset in our past wars when politicians did not have much knowledge about military affairs. Sometimes, out of insecurity, they blustered and bullied officers. At other times, in recognition of their own ignorance, civilian leaders ceded too much control to the Pentagon.

Under the Clinton administration it was felt that an increasingly alienated military exercised too much autonomy, whether in lecturing civilian authorities that gays simply would not work as fully accepted members of the armed forces or in voicing strong initial opposition to the prospect of humanitarian intervention in the Balkans. (See General Colin Powell's "We do deserts. We don't do mountains.")

Militaries, for their part, understand that during "peacekeeping" exercises the rules of engagement change, the cameras intrude, and they are asked to assume civilian roles where their target profile increases, while their ability to fight back without restrictions is checked.

During the past Bush presidency, by contrast, the charge was often just the opposite: A compliant Pentagon had been bullied by its civilian overseers into keeping quiet about doubts over the feasibility of neoconservative nation-building. In fact, in 2006, we witnessed a "revolt of the generals" against civilian leadership of the Pentagon—again, something we had not quite seen since the similar "revolt of the admirals" in 1949, when furious naval officers went on the offensive against Defense Secretary Louis Johnson.

Top brass came forward out of recent retirement to lambaste Secretary of Defense Donald Rumsfeld over the entire civilian conduct in the Iraq War. They complained that there had been too much micro-managing. Too many policy demands, they alleged, were placed on a military that was stretched too thin to carry such burdens, and too much utopian ideology guided the conduct of the war, at the expense of realistic judgments of what in fact was tactically possible. In the topsy-turvy politics of Washington, D.C., liberal critics of the Iraq War applauded the officers as genuine patriots willing to take on errant civilian overseers; many pro-military conservatives saw an ominous breach of defense protocol, and a danger to civilian control of the military.

Why do democratic societies perennially worry about their own military's periodic objections to civilian oversight and larger liberal values? Why, often in response, do military leaders conclude that they are either misunderstood or manipulated by civilian authorities whom they regard as naive or ignorant about military affairs?

Antithetical Cultures

ARMED FORCES ARE inherently hierarchical organizations based on rank and the chain of command. They can serve democracies, but by their very nature are antithetical to democracy. There is no opportunity in military units for decision by majority vote when war begins. Once bullets fly, soldiers can ill afford to debate the wisdom of assaulting the next hill. They cannot worry about the "fairness" of a brilliant private having no influence in the decisions taken by an obtuse or blockheaded commanding officer.

Impatience, resolve, audacity—these necessary military traits are not necessarily those that democratic legislators and bureaucrats prize. Most politicians loathe a loudmouth like George S. Patton in peacetime as much as they relish his swashbuckling style in time of war. What Curtis LeMay said about war during the air assault over Japan reassured Americans that we would break the Japanese; when he voiced the same bellicosity during the Cold War, it scared some to the death.

Occasionally the voting public suspects that professional soldiers like violence and killing, or at least far more than civilians do. And supposed sheep always worry about giving orders to hungry wolves. Read the sad letters of poor Cicero to see how in his arrogance he entirely and fatally misjudged the military minds of Caesar, Augustus, and Antony. Civilian overseers in France and later in Germany sought to solve emerging problems by dispatching Napoleon to Egypt or by throwing Hitler in jail, but they found that ultimately these steps were just the beginning, and not the end, of their troubles.

Democracies have other, even larger problems with their own militaries, especially the ever-present fear of militarism that permeates civilian society—that is, the ongoing worry over the cult of arms transcending the battlefield and becoming an ideology that celebrates power, rigid discipline, or fanatical devotion to a cause. Indeed, this exaggerated dimension of military life often draws the most zealous and dangerous of characters into its orbit, and these can be truly scary folks. The Spartan *krypteia*, the Praetorian guards, Hitler's SS, Serbian paramilitaries—such groups in the past have often interfered with or intervened in politics under the posture of being models of rigorous asceticism for the nation.

Anti-constitutional military coups—and not the idealistic promotion of democracy and liberal values—thus seem the more logical vice of military figures when they intrude into politics. History in some sense is the record of supposedly sober soldiers intervening in times of perceived social chaos to bring society a needed dose of their own order and obedience.

That was the rationale when Caesar in 44 B.C. crossed the Rubicon and put a formal end to the Roman Republic, when Napoleon dismissed the directorate, when Hitler ended the Weimar Republic, and when the twentieth-century Latin America caudillos, Greek colonels, and Middle Eastern Baathist and Nasserite officers staged their various coups. Communist dictators in the Soviet Union and China inserted their own commissars into their militaries to ensure that they were perpetual advocates for Communist ideology and indoctrination, at home and abroad.

Military Liberalism?

B UT THERE IS another and less known tradition of what we might call military liberalism, when militaries have often given birth to, or at least facilitated, the creation of free governments and have been used in turn to promote and extend them abroad. Almost all of our successes abroad in the Second World War, Korea, and Serbia resulted in democratic advancement. Almost all of our failures such as Vietnam—the verdict is still out on Afghanistan and Iraq—were in at least partial pursuit of promoting democratic government.

America's approach to such optional wars for democracy is apparently cyclical: a hard slog like Vietnam followed by a walkover in Grenada followed by a hard slog in Iraq. About every thirty or forty years or so, the United States in idealistic fashion sends troops abroad to promote consensual government, or at least to thwart authoritarianism in rather difficult landscapes, such as the Philippines, Vietnam, Afghanistan, or Iraq. Then it finds itself bogged down in dirty fighting against nonconventional insurgents, and in discouragement finally swears that it will never again intervene in such ambiguous scenarios—until an easy success in Panama or Serbia reassures the Pentagon and White House that America indeed can use its force to effect positive change at relatively little cost.

It seems to be in our national DNA to try to use our armed forces in ways that reflect American values and political aims, and to find maverick officers who will be eager to carry out those objectives. The urge is perhaps more than just an American phenomenon. In fact, democracy has always been nearly synonymous with wars of national expression. Fifth-century B.C. Athens fought three out of four years in its greatest age of cultural achievement—usually goaded on by a vote of the assembly, often to fight some sort of oligarch state. America since the Second World War has seen its troops in combat in, or in the skies above, Afghanistan, Bosnia, Cambodia, Cuba, the Dominican Republic, Grenada, Haiti, Iran, Iraq, Korea, Kosovo, Kuwait, Lebanon, Libya, Panama, Serbia, Somalia, and Vietnam—all with the professed aim of restoring some sort of order by fighting oligarchs, dictators, and autocrats.

Consensual governments ratify wars, and thus rarely can the people successfully argue that they were forced into unpopular and costly fighting by kings or dictators. The historian Herodotus—noting the propensity of democracies to be fickle and ready to fight for idealistic reasons—remarked that it was easier to persuade thirty thousand fired-up Athenian citizens to send aid to the Ionia during the revolt from Persia than to convince a few reluctant Spartan oligarchs to do the same.

Democratic Crusades

IT IS HARD to think of many democracies that were not born in some manner out of war, violence, or coercion—beginning with the first example of Cleisthenic Athens in 507 B.C., and including our own revolution in 1776. The best examples are those of the twentieth century, when many of the most successful present-day constitutional governments were epiphenomena of war, imposed by the victors or coalition partners, as we have seen in the cases of Germany, Japan, Italy, South Korea, and more recently Grenada, Liberia, Panama, Serbia—and Afghanistan and Iraq.

Of course, democracy, as Aristotle outlined its various wide parameters in the *Politics*, is in some sense a relative term. Scholars still argue over its definition—and especially the weight that should be given to the criteria of voting, the degree of constitutional rights granted to the individual, and the relationship of political freedom with concurrent economic and social liberty.

But if we adopt the most expansive sense of the notion of constitutional government, then parliamentary Britain of the nineteenth century would be considered far more consensual than nearly all nations of its time. And British officers sometimes used their overwhelming military superiority to promote a classical sense of liberalism, whether in ending suttee in India or shutting down the African slave trade.

We sometimes forget that the existential global evils of the nineteenth and twentieth centuries—chattel slavery, Nazism, Italian Fascism, Japanese militarism, and Soviet Stalinism—were not only eliminated by force or the threat of force, but exclusively by the might of democratically governed militaries. American armies or the threat of them ended the plantation system, the death camps, the Co-prosperity Sphere, and the gulag. American democratic militaries made possible the future of the new Atlanta, the new Rome, the new Tokyo, the new Berlin, the new Seoul, and the new Warsaw.

Even during Roman imperial times, when the first emperors succeeded in suppressing the autonomy of the senate and central assemblies, there still functioned at the local level the concept of Roman law that allowed all Roman citizens the same rights of habeas corpus, trial by a magistrate, and protections of private property. The armies of the late republic that swept the Mediterranean did not do so solely on the brilliant discipline, tactics, and technology of the legions. They also offered to the conquered the promise that Roman proconsuls and legates would use legionnaries to enforce a sense of equality under the law for indigenous tribes from Gaul to North Africa—a reality that often undermined local nationalist resistance leaders.

It is not just governments per se that democratically inspired armies protect and promote, but often the wider cultures that incubate and nurture them. And that allows armies to be more effective agents of change and custodians of more liberal values. The present-day Turkish armed forces, at last subject to elected officials and the products of military science and professional training, still adhere to the secular statutes that Kemal Atatürk established for the modern state of Turkey. The military is thus paradoxically sometimes the only guardian of liberal values in that country, the one institution that is most likely to resist the insidious imposition of sharia law or the Islamization of Turkish culture. In a July 2009 crisis, the Honduran military arrested and then deported President Zelaya—but only after it was ordered to do so by both the Honduran Parliament and Supreme Court. Both had warned Zelaya that his unconstitutional plans of holding a plebiscite to ensure an unlawful third presidential term would lead to his exile.

Racial integration and gender equality were much more easily achieved in the U.S. military than in civilian institutions, once reformist politicians discovered that the military's chain of command and culture of obedience could be used much more efficiently to impose democratic agendas from on high.

The armed forces of the democracies like fifth-century B.C. Athens, fourth-century B.C. Thebes, and contemporary America all tried not just to promote abroad the values that they cherished at home, but often to replicate their very own democratic structures and institutions. Why should this be so?

Democracy and Military Self-Interest

THE ANSWER IS complex but seems to involve both practical and ethical reasons in seeing as many democracies as possible spread beyond their own shores. Athens's so-called *ochlos*—the voting mob empowered by the radical democracy—felt that its own privileged position hinged on having like-minded supporters in the subject states of the Aegean. So the maritime Athenian empire was patrolled by two hundred imperial triremes with names like *Free Speech* and *Demokratia*, and powered by poor landless *thete* rowers who were paid a generous wage as the muscles of democracy.

The truism that democracies rarely attack each other is mostly valid in the modern era and perhaps often for antiquity as well. Although democratic Athens attacked democratic Syracuse during the Peloponnesian War, such internecine warfare among democratic polities was not the norm. Thucydides saw that the Peloponnesian War pitted the Athenians' democratic allies and subjects mostly against the oligarchies aligned with Sparta. He also observed that Athenian forces did not fight so well against the Sicilians when it was thought that a supposedly hostile Sicily otherwise had something in common with Athenian political culture.

National security was also at least part of the catalyst for the great march of Epaminondas the Theban in 369 B.C. Then the general took a huge democratic army down into the Peloponnese to end the Spartan land empire, free the Messenian Helot serfs, and found the democratic citadels at Mantineia, Megalopolis, and Messene in order to encircle Sparta. After all that, classical Sparta never again marched north of the isthmus at Corinth—a routine occurrence before Epaminondas's invasion.

The European Union apparently has achieved its promised anomaly of a continent of autonomous states that will not attack one another—a dream made feasible only by the institutionalization of democracy, in turn made possible by the Allied victory and democratization after the Second World War and the collapse of the Soviet Union after its defeat in the Cold War.

Democratic militaries are also imbued with the moral logic that there is an inherent ethical inconsistency in protecting democracy at home while undermining it abroad. One of the raging controversies of the Cold War was the criticism that the United States had somehow birthed, often armed, or occasionally supported a rogue's gallery of dictators like Ferdinand Marcos, Georgios Papadopoulos, Augusto Pinochet, the shah of Iran, and Anastasio Somoza—and that this cynicism was a betrayal of American values.

The post–Cold War hope was that the realpolitik that marked U.S. policy during that era was an aberration of sorts, owing to the emergence of the Soviet Union as a nuclear power with expansionist ambitions. The collapse of the Soviet empire thus created the conditions for a new emphasis in U.S. foreign policy. Accordingly, the American intervention in Panama, the 1991 Gulf War, the bombing of Kosovo and Serbia, and the wars in Afghanistan and Iraq (whatever the underlying wisdom or folly of those interventions) were aimed at dictators and autocrats, with the expectation that their removal might be followed by the imposition of democratic rule.

In short, while all democracies worry about right-wing officers seizing control of civilian government, more often right-wing officers follow civilian agendas to promote, rather than to destroy, constitutional governments abroad. Politicians may go after autocracies on occasion for idealistic reasons, but officers apparently understand that the more constitutional societies arise abroad, the less dangers their own militaries face.

Dreams and Realities After the Cold War

WHEN GEORGE H. W. BUSH did not push reform on Iraq or the region as a whole after the defeat of Saddam Hussein in 1991, critics at home alleged that such realism was no longer appropriate in the post–Cold War world. The public, it seemed, was appalled at Secretary of State James Baker's declaration that the war in the oil-rich area was to be fought solely over "jobs, jobs, jobs"—and, later, that a successful war to liberate Kuwait had only led to years of no-fly zones to prevent continual butchery of the Shiites and Kurds. Baker's quip that we "had no dog in that fight" about the Balkans struck many in America as an unwillingness to use moral and military power to thwart the genocide in Bosnia.

Indeed, one of the ironies of the round of attacks on George W. Bush's Iraqi War—too much emphasis on democracy, not enough troops in Iraq, too much confidence in Iraqi reformers, too little fear of Iran, an international coalition that was too small—is that it was advanced by authors and writers like Michael Gordon, Thomas Ricks, Bernard Trainor, Bob Woodward, and others who in the 1990s had critiqued the first Gulf War in books and articles on nearly opposite grounds: that Americans had fought without sufficient idealism, that too many troops were unnecessarily deployed, that too little confidence was placed in Shiite and Kurdish reformers, that the fighting coalition was too large and unwieldy, that the realpolitik strategists had excessive fear of Iran.

Democracies that profess egalitarianism and the freedom of the individual are especially sensitive to charges of cynicism and hypocrisy when their foreign policies do not reflect their own values. At worst in its past, the United States fought its covert, dirty wars on the basis of economic or strategic pragmatism, which meant that it was quite willing to install compliant thugs whom it felt might be better than the alternative, and might in time evolve into something more liberal. But in its more conventional conflicts, which were closely covered by the press and followed by the public on a daily basis (World Wars I and II, Korea, and the contemporary Middle East conflicts), U.S. administrations generally sought to implant those who promised constitutional governments in postwar landscapes.

To the degree that our military has an active consultative role in picking and choosing America's fights, it would not be against, but might indeed support, the concept of promoting democracy as an expression of the national interest. Nor does the broader public oppose such a role for our military. Even in controversial cases like Iraq and Afghanistan, the public is strongly supportive of military efforts, after the fighting has stopped, to nurture consensual government in the wake of the removal of dictators, notwithstanding the difficulties of doing so.

Most Americans understand that the alternative—restoring order by imposing a friendly strongman—would only sharpen the charge of cynical colonialism, imperialism, and corporatism. If it is true that the spread of democracy around the world will make wars less likely and less frequent, then the military might see democratization as a means of reducing the likelihood of its own deployment in dangerous foreign wars to come.

The New Slur of Nation-Building

FOR A FULL generation now, the all-volunteer American military has trained an entire cadre of officers who have received advanced degrees in our finest academic institutions and thus possess proconsul skills that far exceed those necessary to command men in battle. "Winning hearts and minds" is now deemed just as important to the training of military officers as mastering GPS-guided bombing techniques or the proper uses of the Abrams tank.

In far-off diverse areas such as Colombia, Mongolia, and the Philippines, the U.S. military is not only conducting counterinsurgency warfare (what Robert Kaplan has called fighting in "Injun Country"), but it is also training local troops to operate under constitutional government. Special Forces officers administer to the social and economic needs of local constituents for the purpose of stabilizing local governments, so that they will not exploit discontent or use oil or drug revenues to destabilize the global order that has grown up since the Second World War. The United States, obviously, has a vital interest in defending and expanding this order, which promises to extend the sphere of prosperity and democracy.

In the furor over the war in Iraq, however, the entire notion of nation-building, both in small backwaters and at the conclusion of major military interventions—which was relatively unquestioned after Panama, the Balkans, and Afghanistan—is now under intense scrutiny and reexamination. The post-Iraq foreign policy of the United States, to the extent it is not isolationist, will probably see calls for the return of a posture of realism. In other words, we should accept the fact that we have to make arrangements with the world as it is, rather than trying to change it in our own image. By June 2009, the Obama administration had already gone on record that it would not "meddle" by voicing encouragement to Iranian reformers protesting in the streets against Iranian theocracy.

Reactions against nation-building might devolve into the acceptance of an attitude of "more rubble, less trouble," leading to a strategy of standoff bombing to deal with trouble spots in the world. Or yet again, future administrations might accept de facto appeasement of those who threaten our security in the hope that they will go away or their anger will thereby be assuaged. This we have already seen in the past policy that terrorism warrants only an occasional cruise missile or, as a criminal justice matter, a federal indictment.

All these approaches might be tried as alternatives to nation-building or democratization. If the realist right will talk about "American self-interest" as a reason of not getting involved in efforts to stop genocide or remove horrific dictators, the well-intended in the West will struggle with the paradox that most of its idealism about human rights butts up against the very anti-human-rights policies of the likes of Hugo Chávez or Mahmoud Ahmadinejad. Non-judgmentalism may trump abstract support for democracy, inasmuch as most of the transgressors of civil liberties today are not so-called whites, are not native English speakers, and do not reside in the so-called West. President Obama himself has hinted that democracy may not be the best litmus test of foreign governments' success, but rather the degree of freedom among the population from hunger and illness.

Richard Haass, president of the Council on Foreign Relations, remarked in a recent interview, "We're discovering that the conventional military power for which the United States is best known is most relevant to classic battlefields like the first Iraq war [in 1991], but the struggles we're engaged in now and for the foreseeable future are anything but classic." Haass added that battling guerrilla insurgencies and salvaging failing states such as Iraq and Afghanistan with nation-building are not skills at which the U.S. government has excelled. "So we're finding it very hard to translate classic military superiority into stability in these struggles."

In summing up the pessimism that swept New York and Washington during 2007, Haass soberly concluded, "For a number of reasons, I believe we are entering an era where U.S. power and relative influence, in the Middle East especially, is reduced and the influence of others who have anything but a pro-American outlook is increasing, and that trend is likely to continue for decades to come. I predict this realignment will be enduring."

This gloom is now shared by thinkers as diverse as Niall Ferguson and Francis Fukuyama. Both, now, in the fumes of Iraq see only perils in promoting democratization, though they once advocated the military removal of Saddam Hussein. They accept that such idealism abroad is best in tune with our own professed values. And they concede that promoting democracy has worked after other victories in the past, and in theory could contribute to global stability. But their concern centers mostly on the practicality rather than the desirability of implanting Western constitutional governments in today's more chaotic and globalized world, where billions simply have no experience with transferring their accustomed loyalty from a first cousin to a democratically elected parliament.

Freed from the distortions of the Cold War, and after a decade of using our military to promote democracy through the use of arms, has the idea of "military liberalism" run aground in Iraq? Is "nation-building" the new slur? And if so, why?

What Went Wrong?

First, the United States wishes to put the cart of postwar reconstruction ahead of the proverbial horse of defeating—and humiliating—the forces of the enemy. In this regard, in present and future wars of the twenty-first century we are faced with two mutually exclusive propositions. In an era of globalized communications and comfortable populations, it is very difficult to marshal support for a level of violence sufficient to bring wars to their full conclusions—that is, to defeat the enemy and humiliate his armed forces to such a degree that he submits to the dictates of peace.

What moralist wishes to see on television an enemy's power plant bombed to smithereens—when it had provided life-giving electricity not merely to a heartless regime but also to its oppressed victims? (Saddam Hussein's ruling Baathists found ways to smuggle in cognac and caviar while the Iraqi people nearly starved under the U.N.-sponsored oil-for-food boycotts and embargoes of the 1990s.)

And what taxpayer wants to level something when he knows that he will be stuck with the bill for rebuilding it? Yet, had Hitler abdicated in 1943, or had Tojo and his clique left Japan in 1942 to allow a negotiated armistice, it is difficult to envision Germany and Japan today as fully democratic nations at peace with their neighbors for more than six decades.

In the present postmodern age, the carnage necessary to disabuse the enemy of continuing in his present course is often seen as counterproductive or unnecessary—or perhaps contrary to Western moral sensibility itself. In short, democracies should no longer kill off autocratic regimes to promote democracy. Most strategic thinkers thought our pullback in Fallujah, Iraq, in spring 2004 was a costly mistake—a halfmeasure that necessitated a belated reentry by the postelection autumn. Then later in November, after renewed fighting to take the town, which was far bloodier than the initial conflict, our soldiers found torture cells, bomb factories, and a veritable terropolis that had been constructed after our withdrawal—macabre, grotesque revelations that should have shocked the world.

But the siege seems to have provoked almost the opposite reaction in Western popular culture, which highlighted supposed American atrocities inflicted on the insurgents in 2004 rather than real atrocities inflicted on the innocent by insurgents. Lest one think that the demonizing of the U.S. military is simply the province of the far left, consider the review of the well-publicized London play *Fallujah* in the supposedly evenhanded *Economist*, whose critic described the action as follows:

> The audience shuffles about his landscape while the action takes place around them. Soldiers push their way through, swaggering and malevolent; a roving stage light suddenly picks out two women in the audience as Iraqi aid workers. They weave gracefully through the crowd, telling their story, placing a hand gently on someone's shoulder.

The *Economist* concedes that it is an "anti-American drama," but concludes that "*Fallujah* can still be applauded for casting light on a shameful chapter in a disastrous war."

Shameful chapter? This rather easy sermonizing of Western elites obscures two unspoken truths: Privately, no British theatergoers would prefer the world of beheading, gender apartheid, and sharia law that flourished in lawless Fallujah to the legal system and audit that governs the American military. Nor would they have wished to venture there under the earlier "secure" reign of Saddam Hussein, when the population was terrorized by undercover security police and informers.

Yet in the present age, some elites perhaps sense that, on occasion, professional advancement, even psychological well-being and political acceptance, can derive from criticizing the U.S. Armed Forces and their efforts to stop such anti-democratic savagery. Thus to theater directors, the war to establish democracy to replace Saddam Hussein's genocidal rule must be reduced to "swaggering" Americans threatening female "Iraqi aid workers."

In fear of televised collateral civilian damage, in worry over causing casualties, and sensitive to antiwar sentiment at home, the American military is, not surprisingly, ambivalent about using its full arsenal against its enemies. The dragging of naked American corpses in the streets of Mogadishu ended President Clinton's humanitarian efforts in Somalia. And with more than four thousand Americans dead in Iraq, the narrative is the improvised explosive device and the suicide vest, not the purple finger of democratic participants. The rhetoric of Cindy Sheehan, Michael Moore, and former president Jimmy Carter reduced George Bush—whose sermons of "freedom" and "human rights" abroad could have come right out of a 1960s campus free-speech area—to a demonic figure at home during the end of his administration, and our efforts in Iraq to nothing other than a grab for oil, a proxy war for Israel, or a profit-making enterprise on behalf of Halliburton.

The larger point is that in the face of such endemic criticism, the military apparently cannot inflict a level of hurt upon an enemy, or suffer a level of casualties, that in the past were deemed a requisite for victory and hence postwar stability and reconstruction. Saddam Hussein's Baathist army evaporated in April 2003. Yet its shamed officers and conscripts soon learned that a good way to restore Arab pride after such televised humiliation was to go home, strip off their uniforms, and reinvent themselves as patriotic insurgents. Then the odds of safely killing, through remotely detonated IEDs, an American stringing telephone wires or painting a schoolhouse were far better than in the recent past, when meeting an American in a gun battle meant that outright war, not a CNN-televised "peace," governed the rules of engagement.

What worked in the Balkans in 1998, contrary to popular consensus, was not multilateralism. The vast majority of combat sorties were flown by American pilots. The Clinton administration neither asked the U.S. Congress for approval nor even approached the United Nations. It had allowed NATO forces to languish on the sidelines watching a ten-year holocaust that took a quarter million lives.

Instead the key to eventual success was that a liberal Democratic American president was able to use the U.S. Air Force, safely thousands of feet in the sky over Serbia, to drop its new precision munitions on the very capital of a right-wing Christian white European dictatorship without sacrificing a single American life—with the veneer of world support given the nominal, but well-publicized, participation of liberal European states.

A war for democratization, it seems, will still work in the messiest of places—if thousands of civilians have first been butchered by autocrats, if it costs no American lives, if the media do not have easy access to the enemy, if it is part of a war against right-wing nationalists, if it does not involve multiethnic or multiracial fault lines, if it is conducted by a liberal American administration, and if it is sanctioned by liberal Europeans. That is a lot of ifs—especially the most critical: not costing American lives.

But the stars seldom line up so perfectly. Our wars to come will sometimes have to be waged by conservative administrations against enemies in the former third world—sometimes of different religions and colors than many of our own—and on the ground in messy primordial failed states, far from Europe, and without scores of journalists broadcasting collateral damage and empathetic stories of misunderstood insurgents.

Democratic What?

A LONG WITH A war's military concerns, another worry is the postbellum practicality of extending democracy to traditional, non-Western societies that have little or no experience with liberty, equal rights, the rule of law, or representative government. After all, the easy cases for democracy—Europe, the former British commonwealth, North America, and the prosperous Asian capitalist economies—have worked and now have all been exhausted. We are left with the more problematic states with no prior heritage of either constitutional government or free market economics—or no past humiliating defeat by the United States in a catastrophic war.

Volumes have been written on the prerequisites—economic, social, cultural, and psychological—necessary for democratization. I argued in *The Other Greeks* that Athenian democracy—the West's first—was an epiphenomenon, impossible without two centuries of prior limited consensual government that first saw the establishment of rights of property-holding and inheritance and a solid middle class (the *mesoi*) of freeholding Attic citizen-hoplite farmers. Then, and only then, was it possible to put into place the key attributes that we associate with Athenian democracy, such as the principle of one free male, one vote, and full political participation without regard to wealth.

The contemporary enigma in the Middle East, however, revolves around the question of to what degree, if any, globalization—the intrusion into traditional tribal life by television, DVDs, the Internet, and cell phones, along with the large numbers of contemporary democracies in the world at large—has collapsed the period of preparation necessary for reform. And while Islam, for example, seems not incompatible with democracy per se in countries like India, Indonesia, Malaysia, and Turkey (where more than half of the world's Muslims live), the Arab Islamic world may prove to be a different story altogether.

There the obstacles to democracy and Western ideals of liberty and equality seem more profound than elsewhere. These include a deeply entrenched tribal culture and endemic anger at modernity combined with a paradoxical desire for the fruits of Western progress. Feelings of pan-Arabic chauvinism are nursed on transnational solidarity. There is plenty of scapegoating of foreigners and foreign influences, and intense feelings of grievance over a grand past juxtaposed to a perceived miserable present. Dislocations brought about by the huge wealth of exporting a third of the world's daily petroleum consumption make the community less than stable. All have combined to produce the antiliberal practices and attitudes that are prevalent in the region: fundamentalism, terrorism, and a kind of nihilistic violence against any foreign influence, however well meaning or constructive it might be.

In other words, it is redundant now to advocate democratization in the regions of the world where it is easiest to promote or is already under way—eastern Europe or a prosperous capitalistic Asia especially. When we talk of nation-building in the future, it will frequently be in the context of the Middle East, where there is uniform autocracy, plenty of petroleum, radical Islamism, terrorism, promises to annihilate Israel, and soon, nuclear-tipped missiles—in other words, a complete mess.

A Future for Nation-Building?

So where does all this leave us?

We need no more lectures about the truth we all know: Mere plebiscites are not democracy; such desirable government emerges ideally in concert with some sort of institutionalization of human rights, transparency, a free press, and an independent judiciary; and war and democratization should not be preemptory but rather the last resorts, taken only when such idealism is subservient to our national interest and survival.

We all know that there are simply too many Miloševićs, Saddams, Talibans, Chávezes, Castros, Gadhafis, and Kim Jong-Ils to remove, both practically and politically, and a reluctance to spend much American blood and treasure on those who may be more prone to criticize than praise our sacrifice. We all know that "supporting democracy" should not result in a "one vote/one time" coercive plebiscite that brings thugs like Hamas to power in Gaza. And we also know that in some cases such "wisdom" doesn't offer much guidance in a world not of our own choosing.

Yet the future for the West at war will be often one of just these poor choices. The worst may be to allow anti-Western dictators to commit genocide at will as they divert national wealth into alliances and weapons that threaten the postwar global order; the bad alternative is to try to remove them and in their places encourage democratic reforms under nearly impossible conditions.

But it will not be quite so easy to close the book on "democratization" and resurrect George W. Bush's 2000 pre-Iraq campaign promise not to use the American military for nation-building. The problem will not be refuting the argument for nation-building but finding the requisite resources and will among an exhausted American people—who wish to do the right thing abroad but, increasingly and for a variety of reasons, will be convinced they cannot.

First, we must remember that realism—whether close ties with the House of Saud or offering encouragement to former Pakistani "president" Musharraf—has been tried before and did little to circumvent either the attacks of September 11 or nuclear proliferation. Both autocracies have plenty of grandees—Saudi and Pakistani—who stealthily continue to either fund or offer sanctuary to al-Qaeda terrorists.

Nor did appeasement prove successful—as we are reminded by those often-cited two-decades-long serial assaults from the 1979 Tehran hostage-taking to the 2000 attack on the U.S.S. *Cole*. For more than three decades, the Carter, Reagan, Bush I, Clinton, Bush II, and Obama administrations have reached out—both overtly and covertly—to the Iranian theocracy, with offers of economic assistance, weaponry, restored relations, private live-and-let-live deals, and serial apologies.

But by 2009 the clerics were as anti-American as they were in 1979. And they were still rounding up, killing, and torturing dissidents in the same manner that they had consolidated power after the fall of the shah. In 1983 the theocrats began sponsoring those who were killing Americans abroad in terrorist operations, and they were doing the same thing in 2003 in Iraq. What separates the contemporary Mahmoud Ahmadinejad from the founder Ayatollah Khomeini is that the former, through the acquisition of nuclear weapons, may at last realize their long-shared desire to see Israel's end.

Second, supporting nation-building does not mean, at a time of record American debt, supporting *all* nation-building. Several truths are evident about the controversial but atypical Afghanistan and Iraq endeavors: The Taliban were directly responsible for harboring the architects of September 11, and they had turned a ruined Afghanistan into a Neanderthal-like ruined terrorist state. Saddam Hussein was not just the average Middle East thug in the Assad or Gadhafi mold. Rather he had attacked four neighboring states, had slaughtered hundreds of thousands of his own, had subsidized a variety of terrorists, and had fought the United States in a variety of theaters from 1991 to 2003.

In other words, the United States did not embark on a serial neoconservative crusade to remake the Middle East by arms, but limited its military efforts at removing just two odious dictatorships.

What has evolved for the present is not so much our policies or goals. Instead, in the cauldron of Iraq and Afghanistan, it is we ourselves of the present generation who have changed to the point that we have lost the confidence to enact positive reform abroad *at a price in blood and treasure deemed worth the objectives.*

It matters little that our present aspirations are far less grandiose in Iraq, and our losses far fewer, than were those in democratizing Germany, Italy, Japan, or Korea. The key, instead, is our current perceptions of what constitutes a foreign endeavor that is too costly or painful to endure. In our postmodern, globalized present, the challenge is not so much to use the American military to thwart autocracies and help foster constitutional government in their place, as it is to convince the American people that in some instances we have little long-term choice—and that we have done so in the past with success, and can do so again in the future.

During the dark days in Iraq between 2006 and 2007, many Americans grumbled that we had taken our eyes off the "good" war in Afghanistan—once home to the Taliban and Osama bin Laden—for an optional "bad" war to remove Saddam Hussein. But when Iraq quieted down after the 2007–8 surge, while Afghanistan unexpectedly flared up in 2009, suddenly there were renewed calls to exit Afghanistan, while little opposition remained over the now largely peacekeeping effort in Iraq. The common theme: In the place where Americans are dying, the war is probably misguided and unnecessary.

In short, most potential trouble abroad will be seen as far too dangerous and distant, requiring problematic American correctives that will always be deemed as marginally "optional" interventions. Any limited wars will be harder to bring to their full completion. The nature of our defeated enemies will make it far more difficult to democratize them. Western democratic publics will be far more reluctant to spend even a fraction of the blood and treasure that were needed to rebuild Europe and Japan into successful democratic societies. And the specter of massive, unprecedented American debt will loom, as our unchecked appetites have ensured an annual budget deficit for the next decade that exceeds all the money spent annually on defense.

In response, the immediate future will be not more of Afghanistan and Iraq, but more Rwandas and Darfurs, where the rhetoric of idealistic intervention increases even as our willingness to use our military to enact desirable reform erodes.

CHAPTER 13

Who Is the Enemy?

Fighting Ourselves[*]

The Alternative to Punitive War

THE NATURE OF American military power in our age is defined by how it is constrained—through nuclear deterrence, political realities, and cost-benefit analysis. How, then, on rare occasions,
does the United States employ its overwhelming military superiority to
achieve political aims, especially when even friends and neutrals often
wish us to stumble—if for no other reason than to see the world's sole
superpower occasionally humbled?

Our nuclear arsenal deters enemy states from using like weapons
of mass destruction against us. In the rare cases of lunatic regimes that

---

[*] This essay incorporates some ideas that first appeared in the June 2006 *National Review Online*
and others that were delivered as the Margaret Thatcher Lecture, on June 3, 2008, at the Heritage
Foundation.

appear suicidal and are immune to the protocols of mutually assured destruction—or at least, like North Korea and perhaps Iran, pose as such—we try to ensure they do not get the bomb. And when they do, we will apparently rely on future missile defense.

The more rational among our enemies know that they would lose either a nuclear or a no-holds-barred conventional struggle against the United States, so they seek to wage asymmetrical warfare. All such initiatives are based on the premise that America, in its wealth and comfort, is more concerned about suffering than inflicting losses, more worried about what others think of it than what it thinks of others.

In the recent past, we have dealt with bothersome threats through punitive bombing. When terrorists attacked Americans or general U.S. interests abroad, we launched air attacks—the four-day bombing of Iraq in 1998; the bombing campaign against Milošević in 1998; sending cruise missiles into Afghanistan, once again, in 1998. The Clinton administration referred to this sort of occasional missile shooting and GPS-guided bombing as "keeping [the enemy] in his box."

The upside to these campaigns apparently is that there is usually only a monetary rather than a human cost. One does not have to be a cynic to see that the window of political support for these operations is considerable since Americans rarely perish on television. Indeed, a hostile media is often neutralized: Devastation that we inflict is seldom filmed on the ground in a targeted police state, especially given the possible proximity of reporters to falling American bombs. Journalists who did go to Saddam's beleaguered Baghdad in 1990 or to a Belgrade under NATO air attack, either didn't get free access or, if they did, came under the suspicion that their full coverage was censored.

There are a few limits to punitive bombing. First, we avoid nuclear states such as North Korea and Pakistan because we don't want to risk a dangerous nuclear regional response. Second, we try to prevent a long war that results in images of carnage broadcast back to the United States. And third, our planes are *not* to be shot down.

Even when air raids are said to have gone well, the drawback, as we saw throughout the 1990s, is that the results are by definition mostly punitive, since we have no presence on the ground to affect political events in a more constructive fashion. And even the degree to which standoff bombing is successful in temporarily deterring a Saddam, a Gadhafi, or the Taliban from supporting terrorists depends on the accuracy of American bombs, the nature of the press coverage, and whether a population is restive and blames its pain on its own autocracy (e.g., Serbia) or on the American perpetrator (e.g., Iraq). Such wars can be relatively short (Libya, Operation Desert Fox) or go on for months (Serbia) or even years (the Iraqi no-fly zones).

A riskier proposition is to employ American ground troops to change the political situation—that is, to flip a hostile government on the theory the people are desirous of freedom and would welcome liberation. Invasions to remove autocrats are easy in a small Panama or Grenada, less so in large countries in the Middle East or Asia with well-entrenched political or religious movements that can pose as nationalists uniting various groups against the Western infidel or interloper.

Once America enters such a landscape, the clock ticks. The question of victory or quagmire is decided by whether we can defeat the insurgents and set up a local government before the enemy can erode U.S. public opinion. The enemy can accomplish this either by killing enough Americans, with footage shown on the evening news, to make us doubt the cost is worth the gambit or by suggesting that the vaunted values of Western bourgeois society have become sullied in the conflict at places like My Lai or Abu Ghraib.

The key again in any such effort is mostly political: Can indigenous forces, with American aid and the promise of democratic government, take the lead in the fight, ensuring fewer American losses while offering their countrymen something better than the past that resonates with sympathetic Westerners—and sell all that to a deeply skeptical cadre of Westernized elite journalists?

That an odious enemy beheads or tortures the innocent means little. Indeed, in such asymmetrical warfare, it is at times to the advantage of the terrorists to embrace barbarity—either to terrify suburban America or at least to galvanize antiwar opposition by opening a Pandora's box of horrors that inevitably "follow" from America's "aggression."

In the contemporary arithmetic of war, not only do Westerners count their own losses as a sign of misguided war making but also usually compute enemy deaths as proof of their own wrongheadedness or barbarity. In addition, even if "collateral damage" is a result of deliberate killing on the part of insurgents, or of their use of human "shields," the generic civilian "death count" is attributed nevertheless to Western culpability for creating the overall landscape of such turmoil. In military terms, that means a Taliban jihadist or an al-Qaeda terrorist in Anbar province can blow up civilians, in expectation that responsibility for hundreds of the resulting innocent dead will be charged to the U.S. military by many in the Western media.

Security Versus Freedom

WHAT ABOUT THE relationship between the need for security and democracy on the domestic front? Much of the confusion in military thinking of the present day derives from the juxtaposition of traditional measures to establish security and new, expanded ideas about civil rights and personal expression. This is an old paradox in the West. The Greeks from the very beginning understood this symbiosis between security and freedom, and framed the nature of the relationship—and occasional antithesis—between these necessary poles. The historian Thucydides, for example, makes Pericles, in his famous funeral oration, talk in depth about the nature of democratic military service and sacrifice, which are the linchpins of the freedom of Athens—and how any short-term disadvantages that may harm an open society at war are more than compensated by the creativity, exuberance, and democratic zeal that free peoples bring to war.

Because, like all democratic leaders, Pericles knew the charge that liberal peoples were prone to indiscipline and incapable of collective sacrifice in times of peril, he made the argument that consensual societies in extremis fight with as much discipline as closed, oligarchic communities, and yet still enjoy the advantages that accrue to liberal societies.

> We throw open our city to the world, and never by alien acts exclude foreigners from any opportunity of learning or observing, although the eyes of an enemy may occasionally profit by our liberality; trusting less in system and policy than to the native spirit of our citizens; while in education, where our rivals from their very cradles by a painful discipline seek after manliness, at Athens we live exactly as we please, and yet are just as ready to encounter every legitimate danger.

In contrast, authors as diverse as Herodotus, Xenophon, and Aristotle remind us that the king, tyrant, and autocrat live insecure lives, since their reign is based on fear and instilled terror. Thus they dare not ever lessen their grip for an instance, lest both the people and the military turn on their despised government.

The long history of Western civilization—the Persian War, the Punic Wars, the Napoleonic Wars, World Wars I and II, the Cold War—often suggests that free peoples, if slow to confront enemies on the horizon, nevertheless have been able more often than not to defeat their autocratic enemies. That is why today the West is defined by consensual governments rather than something more akin to the Napoleonic, Hitlerian, or Stalinist modes of rule that combined Western science with autocracy.

The key for Western societies in times of peril has been to calibrate the proper balance between personal freedom and collective military preparedness. Often authoritarianism has sacrificed personal liberties in preference for security concerns and militarist cultures. Yet just as often, in reaction to bloody wars, other Western societies have erred in the opposite fashion on the side of disarmament and appeasement, and lost their liberty as a consequence of not being able to provide security for their own peoples. Here one thinks of the fate of Athens in the age of Demosthenes or France of 1940.

But the quandary is not so black and white. Abraham Lincoln, and later Andrew Johnson, suspended habeas corpus in some border states to detain pro-Confederate sympathizers, and later Ku Klux Klan organizers. In the Second World War, the United States censored news from the front, hid information about military disasters, tried and executed German saboteurs in secret military tribunals, and wiretapped without warrants the phones of suspected enemy sympathizers—and yet preserved the Constitution while fighting a global war with a military of more than twelve million. Woodrow Wilson, more so than any American wartime president, eroded many elements of the Constitution—most frighteningly with federal sponsorship of the American Protective League, a private-public joint effort to spy on and intimidate potential critics of Wilson's wartime decisions.

Since September 11, Western societies have struggled with this age-old tension between freedom and security concerns, and a number of dilemmas have arisen. With passage of the Patriot Act, the establishment of the Guantánamo detention center, court-approved wiretaps, military tribunals' renditions of terrorist suspects abroad, and systematic surveillance, some Americans have often casually alleged that the Constitution has been sacrificed to unnecessary security concerns. But it is far more difficult to calibrate this supposed loss of civil liberties than it is to appreciate the absence of a post–September 11 terrorist attack.

During the 2008 presidential campaign, candidate Barack Obama made the argument that the Bush administration's security protocols had perhaps unduly deprived American society of its constitutional protections. Yet after being elected commander in chief, Obama quietly kept intact the past Bush practices of wiretaps, renditions, military tribunals, Predator drone attacks in Pakistan, and large troop deployments in Afghanistan and Iraq. Western societies demanded that the United States shut down the Guantánamo Bay detention center, as an abhorrent place that housed those convicted of no crime. Yet by winter 2009 no countries, despite American encouragement, had come forward to extradite their own supposedly benign suspected terrorists back to their home ground for scheduled release among the general public—an act that would allow an almost immediate closure of the facility.

Instead the worry about free speech in these chaotic times of conflict abroad may not be so much that our government has trampled the Constitution, but rather that we, the people, are insidiously self-censoring our own speech—as a result of Western public opinion that itself is willing to sacrifice unfettered expression out of good intentions—or is it sheer fear? In this regard, pose a few rhetorical questions about the nature of freedom and security in the public realm. Take a variety of contemporary genres of Western expression:

Film—Is it now safer for a Westerner moviemaker—not just in career terms but also as a matter of life and death—to produce a controversial feature-length film attacking the former president of the United States (as in Michael Moore's *Fahrenheit 911* or Gabriel Range's prize-winning *Death of a President*, which offered a dramatic version of an assassination of George W. Bush) or a short clip questioning radical Islam, such as Geert Wilders's *Fitna* or Theo van Gogh's *Submission*?

Literature—Is a Western writer more in danger for writing a novel contemplating the assassination of a former sitting American president (such as Nicholson Baker's *Checkpoint*) or one, in allegorical fashion, caricaturing Islam (such as Salman Rushdie's *The Satanic Verses*)? And would a publisher worry more about publishing a book critical of Islam or one envisioning the murder of George Bush? The recent decision by Yale University Press not to publish cartoon caricatures of Muhammad in a book devoted to the Danish cartoon crisis revealed that the university and editorial board were far more worried about safety concerns than the freedom of expression of one of their authors.

Journalism—Is a Westerner more constrained from hating in print a former sitting American president (such as Jonathan Chait in his 2004 *New Republic* article "The Case for Bush Hatred," whose first sentence is "I hate President George W. Bush") or drawing editorial cartoons mocking Muhammad (such as those initially published in 2005 in the Danish newspaper *Jyllands-Posten*)?

Religious expression—Is a Western religious figure more in danger after damning the United States (such as Reverend Jeremiah Wright calling the United States "the USKKK of A," urging his congregation to "Goddamn America," and suggesting that the United States deserved the September 11 attacks) or after referencing the historic relations between Islam and Christianity (such as Pope Benedict's quotation from a fourteenth-century Byzantine treatise about a letter from Manuel II Paleologus to leaders of the Ottoman Empire)?

Public dissent and expression—Would a citizen of London or Amsterdam feel more secure in violent public protest of Israeli foreign policy or in peacefully criticizing Islamic sharia law and its contributions to terror abroad and repression at home? Note again in this regard how the Swedish newspaper *Aftonbladet* ignored Israeli protests and published a controversial blood libel article alleging that Israelis harvest the organs of Palestinian dead, but it would not publish the incendiary Muhammad caricatures.

Each age has its demons of either laxity or authoritarianism. But our era in the West has fostered a peculiar form of self-censorship that far exceeds anything dreamed up by the Department of Homeland Security, the FBI, or the Pentagon. The only mystery about our reluctance to speak honestly and freely about particular issues is why we are so eager to give up on free expression, especially when it comes to radical Islam, which fuels much of the world's terrorism in the post–September 11 landscape?

The New –isms

OTHER THAN FEAR of bodily harm, one reason for curbing criticism of radical Islam surely is contemporary postmodern ideologies such as multiculturalism (the notion that the West is just one of many cultures, no better or worse than any other); utopian pacifism (wars can be eliminated through diplomacy and the teaching of nonviolent arbitration); and moral equivalence (those with power and influence in the West, given its own sins, cannot legitimately calibrate, much less condemn, the distasteful practices of other cultures).

What these notions have in common are particular views of radical egalitarianism and Western culpability for the inability to achieve equality on a global scale. Multiculturalism—whether found in Edward Said's *Orientalism*, or "black liberation theory," or various indictments of European colonialism of Africa and the Americas—grew up in an age of postwar affluence. It perhaps was fueled by Western guilt over past colonialism, imperialism, and global exploitation. And it argues that the sins of humankind—slavery, sexism, racism, and imperialism—are to be more emphasized as Western-inspired rather than equally innate to all cultures. Therefore, we could hardly use our own arbitrary standards of freedom or equality to judge other cultures, a practice that in the past had led to the subjugation and oppression of others under dishonest banners such as "civilization."

In its most radical manifestation, the idea that all cultures are de facto of equal pedigree and moral thought would mean that Westerners could not arbitrarily define what distinguishes the methodology of a contemporary Islamic terrorist from, say, the revolutionary generation of 1776 or a B-17 bombardier over Dresden or an American G.I. at Hue. Or more broadly, the multiculturalist alleges that the West has neither the moral capital nor the intellectual deftness to condemn foreign practices such as suicide bombing, religious intolerance, female circumcision, and honor killings, and so must allow that these endemic practices and customs are merely different rather than necessarily repugnant across time and space.

The practical consequence is that millions in the West have been taught not to believe in Western exceptionalism, and thus insidiously convey that message to millions of immigrants who seek to enjoy the benefits of European and American life, but who feel no pressing need to fully assimilate into it, and in some cases, thrive on being antithetical to it, albeit without forfeiting the undeniable material benefits that residency within Western borders conveys.

Many Westerners are now hesitant to condemn something like sharia law in abstract terms as an enemy of freedom, or to say Islamic suicide bombers kill barbarously for an evil cause. Some in the West don't think jihadists necessarily pose any more of a threat than their own industrial capitalist state, abortion protesters, or right-wing militias. And some who do simply feel that they lack the knowledge, or have previously lost the moral capital, to do anything about it.

Utopian pacifism was always innate in Western civilization, given its propensity to wage horrific wars, and in response to seek transnational legislative means to prevent the reoccurrence of such catastrophes.

From classical times, there has been a strain in Western letters and thought that a natural human, freed of the burdens of an oppressive civilization, might find a blissful existence without war, hunger, injustice, or the stress of the nation-state—should he be properly educated and replace wild emotion with a certain sort of pseudo-reason that borders on romance. Elite urban Romans often romanticized shaggy Germans bathing in ice-cold, pure mountain rivers. Plato's *Republic* was the beginning of a number of never-never speculations about how properly educated and trained elites could construct a society without war and poverty.

In revulsion at the carnage of the European twentieth century, and given the respite at the end of an existential threat from a nuclear Soviet Union, these old ideas about the perfectibility of human nature through education, energized by a vast increase in national income, have again taken hold. Sometimes we see these hopes manifested in world government. Many Westerners advocate sharing some national sovereignty with the United Nations, or allowing American soldiers to be subject to edicts arising from the World Court at The Hague.

Sometimes they are more pedagogical and more ambitious, establishing "peace studies" programs to inculcate our youth that, with proper study and counsels, war can be outlawed, as if the carnage is a result of misunderstanding rather than evil leaders knowing exactly what they want and planning how to get it. At other moments, diplomats convince themselves that controversial leaders of autocratic states—Mahmoud Ahmadinejad of Iran, or Bashar Assad of Syria, or Kim Jong-Il of North Korea—either may have some understandable complaints against the West, which explains their hostility, or appear more bellicose than they really are, largely through misunderstanding and miscommunication or the efforts of Western rightist zealots. In fact, the utopian believes that such autocrats may no more wish to harm us than we do them. Such bogeymen perhaps resort to the alarmist rhetoric of armed threats largely as a legitimate reaction to the military preparedness of the United States.

Utopian pacifism has had the effect within Western societies of defining difference down. In the present post-9/11 world, it deludes Western publics into thinking that problems with radical Islam are as much of our own making as they are a result of aggressive jihadist doctrines. In practical terms, utopianism translates into an influential segment of the public that does its best to convey the message that Western and radical Islamic cultures are roughly similar—and that any differences that arise can be adjudicated through greater understanding and dialogue. Therefore, novelists, filmmakers, journalists, or politicians who believe otherwise should not voice their sentiments out of concern for the greater ecumenical good—or at least exercise prudence by curtailing free expression, in recognition that their blunt talk may evoke a counterresponse quite injurious to the Western public in general.

As for such moral equivalence, or the inability to discern Western and non-Western pathologies, it begins as a strain of cultural neutrality. "They do it, but we do it" thinking seeks to do away with any notion of relative magnitude in hope of achieving global ecumenicalism—and yet thereby places impossible burdens of perfection on Western societies.

Sometimes the Western misdemeanor is defined as equivalent to another culture's felony. Prisoner abuse at Abu Ghraib, for example, was rephrensible and abhorrent to any sense of decency, but no Iraqi detainees were seriously injured nor perished. Nevertheless, it was treated in popular media as the equivalent of either a Nazi stalag or Soviet gulag, or a continuation of Saddam Hussein's torture center, where thousands were tortured or executed. Evidently, all were penal camps and therefore roughly all equivalent in ethical terms. Thus Senator Ted Kennedy fulminated, "Shamefully, we now learn that Saddam's torture chambers reopened under new management: U.S. management."

Context must become less important. The invasion of Iraq—approved by an elected Senate and House, argued over at the United

Nations, intended to remove a genocidal dictator and leave a constitutional government in its wake—becomes not much different from the Soviet invasion of Afghanistan, the result of a Communist dictatorship's desire to crush an anti-Soviet neighbor, waged ruthlessly against a civilian population, and resulting in the installation of an authoritarian puppet government. When the Russians went into Georgia in summer 2008, an autocracy seeking to destroy a republic, many in America said they were emulating our example in Iraq—a democracy trying to destroy a dictatorship in order to foster a democracy.

Standards of censure are never quite equally applied: We worry whether an errant bomb killed Iraqi civilians; silence ensues when Russians nearly obliterate Grozny and kill tens of thousands of civilians. The mishandling of the federal government's response to Hurricane Katrina, one of the five worst natural disasters in the nation's history, in which 1,836 Americans were killed, is singular evidence of American racism and incompetence. Yet not much later, 300,000 were lost in an Indonesian tsunami, a Burmese hurricane accounted for 100,000 dead, and a Chinese earthquake took 50,000 lives—and few remarked on either the incompetence of those governments in reacting to such a staggering loss of life or the failure of such states to provide safe and adequate housing for their populations in the first place.

Despite the veneer of internationalism and caring, moral equivalence is predicated on a sort of condescending notion of low expectations—that an educated and affluent Western society must not err, while the "other" is apparently always expected to commit felonies. Once the doctrine of moral equivalence is adopted, it becomes again impossible to abide by any abstract standards of censure or calibration of blame.

We circumcise infant males, so why shouldn't the Sudanese "circumcise" female infants? We have bombed civilians from Tokyo to Hanoi, so why shouldn't suicide bombers do the same? Timothy McVeigh was a religious, right-wing terrorist, so why are the thousands of Islamic terrorists deserving of any special censure? Much of the effort to hold the West to an unambiguously higher standard of being near perfect to qualify as being merely good speaks well of our values and aspirations. But in times of war, such requisites can endanger the lives of those entrusted with ensuring that we the public can entertain such exalted moral ambitions.

The aggregate result of multiculturalism, utopian pacifism, and moral equivalence among its cultural elites and leadership is that philosophically and ethically the Western public becomes less well-equipped to condemn antithetical ideologies and to defend itself against their aggression. In Western consensual societies this so-called political correctness likewise permeates the legislative, executive, and judicial branches of government. For a variety of reasons we voluntarily restrict our own free speech and expression; and we do not expect our governments to have the intellectual and moral wherewithal to protect the safety of writers, filmmakers, intellectuals, and journalists who choose to express themselves candidly and incur the wrath of radicals abroad.

But Why Now?

A QUESTION LOOMS: Why have these doctrines become so popular in our own era? First, in the general sense, the wealthier, freer, and more leisured a society becomes—and none is more so on all three counts than twenty-first-century America—the more its population has the leeway, the margin of error, so to speak, both to question and to feel guilty over its singular privilege.

Abstract doctrines that allow one to vent remorse over our riches, without denying our enjoyment of them, satisfy a psychological need to reconcile what is intrinsically irreconcilable. We see the same sort of phenomenon in early Roman imperial literature—Petronius, Juvenal, Suetonius, and Tacitus—where wealthy elites engage in a sort of nihilism or cynicism in matters concerning their own culture, as if ridiculing luxury means that they are exempt from criticism of enjoying it.

Second, with the collapse of Communism and the rise of globalized capitalism, Marxism as a formal doctrine was formally discredited. But its underlying and more vague assumptions that the state must enforce an equality of result among all the citizenry remain attractive to many, especially once the doctrinaire baggage of the millions killed by Soviet and Maoist Communism is removed.

One way of encouraging Western societies to redistribute their wealth both at home and abroad is to argue that it is not earned—or the result of practices not at all different from, much less better than, what is found in non-Western societies. And if non-Western societies appear to us to be more violent and unfair than our own, such perceptions need to be contextualized as legitimate responses to prior Western sins, ranging from colonialism and imperialism to unfair commercial protocols arising from globalization.

The Western military tradition assures Western states that they could, if they so wish, become almost immune from foreign attack. Consensual governments can, in extremis, craft security legislation consistent with constitutional principles that will protect citizens without eroding their rights. But government has no remedy once citizens voluntarily begin to abandon freedom of expression out of fear or guilt—or misguided ideologies designed to deny the singularity of their civilization. More important still, as the use of military force in unconventional landscapes becomes increasingly problematic, the power of rhetoric, sloganeering, and public opinion in the conduct of wars becomes even more critical.

Asymmetries Everywhere

T HE ENEMIES OF Western democracies grasp these contradictions in postmodern life in American and Europe perhaps better than we do ourselves. Once the jihadists understood that America was no longer content with punitive retaliation, largely by air, but would instead fight on their own turf to achieve larger political aims by winning hearts and minds, the terrorists subtly changed their tactics. So successful have they been that, after years of combat, much of Afghanistan is still not secure. And in Iraq, the U.S. military only recently was able to secure Baghdad. Saddam is gone, and our ground troops are backed by billions of dollars, the finest air force in civilization's history, sophisticated technology, and advice from seasoned counterinsurgency veterans. Yet for years the Sunni Triangle was not safe for anyone.

The same dilemma frustrates even Israel, that veteran of counterterrorism. We were told that, after nearly a month in Lebanon, the Israeli Defense Forces were no closer to destroying Hezbollah's Katyusha missiles than they were to eliminating the even more primitive Kassem rockets Hamas launched from Gaza—notwithstanding the Arab fear of taking on the IDF as in the conventional wars of 1967 and 1973. It almost seems that the less the United States and Israel worry about a Syrian armored corps or an Iranian air wing, the more loath they are to fight Iraqi insurgents or Hezbollah, because of the difficulty of cleaning up terrorist enclaves and the public relations fiascos that follow in the global press.

There are relatively easy conventional military methods of removing Iranian centrifuges and nuclear installations; there are less easy remedies in countering the resulting terrorist response that an Iranian-backed Hezbollah, Hamas, or other Islamic organizations would unleash regionally as well as globally—not to mention attacks on tankers passing through the Persian Gulf.

Why, critics moan, can't prosperous Western societies, sobered by September 11 and possessing superb conventional militaries and sophisticated antiterrorism forces, overwhelm this latest generation of ragtag jihadists—and convey the importance of victory to the world at large? After all, aren't the terrorists' arsenals limited to cobbled-together improvised explosive devices, outdated and underpowered missiles, suicide bombers, and rocket-propelled grenades?

The West's GPS- and laser-guided bombing was supposed to usher in a new age of warfare in which Western arms could reach the most distant mud-brick hut in the Hindu Kush. Islamic terrorists even in faraway Afghanistan were no longer immune to missiles that could appear from nowhere and shatter their remote caves. And precision weapons allowed us to minimize civilian casualties and avoid the collateral damage of Vietnam-style bombing. On some occasions all of the above may well be true.

But the ongoing fighting in Afghanistan, Iraq, Gaza, and Lebanon—and even NATO's 1998 bombing campaign in Serbia—suggests otherwise. As the Americans have learned in Baghdad, and the Israelis in southern Lebanon, it is not easy to use commandos and specially trained antiterrorist forces to quickly defeat insurgents who know that time is on their side and that any death—enemy or friend, civilian or combatant—advances their cause. It is much easier to create misery than to prevent it, easier to blow up a marketplace than reconstruct it with proper wiring, plumbing, and drainage—especially when the general suffering of the people is blamed on the prosperous Western interloper and so aids the cause of the terrorist. And missiles cannot always change hearts and minds, much less distinguish on the ground between a terrorist, his ten-year-old girl, his civilian sympathizer or shield, or his principled opponent.

In short, for a variety of reasons, many of the advantages of contemporary warfare seem to lie with the insurgents and terrorists who would challenge the postmodern West. First, it matters less than ever that the global arsenal of munitions is largely designed in the West. While all the world's militaries are parasitic on technologies and weapons expertise that originate in Europe and the United States, it is now far easier to steal, buy, or be given weapons suitable for terrorists than to acquire those suitable for traditional armies.

Tanks, jets, and missiles are expensive and hard to operate. True, the Syrians and Iranians may not be able to field them in such a way as to establish operational equivalence with the Americans or Israelis. But they can buy off-the-shelf surface-to-air missiles, rocket-propelled grenades, mines, and machines guns. These are all cheap, require little expertise, and, in the right urban landscape of hit-and-run attacks amid civilians, can provide a sort of parity against a Merkava tank or an Apache helicopter. As September 11 demonstrated, sometimes a few hundred thousand dollars' investment and a score of terrorists can do more human and material damage inside the continental United States than all the deadly conventional arsenals of the Nazis, Fascists, Japanese, and Soviets put together.

A second challenge is the widening gap between the quality of life in a successful West and that in a failed Middle East. Other than a few Gulf principalities, globalization has passed by most of the latter, whose governments resist modernity and the bounty that accrues to open societies. Oil wealth epitomizes this dilemma and ensures the worst of both worlds: Petrodollars have a way of circulating to terrorists and paying for their weapons, but they do not filter down to the Middle East street, and so create social tensions rather than alleviate the general poverty that fuels Islamic fundamentalism.

Blaming the West for the Middle East miasma—which is actually induced by autocracy, statism, fundamentalism, and gender apartheid—lies at the heart of the radical Islamic creed. Yet we often forget the military consequences of the wide gap between our own wealth and theirs, as affluence in strictly military terms can almost become a liability, while poverty transforms into a weird sort of advantage. Rarely have the criteria of victory and defeat been so radically redefined, with the mostly secular combatants on our side having so much to lose, while the enemy dreams of an Islamic paradise of sexual pleasure and riches far more enticing than the slums of Sadr City or Jericho.

The more leisured and affluent an America at war becomes, the less willing it is to endure the deaths of its youths seven thousand miles away, in awful places like Somalia and the Sunni Triangle, in fighting deemed not immediately connected to the survival of the United States. The result is that the West assumes it need not mobilize much of its enormous military strength to crush the impoverished enemies, who in fact continue to grow as formidable as before.

The West's revulsion at losing lives in such distant and unfamiliar theaters is only magnified by the televised savagery of beheading and mutilation. Most Americans—already tired of high oil prices, the spiraling debt, the monotony of the fist-shaking Arab street, and the lack of sympathy from our so-called Muslim friends from Jordan to Iraq—are returning to the 1990s mood of punitive isolationism. The result is that four thousand war deaths in Iraq eroded public support for war much more quickly than did the much more numerous losses in Vietnam. The message conveyed by the terrorists to the West when dead American contractors are strung up and mutilated outside Fallujah or Israeli corpses are dismembered in Lebanon is something like, "Go back to your twenty-first-century suburbs and leave the seventh century to us."

Third, not since the early twentieth century has the West been more chaotic, disparate, and divided. In the present age, Hezbollah's best chance of reining in the Israeli Defense Forces is not through a cascade of missiles, but rather through E.U. and U.N. pressure. The French foreign minister flew to Lebanon to praise Iran as a force for "stability in the region"—the very regime that has promised to wipe Israel off the map and given Hezbollah rockets to try to do just that.

Indeed, condemnation from U.N. Secretary-General Kofi Annan

or U.N. envoy Javier Solana during the summer 2006 invasion of southern Lebanon may have ultimately harmed Israeli operations more than a dozen suicide bombers could. Wealthy cosmopolitan Israelis worry when the Westernized world shuns their country; poor and often bitter Shiite Muslims care little. An Israeli does not like stares at Frankfurt Airport when he shows his passport, a Lebanese Hezbollah operative may well not have a passport—or if he does, care little about the reaction of a German official.

A largely unarmed Europe worries over reliable supplies of oil, and desires to recycle petrodollars through arms sales. Europe also fears Islamic terrorism and the ominous presence of unassimilated Muslim minorities in its midst. Add in its envy of America the hyperpower and old anti-Semitism, and Europe, with its economic and cultural clout, often sides with anti-Western belligerents. And this fact is well known to jihadists, who simply add an Islamic touch to a preexisting well-established European anti-Americanism.

Fourth, the antiwar movement has become more sophisticated than in the days of Vietnam. Of course, there has been dissent for Western wars from the days of Aristophanes' *Acharnians* and Euripides' *Trojan Women*. But today modern and postmodern ideologies question not just the wisdom or morality of particular wars, but also, as we have seen, the entire notion of war itself. Once more such doubts conspire with instantaneous media to make it arduous to fight in the Middle East on the terrorists' turf.

The point is not merely that Americans should not die in wars deemed "optional," given their great distance from the United States, but also that Americans should not kill the "other." The fallen terrorist is usually not in uniform, and pictures of his charred remains can be beamed around the globe as proof that another underprivileged civilian has been murdered by bullying American troops. Note that the media usually distinguish between civilian and military Israeli losses to suicide bombers or incoming rockets. Not so with Hezbollah or Hamas:

Almost everyone who dies in Lebanon or in Gaza is portrayed as a "civilian." Remember, also, that the anti-Western Hezbollah has a very Western media-relations department, whose director, for all his hatred of America, issues American-style business cards complete with e-mail addresses, and in times of war is in hourly contact with Western news services. Again, so strong is the tug of cultural neutrality that it trumps even the revulsion of Western progressives at the jihadist agenda, with its homophobia, sexism, religious intolerance, and racism. The poor, the nonwhite other, the non-Christian, and the former colonial may seem at times illiberal to suburbanites in the West, but who would not, given prior exploitation and present-day global inequality? Westernized Hezbollah elites understand Western media and Western public opinion, and thus how to package their own "narratives" in such a way as to draw on our well-intentioned sympathies.

But there is another unspoken challenge. The United States has usually waged war more easily with Democratic presidents—Wilson, Roosevelt, Truman, Kennedy, Lyndon Johnson—who appear as reluctant warriors forced to fight, rather than with supposedly bellicose right-wingers who "enjoy" settling issues by force. Again, note the absence of much criticism when Clinton failed in 1998 even to approach Congress or the United Nations, and instead unilaterally ordered American planes to war.

Many of Osama bin Laden's and Ayman al-Zawahiri's talking points come right from the Westerners—from the myth that the Iraq War was about oil, to the evils of Halliburton, to the "war crimes" at Abu Ghraib and Guantánamo. Bin Laden often issues not mere communiqués, but even lists of suggested readings, ranging from the works of Noam Chomsky to those of Jimmy Carter. When a U.S. senator claims that we are continuing the work of Saddam Hussein or another compares our actions to those of Hitler, Stalin, and Pol Pot, the jihadists fathom all too well that it matters little to the West that its enemies are politically incorrect—since the West at times seems happy to declare itself worse.

Western Advantage?

So, in the future, how will a confused America—particularly under presidents who cannot posture as reluctant liberal warriors—fight well-trained terrorists and insurgents who have access to lethal weapons and who use the media to portray themselves as sympathetic victims?

The West has always found ways of overcoming these checks on its conventional power. And its options extend beyond improvements in military technology that can lessen both its own losses and collateral damage. In an interconnected and globalized world, the example of Western consensual law and economic prosperity can, in fact, undermine insurgents by winning over the proverbial hearts and minds of their countrymen.

For all the negative press concerning neoconservatism's naive trust in the universal appeal of free institutions and personal liberty, it is to America's advantage that we are now more likely to be caricatured as dreaming idealists than as cynical realists. And if in the short term, terrorists find it helpful that explosions and mayhem are aired daily on Western television, then in the long term, globalization, democratization, and international communications will undermine the parochial world of the Islamic fundamentalist and the Middle East patriarch.

We forget as well that Western popular culture is radically egalitarian. Its video games, pop music, informal dress and manners, diction, and easy and cheap fast food all conspire to destroy hierarchies and break down traditional protocols and prerequisites. The result is a sort of undermining of tribal culture. For good or evil, Middle Easterners are more likely to wear Princeton sweatshirts and listen to iPods than Westerners are to don burqas and establish all-male coffeehouses.

In free societies, the best weapon against those who choose not to fight an aggressive enemy is simply to tell the public—constantly and candidly—why we should fight. This is true even in ugly wars that present only bad and worse choices. Western armies always do better when a Pericles or a Franklin Roosevelt explains—rather than asserts—how difficult the task is, what the enemy is up to, and how we will, as in the past, ensure its defeat.

For all the talk of Vietnam redux, one forgets that America has so far been quite successful in preventing another 9/11 and removing illiberal governments from Afghanistan and Iraq, and that its subsequent efforts to establish lasting democracies may yet prevail. The conventional wisdom between 2003 and 2008 was that the Iraqi quagmire had weakened Iran's traditional Arab rival, and thus empowered the clerics in Teheran to take even greater risks. But it is countenanced somewhat by the notion that a successful democratic Iraq can be equally destabilizing to theocratic Iran across the border. By June 2009 hundreds of thousands of Muslims took to the streets, not in Baghdad to complain of American occupation, but in Teheran to demand the sort of freedoms for mostly Shiite Muslims that they had sensed were possible in Iraq.

Unfortunately, the United States will probably have to fight more wars, in places and in ways it would otherwise not choose, and against ever more sophisticated terrorists. What we have seen in Afghanistan and Iraq suggests not only that the battlefield has become often bizarre, but also that the home front is even more confused.

Western militaries adapt rapidly and can prevail often in the most inhospitable landscapes. But the future challenge for beleaguered Westerners will be more at home than in the field abroad. The western Europeans—who have experienced, and are currently threatened by, terrorist attacks on their home soil—could outfight Islamic terrorists even in the distant Afghanistan borderlands. But the answer to the question of whether they can convince themselves that such concomitant sacrifice would be justified seems increasingly unambiguous: no.

I am not worried about a twenty-first-century America losing its edge in technology, military organization, and logistics, or a loss of spirit among the ranks. The worry is instead that the public at large is becoming ever more sophisticated, nuanced, and cynical—postmodern, if you will—even as the majority of our enemies remain unapologetically uncomplicated, single-minded, and zealous, attitudes that can prove advantageous when war breaks out. War is not litigation, regulation, or adjudication; rather it's a primitive nasty business, in which the greater force of one side prevails over the other—force often defined as much by morale and commitment as material strength.

An increasingly prosperous United States is redefining age-old battle not as a tragic experience in which human error, primordial emotions, and chance always conspire to ensure terrible mistakes, unforeseen setbacks, and uncertain progress as requisites to ultimate victory. Instead the public and its leaders assume their wars in awful places like Afghanistan and Iraq can be switched on, progress reliably, and be turned off in predictable fashion. They cannot—a fact accepted by others less fortunate, whether in post-Soviet Russia and Communist China or Islamabad and Tehran. We the people—not just the First Marine Division or an array of satellite lasers—will keep us safe. And finally that means sometimes we must wage war to defeat our enemies, even as we lament that they are our enemies and that our good enough soldiers prove to be not quite perfect.

EPILOGUE

The Paradoxes of the Present

WHAT HAS WAR become in the present age?

The first decades of the new millennium saw deadly wars in the non-West—and a United States divided over whether its ongoing fighting is existential or optional. Between 2000 and 2010 conflicts raged in Afghanistan, Congo, Gaza, Georgia, Iraq, Kashmir, Lebanon, Nigeria, Somalia, the Sudan, and Wazirstan. The United States itself on September 11, 2001, suffered its first major foreign attack on its continental homeland. Nearly three thousand perished at the World Trade Center, at the Pentagon, and on passenger aircraft. North Korea exploded a nuclear bomb and threatened its neighbors; theocratic Iran seems to be gravitating in the same direction.

The world's potential hot spots—whether the Middle East, the

38th parallel in Korea, the Pakistani-Indian border, the republics of the former Soviet Union, Taiwan, Cyprus, or the Venezuelan-Colombian border—could erupt into fighting at any time. Such conflict could very quickly draw in either nuclear players or patrons. Unlike an Iraq or Afghanistan, both sides in any of these wars would have recourse to large conventional militaries with plentiful air or naval support.

Yet at the same time, rarely has the majority of people on the planet been more peaceful and more prosperous. As a cause of the daily loss of human life, war's toll pales in comparison with both age-old scourges like malaria and hunger and new worries like the AIDS virus or virulent new forms of swine or avian flu. So are we more or less violent than ever?

True, globalization has disseminated widely the singular Western methodologies of war making. But it presents plenty of paradoxes. High technology, capitalist forms of production, and instant communications also have spread worldwide, unifying billions through common tastes and appetites. The resulting better life has reminded many from Dubai to Chile of shared interests in resolving disputes peacefully, given the new dividends of a global economy. Meanwhile, the enormous military power of the United States—so often blamed in prompting wars in the Middle East—in fact, plays a stabilizing role in discouraging state aggression well beyond the perimeter of the NATO alliance.

Remember, most of the world's attention over the past quarter century has been directed at wars involving Western powers. America, Britain, or the European nations—or all combined—fought in the Balkans, the Falkland Islands, Iraq (twice), and Afghanistan. Yet in terms of lethality, the real carnage was elsewhere and has gone almost unnoticed. Several millions perished in the Cambodia, Congo, Chechnya, Darfur, East Timor, Rwanda, and Iran-Iraq wars, where Westerners were not involved and not really interested. This asymmetrical awareness of these wars is not new: Thanks to Livy and the science of Western historiography, we know some of the gruesome details of Rome's Punic Wars, but we know almost nothing about roughly contemporary tribal bloodbaths throughout most of Africa and Asia where there were no historians.

What, then, are to we to make of the chaos of contemporary conflict? Perhaps it is best summarized as a tension between the globalized spread of Western-inspired affluence, and the simultaneous proliferation of Western arms. And what a dilemma these two developments present: Globalization creates new wealth that lifts millions out of poverty and thereby mitigates conflict—but it does so in inequitable fashion, encouraging unfairness, resentments, and reactionary envy, the age-old catalysts for war.

The practice of Western warfare is not only more lethal but also increasingly protective and defensive. Tens of thousands of soldiers have been saved—through the use of drones, armor, defensive weapons, instant communications, and advanced medicine—who just a few years ago would have been doomed. Yet as NATO troops go to war enhanced by Predators, Kevlar, robots, computers, and IV drips, so too their enemies have graduated from AK-47s to sophisticated roadside bombs, along with Internet mustering sites. In short, the best way to sort out the confusion of present-day war is to fathom how its Western strain is evolving and mutating—and yet also remaining predictably reflective of its origins.

The Old in the New

TODAY'S CONVENTIONAL MILITARIES are not only equipped with Western-designed weaponry and organized along Western lines, but they even look uniformly Western—if we can judge by Chinese boots, Egyptian camouflaged tanks, and Venezuelan officer caps. Apparently there is universal consensus that the best way to marshal manpower and material for conventional war is to emulate the system that originated on the killing fields of Greece and Rome.

Indeed, for some 2,500 years the piecemeal application of Western notions like consensual government, capitalism, personal freedom, and secular rationalism to the battlefield has led to dynamic militaries. Their successes were not explicable by the relative population, territory, or natural resources of Europe or North America. Most nations know that, and now believe that they can adopt mostly the military fruits of Western culture rather than emulate all of its bothersome political, economic, and social roots. While they agree Western war is unsurpassed, they are not so convinced about the larger system that created it. The result in military terms is that there is no "West" and "non-West" anymore, but more often a "sort of West."

As we have seen, Western military successes never progressed in linear or predetermined fashion. There was always some recourse to check Western military power, at least for a while. That has been especially true given the propensity of Westerners to fight far from home in optional wars of questionable public support. The present Afghan conflict is not the first time an outnumbered Western army, thousands of miles from its home bases, has battled over Kabul in a fashion and on terms not to its liking. What is new, however, is that someone who trained in a cave in Afghanistan ended up at the controls of a sophisticated airliner, ramming it into America's best-known skyscrapers, with a kiloton's worth of destructive force.

From the Greeks' efforts to curb missile weapons to the current protocols of mutually assured destruction, there have been efforts—both legal and de facto—to limit the unbridled expressions of Western warfare. We presently witness the absurd situation in which a lunatic Iranian regime uses its oil wealth to spin thousands of imported centrifuges to enrich uranium, while peaceful, democratic Germany, where nuclear physics originated, could well be soon blackmailed by the threat of losing a Munich or Hamburg—despite its ability to build within a year hundreds of fusion bombs as predictably lethal as a BMW or Mercedes is reliable. And Germans, whose soldiers once inflicted on the world such destruction, now peacefully and lawfully follow the proto-cols of global nonproliferation. Those far more eager to make war usu-ally do not care much for either international laws or public opinion.

Military traditions that gave us both Napoleon and Rommel now worry whether their troops should fight at night, or should kill terror-ists when in theory they might better be captured. These are optional self-constraints that reflect a variety of historical and contemporary considerations about the appropriateness of conflict itself—and yet they are completely unshared by our armies' likely enemies. Westerners now talk of a new, but often baffling, concept of "proportionality" in war-time. Their statesmen worry not so much about the supposedly obsolete notion of victory, but rather about the appearance of evenhandedness in the court of elite international opinion—of not hurting an aggressive enemy any more than it has harmed them.

We should also not assume that there has always been a mono-lithic West. The world's most lethal wars have been fought in Europe between Europeans. For nearly the past five hundred years, Orthodoxy, Catholicism, and Protestantism trisected the West, as we see from the religious wars of the sixteenth-century to fighting in the Balkans at the turn of the millennium. The rise of the Ottoman Empire is explained not just by Islamic zealotry, but also by European division—and by di-rect help to Istanbul in its wars with other European rivals. The best way to call off a Western powerhouse is to get a more powerful Western powerhouse on your side.

The toll climbs considerably in West-on-West fights. A Union vic-tory at Antietam or a French win at Verdun were far more costly than the infamous American loss at Little Big Horn or the French disaster at Dien Bien Phu. Currently the crux of defeating radical Islamists abroad is not an absence of manpower or material resources, but winning ratification from NATO members, ensuring moral support from the European Union, and using both shame and rhetoric to chastise those who wish to profit by selling nuclear or biological expertise to unsavory actors.

242 // *How Western Wars Are Lost—and Won*

It is relatively easy today for non-Westerners to obtain a sort of military parity, either through theft, purchase, or emulation of European arms. And while using a weapon is not the same as designing, fabricating, or repairing it, at critical moments on the battlefield such considerations would appear more abstract than real to those obliterated by Turkish cannons at Vienna. It matters little, after all, to Americans in Anbar that none of al-Qaeda's killers could design the improvised explosive materials of a suicide vest—just as it mattered little to the British soldiers who were shot by Indian mutineers with British Enfield rifles during the Sepoy revolt.

New restrictions on the application of Western force augment these old familiar ones. As we have also seen, the affluence and security that accrued from capitalism and consensual government often proved a mixed blessing in nasty wars against those who were far poorer, far more used to violence, often far more numerous—and usually had far less to lose. During the Peloponnesian War, if a hoplite of imperial Athens fell in the wilds of Aetolia, his death hurt the Athenian cause far more than the loss of the ten tribesmen it took to kill him harmed the cause of Aetolia.

So too it is again with the present. Western medical science not only ensures longer life, but, through the use of sophisticated pharmaceutics and artificial body parts, also promises an *enjoyable* longer life. Those advances will make it ever harder to ask a small minority of our citizens to lose their lives to ensure longer and better ones for the rest of us. Most twenty-first-century Westerners do not see death on their streets. They do not butcher the animals they eat. And they do not lose a large minority of their children to disease and hunger before the age of twelve. But they will increasingly fight those who do.

Those in the First Marine Division who outfought the Japanese, often hand to hand, in horrific places like Peleliu or Okinawa, grew up in more comfortable surroundings than did their Asian enemies—but not that much more comfortable given the ravages of the Great Depression. Today we are even richer and our enemies in comparison are even poorer, whether in Mogadishu or Kandahar. And the gap may widen even further.

Because there was a greater tendency of Western militaries to hear criticism, or to depend on some sort of consensus to ratify their musters, the European public had wider opportunity to oppose and even limit operations deemed too costly or too immoral. That antiwar tradition that started with Homer, Euripides, and Aristophanes accelerates as well. Again, the problem in securing Iraq was not the poverty of American manpower, know-how, or wealth. Instead the challenge was winning over diverse groups of free citizens, who were often not convinced that, in their cost-to-benefit calculations, losing four thousand Americans was worth the price of removing Saddam Hussein and fostering constitutional government in his place in one of the world's most important—but volatile—regions. These skeptics were not just fringe critics, but also local, state, and national voters, organizers, pundits, donors, and lobbyists.

Contradictions, Paradoxes, and Resolutions

THE PRESENT AGE experiences these age-old tensions—both globalized Western military practice and the traditional checks against it—but intensified as never before. Given human nature, there will be no perpetual peace or lasting international consensus. Instead, as in the past, we will witness cycles and trends that can favor either set battle or unconventional fighting, or something new altogether. The difference in the present age, however, is that far more diverse players are participating in Western warfare and at a far more rapid pace.

The onset of globalization, nuclear weapons, and enormous influxes of capital to the non-West has for a time tipped the scale in the favor of the those seeking to check the application of conventional Western power. True, the great slaughterhouse of civilization—Europe—is now united and quiet in loose alliance with America. Yet cross the Yalu River, bomb Hanoi, pursue over the Pakistani border—any such escalation in the last half century raised the specter that some nuclear power, deliberately posing as less predictable or concerned than an America, a Britain, or a France, might well draw nuclear red lines. The reaction to the implicit threat of a wildcard use of the bomb is to pull back rather than to roll the nuclear dice.

Given the increasing scarcity of oil, and the vast amounts of money its purchase transfers to numerous nations in the Middle East, Russia, Africa, and South America, terrorists and insurgents can easily purchase weapons comparable to those fabricated in America, France, or Sweden. To supply al-Qaeda terrorists does not require the supporting structure of industry, manufacturing, or sophisticated knowledge. Bin Laden only needs the income ultimately derived from a few dozen oil wells and a checking account. What does it matter that the petroleum was originally found and exploited by Westerners in hire to Middle East regimes—or sold and banked through Western finance?

The possession of nuclear weapons by the non-democracies—China, North Korea, Pakistan, Russia, and perhaps soon Iran–means that global flare-ups often will not necessarily be decided by the superiority of Western militaries per se. The stalemates, defeats, and hard going in Korea, Vietnam, and perhaps Afghanistan and Iraq prove that well enough. Soon war almost anywhere will invoke the specter of an aroused new nuclear power—one that claims it is more unpredictable, has less to lose, or harbors more grudges than a nuclear and democratic America, Britain, France, or Israel. The result is not just that Western war will therefore be limited, but rather it will more likely be fought in unconventional ways more favorable to non-Western societies.

The onset of the Internet and the instant dissemination of knowledge have also leveled the playing field. Again, who cares that Dr. Zawahiri's suicide bombers draw on no innate tradition of either European physics or munitions? With money from a rogue Saudi prince, a terrorist soon may Google "dirty bomb" and download the necessary expertise to easily assemble a brew of Czech explosives and radioactive medical waste. If one such suicide bomber blew himself to smithereens inside the lobby of the U.S. Congress, he could do far more comparative damage to the confidence of the United States than a fleet of sophisticated B-2 bombers might do to the terrorists hiding among civilians in mud-brick villages in Pakistan.

Does all this depressing news mean the end to dominance of Western warfare, and with it the very security of the West?

Not quite. There always looms the next cycle, the classic response to the last round of such contemporary challenges. At this moment, missile defense is being deployed, with promises that such countermeasures will venture beyond the stratosphere and knock down missiles and planes in their initial takeoff.

Should a series of 9/11-type terrorist attacks hit the West, gone will be the present intramural bickering. Amid the civilian carnage few will warn that we cannot wage war as effective warriors because we are not proper moralists. Fewer will protest that we are too precious and prosperous to fight those who are not. The Somme, Dresden, and Tokyo remind us how quickly Western pieties about the moral limitations of Western arms dissipate when wars are no longer seen as optional, but are deemed existential.

At present—nearly a decade after the fall of the World Trade Center and the attack on the Pentagon—the United States may no longer wish to send affluent twentysomething college graduates into the Waziristan to fight the Taliban. In such climates, a suburbanite private at breakfast can text-message his girlfriend in Houston, and yet be blown up by noon by an illiterate Afghan with a Soviet-era rocket-propelled grenade. But should we lose a series of iconic buildings, see the government derailed by a dirty bomb in the capital, or experience serial explosions on our transatlantic flights, then hundreds of thousands not only will be willing to go after terrorists, but will also fight with a supportive public without much worry about constraining the frightening arsenal of sophisticated Western warfare.

Where does this all leave us as we begin the millennium? Not in as gloomy a state of mind as we might think—given that we can still relearn a once-common knowledge that has ameliorated danger over the centuries. The peril is not in accepting that the innate nature of war lies in the dark hearts of us all, but rather in denying it. History is our great ally. It offers as much hope as does high-tech shields, innovative new methods of diplomacy, or ecumenical world governance.

Some believe that an unchanging human nature is cause for depression, given history's woes. I do not. Instead, I find solace in the fact that we remain the same as the Greeks, but have 2,500 years of experience, trial by error, and tragedy to draw on, and thus predict the general outlines of what men and women are likely to think and do in times of crisis.

Study of the past provides both instruction and comfort about preventing lethal wars. If we know the nature of our society and the fashion of our war making—its deadly advantages and the complex ways in which it has been sometimes checked—then we can always understand ourselves on familiar ground, no different from those who fought at Marathon or Iwo Jima.

Our great hope is not just that we will fight as well as did the Athenians who saved their civilization at Salamis, or the Marines who stormed Okinawa's Shuri Line, but also that we will have learned what prevents such bloodletting in the first place. That knowledge, it is true, accepts the ubiquity of war. But our own past experience with war also reminds us that through preparedness, deterrence, and tough diplomacy, those who seek to profit by aggression can be restrained, but only while they are still relatively unsure of their power—before they gain greater strength, and thus prove both uninhibited and far more costly to subdue.

Hitler, Adolf (*continued*)
U.S. actions compared with, 232; and
utility of military history, 14, 15, 16; way of
war of, 143, 144; where to start studying
about, 29
Holocaust, 119
Homeland Security Department, U.S., 220
Homer, 27, 119, 243
Honduras, 195
Horne, Alistair, 28, 29
Hostage-taking, 39–40
hot spots, potential, 237–38
human nature: and American way of war,
154–57, 181; and future of war, 243, 246; and
military error, 162; and reasons for war, 7;
and roots of war, 40; Sledge's views about,
72; and study of military history, 7, 27;
Thucyides's assessment of, 57, 66, 90; as
unchanging, 81, 133, 243, 246; and war as
"human thing," 91, 154–57
"human thing," war as, 91, 154–57
Huntington, Samuel P., 28, 189
Hussein, Saddam: and alternatives to punitive
war, 214; capture of, 182; and nation-
building, 209; and reasons for war, 18;
removal of, 14, 21, 22, 148, 201, 210, 243; and
renewal of interest in Xenophon, 67; and
utility of military history, 14. *See also* Gulf
War (1991); Iran-Iraq War; Iraq War

idealism, 29, 211, 233
India, 113, 114, 207, 238, 242
Indonesia, 207, 224
insurgencies: and alternatives to punitive war,
214, 215; and American way of war, 150; and
asymmetrical wars, 228–29; and contradictions and paradoxes about war, 244; and
decisive battles, 109; and demonization of
U.S. military, 203; in Iraq War, 124, 162,
178–79, 203; and military error, 162, 178–79;
and military liberalism, 192; and nation-
building, 201; and spread of democracy, 192,
201, 203; and technology, 124; and Western
advantages, 233
intelligence, failure in, 163, 164–67, 183
international law, 241
International Year of Peace (1986), 44
Internet, 47–48, 115, 126, 206, 239, 244
interrogation techniques, 156
Ionian War, 36, 41

Iran: anti-Americanism in, 209; and
asymmetrical wars, 227, 229, 230; and
constraints on military power, 213; and
contradictions and paradoxes about war,
244; and decisive battles, 112; and democracy, 197, 198; and future of battles, 117, 120;
hostage-taking by, 39–40, 209; and military
errors, 163, 168, 183, 184; and military liberalism, 193; and nation-building, 200, 209;
nuclear power of, 227; and present wars as
reflective of origins of war, 240; and return
of battles, 121; and roots of war, 38–39; and
technology, 125; and *300* film, 51; U.S.
relations with, 38–39; and Western
advantages, 234
Iran-Iraq War (1980–89), 108, 167, 238
Iraq: boycotts and embargoes on, 202; and
future of battles, 114, 117; 1998 bombing of,
213; peacekeeping in, 210; sectarian violence
in, 114
Iraq War: and alternatives to punitive war, 213,
214; as asymmetrical war, 227, 228, 230, 232;
casualties in, 13, 16, 24, 166, 183, 204, 210,
230, 243; and civilian-military relationship,
190; and classical lessons about modern
wars, 67, 85; and contradictions and
paradoxes about war, 244; criticisms of U.S.
concerning, 203–5; and decisive battles, 109;
and democracy, 190, 193, 197, 198, 199, 203,
204–5, 234, 243; as "different," 162;
insurgency in, 124, 162, 178–79, 203; and
military errors, 162, 163, 164, 173–74, 175, 176,
177–79, 181–82, 183, 184, 185; and military
liberalism, 192, 193, 202; and nation-
building, 200, 201, 202, 209, 210; and
new-isms, 223–24; and paradoxes of the
present, 237, 238; and present wars as
reflective of origins of war, 243; public
sentiment about, 23–24, 230, 243; and
redefinition of war, 235; and roots of war, 36,
42, 43; and security versus freedom, 218; and
study of military history, 9, 12, 13; and Syria,
17; and technology, 124, 125, 126, 127, 128–29;
terrorists in, 124; *300* as allegory for, 51; and
utility of military history, 14, 15; and
varieties of war, 25; victory in, 20, 22; and
way of war in America, 143, 149; and
Western advantages, 234; and WMD, 164,
182; World War II compared with, 13.
See also Hussein, Saddam

A NOTE ON THE AUTHOR

Victor Davis Hanson is the Martin and Illie Anderson Senior Fellow in Residence in Classics and Military History at the Hoover Institution, Stanford University, and the codirector of the Group in Contemporary Conflict and Military History, a professor of classics emeritus at California State University, Fresno, and a nationally syndicated columnist for Tribune Media Services. He is also the Wayne and Marcia Buske Distinguished Fellow in History, Hillsdale College, where he teaches each fall semester courses in history and classics.